DevOps for VMware® Administrators

VMware Press is the official publisher of VMware books and training materials, which provide guidance on the critical topics facing today's technology professionals and students. Enterprises, as well as small- and medium-sized organizations, adopt virtualization as a more agile way of scaling IT to meet business needs. VMware Press provides proven, technically accurate information that will help them meet their goals for customizing, building, and maintaining their virtual environment.

With books, certification and study guides, video training, and learning tools produced by world-class architects and IT experts, VMware Press helps IT professionals master a diverse range of topics on virtualization and cloud computing and is the official source of reference materials for preparing for the VMware Certified Professional certifications.

VMware Press is also pleased to have localization partners that can publish its products into more than 42 languages, including, but not limited to, Chinese (Simplified), Chinese (Traditional), French, German, Greek, Hindi, Japanese, Korean, Polish, Russian, and Spanish.

For more information about VMware Press, please visit **vmwarepress.com.**

DevOps for VMware® Administrators

Trevor Roberts, Jr.
Josh Atwell
Egle Sigler
Yvo van Doorn

vmware® PRESS

Upper Saddle River, NJ • Boston • Indianapolis • San Francisco
New York • Toronto • Montreal • London • Munich • Paris • Madrid
Capetown • Sydney • Tokyo • Singapore • Mexico City

DevOps for VMware® Administrators

Published by Pearson Education, Inc.

Publishing as VMware Press

ISBN-10: 0-13-384647-4

ISBN-13: 978-0-13-384647-8

Library of Congress Control Number: 2015900457

Printed in the United States of America

First Printing: April 2015

Warning and Disclaimer

Every effort has been made to make this book as complete and as accurate as possible, but no warranty or fitness is implied. The information provided is on an "as is" basis. The authors, VMware Press, VMware, and the publisher shall have neither liability nor responsibility to any person or entity with respect to any loss or damages arising from the information contained in this book or from the use of the CD or programs accompanying it.

The opinions expressed in this book belong to the author and are not necessarily those of VMware.

Special Sales

For information about buying this title in bulk quantities, or for special sales opportunities (which may include electronic versions; custom cover designs; and content particular to your business, training goals, marketing focus, or branding interests), please contact our corporate sales department at corpsales@pearsoned.com or (800) 382-3419.

For government sales inquiries, please contact governmentsales@pearsoned.com.

For questions about sales outside the U.S., please contact international@pearsoned.com.

VMWARE PRESS PROGRAM MANAGERS
Erik Ullanderson
Anand Sundaram

ASSOCIATE PUBLISHER
David Dusthimer

ACQUISITIONS EDITOR
Mary Beth Ray

VMWARE PRESS PROGRAM MANAGER
David Nelson

DEVELOPMENT EDITOR
Jeff Riley

MANAGING EDITOR
Sandra Schroeder

PROJECT EDITOR
Mandie Frank

COPY EDITOR
Keith Cline

PROOFREADER
Chuck Hutchinson

INDEXER
Cheryl Lenser

EDITORIAL ASSISTANT
Vanessa Evans

DESIGNER
Chuti Prasertsith

COMPOSITOR
Mary Sudul

This book would not have been possible without significant support. So, I dedicate this book to the following influences in my life: To God, for giving me the capability and the opportunities to work in a field that I love. To my wife, for putting up with the many hours of lab time spent in making this book. To my grandfather James, who left his home country of Trinidad and Tobago to make a better life for his children in America. To my parents, Trevor Sr. and Marva, for encouraging me to succeed and do my best, even when I didn't want to. To my brothers, Michael and Alfonso, for supporting any initiative that I set my mind to. To two special girls who inspire me to do what I do every day: Isla and Yazmine.
—Trevor Roberts, Jr.

This book is dedicated to my family, who continue to support me in everything I pursue. I especially want to thank my wife, Stephanie, who continues to be my greatest supporter and friend. I can always count on her to keep me grounded, focused, and inspired when I get frustrated.
—Josh Atwell

To my husband and love, Roy, for always providing moral, mental, and technical support.
—Egle Sigler

This is to you, Jackie. I wrote everything in Vim, you converted everything to a Word document.
—Yvo Van Doorn

Contents

About the Authors

Trevor Roberts, Jr. is a Senior Technical Marketing Manager for VMware. Trevor has the CCIE Data Center certification, and he is a VMware Certified Advanced Professional in the Data Center Design and Administration concentrations. In his spare time, Trevor shares his insights on data center technologies at http://www.VMTrooper.com, via the vBrownBag Professional OpenStack and Professional VMware podcasts, and on Twitter (@VMTrooper). His contributions to the IT community have garnered recognition by his designation as a VMware vExpert, Cisco Data Center Champion, and EMC Elect.

Josh Atwell is a Cloud Architect for SolidFire, focusing on VMware and automation solutions. Over the past 10+ years, he has worked very hard to allow little pieces of code to do his work for him through various automation tools. Josh is a father of two boys with wife Stephanie, and a daughter is on the way in early 2015. Based in the Raleigh, North Carolina, area, he enjoys time with his family, golf, audiobooks, and trying new bourbons. Josh has been highly active in the virtualization community, where he's been a leader of technology-based user groups such as CIPTUG, VMUG, and UCS Users Group. Josh has worked with others on preparing for their professional development pursuits through the vBrownBag podcast and the Virtual Design Master competition. Josh is also a regular public speaker and contributing author to the Mastering vSphere series. Never known for lacking an opinion, he blogs at vtesseract.com and talks shop on Twitter as @Josh_Atwell.

Egle Sigler (@eglute, anystacker.com) is currently a Principal Architect at Rackspace. She started her career as a software developer, and still has a soft spot for all the people that write, test, and deploy code, because she had a chance to do all of those tasks. Egle dreams about a day when writing, testing, and deploying code will be a seamless and easy process, bug and frustration free for all. Egle believes that knowledge should be shared, and tries to do so by writing this book, giving talks and workshops at conferences, and blogging.

Yvo van Doorn has more than a decade of system administration experience. The first part of his career, he manually built out and configured bare-metal servers. At Classmates, Yvo became a champion of configuration management and virtualization. Before joining Chef, he learned firsthand the power of VMware's products when he moved a small Seattle technology company's complete production stack over to its virtualization platform. He's a strong believer in the culture change that comes with DevOps. When he isn't busy spreading the gospel of Chef, he's probably enjoying a hoppy IPA, exploring the great outdoors, or celebrating his Dutch heritage while eating a wheel of gouda and watching Oranje lose the World Cup. Yvo lives with his wife and black lab in Seattle, Washington.

About the Reviewers

Scott Lowe, VCDX 39, has been in the IT industry for more than 20 years. He currently works as an engineering architect for VMware focusing on the intersection of network virtualization, open source, and cloud computing. He also spends time working with a number of DevOps-related products and projects.

Randall "Nick" F. Silkey, Jr. is a Senior Systems Engineer at TheRackspace Cloud. His passions revolve around both infrastructure automation and release engineering. He enjoys organizing several professional technical organizations in the Austin, Texas area. Nick has also spoken at local and national conferences about continuous integration and operations engineering. Apart from work, Nick enjoys spending time with his wife Wendy and raising their three children.

Matt Oswalt is an all-around technology nerd, currently focusing on bringing automation tools and methodologies to networking. He started in IT as an application developer for a large retail chain. After that, he spent four years as a consultant in the area of network infrastructure. He is now using both of these skillsets together in order to create more flexible, resilient, network infrastructure. He is heavily involved with automation and DevOps communities to help drive the conversation around network automation and SDN. He publishes his work in this space, as well as with traditional infrastructure, on his personal blog at keepingitclassless.net, and on Twitter as @Mierdin.

About the Contributing Author

Chris Sexsmith is a contributing author for the *DevOps for VMware Administrators* book. Chris has been a Staff Solutions Architect at VMware in the Global Center of Excellence for the past four years, focused primarily on automation, DevOps, and cloud management technologies. Chris lives in Vancouver, British Columbia, where he is working toward his MBA while watching as much hockey as humanly possible. Chris and his team lead the LiVefire program, focusing on specialist and partner solution enablement across the software-defined data center (SDDC).

Acknowledgments

Many people helped make this book possible, and I would like to thank them for their direct and indirect influence in getting the job done:

Gene Kim, for taking time out of his busy schedule with his own book project (*The DevOps Handbook*) and planning the DevOps Enterprise Summit to provide guidance on content for this book as well as on various aspects of the book production process.

Nick Weaver, for getting me started on my own DevOps journey by introducing the VMware community to Puppet through his work on Razor.

Joan Murray, for her strong support at VMware Press to get this book project off the ground.

Kelsey Hightower, for providing expert knowledge on Linux containers and how to orchestrate them at scale.

Aaron Sweemer, for providing contacts within VMware to share the company's DevOps vision with the readers of this book.

My co-authors, for their patience and continued support with my leadership of the book project.

Scott Lowe, Nick Silkey, and Matt Oswalt for providing invaluable feedback on my content in the book.

—Trevor Roberts, Jr.

I would like to acknowledge and thank a few individuals for their assistance in the writing of my portion of this book. Don Jones, Steven Murawski, and Alan Renouf provided me important guidance and feedback as I worked through various ways VMware administrators might benefit from PowerShell DSC. Without their insight and perspective I would likely still be playing in the lab and scratching my head. I would also like to thank Trevor Roberts, Jr. for inviting me to participate in this project. Finally, I'd like to thank the VMware community at large for their considered support and interest in this book. I hope you enjoy it as much as I do.

—Josh Atwell

The open source community, without you, we would not have these wonderful and amazing tools.

—Egle Sigler

First and foremost, I want to thank Trevor Roberts, Jr. for giving me the opportunity to participate in creating this book. To Mark Burgess, co-author of *Promise Theory: Principles and Applications*. Mark wrote the science behind today's configuration management that many of us use every day. Finally, I am grateful for everyone at Chef and in the Chef community that I was able to bounce ideas off of.

—Yvo van Doorn

We Want to Hear from You!

As the reader of this book, *you* are our most important critic and commentator. We value your opinion and want to know what we're doing right, what we could do better, what areas you'd like to see us publish in, and any other words of wisdom you're willing to pass our way.

We welcome your comments. You can email or write us directly to let us know what you did or didn't like about this book—as well as what we can do to make our books better.

Please note that we cannot help you with technical problems related to the topic of this book.

When you write, please be sure to include this book's title and author as well as your name, email address, and phone number. We will carefully review your comments and share them with the author and editors who worked on the book.

Email: VMwarePress@vmware.com

Mail: VMware Press
ATTN: Reader Feedback
800 East 96th Street
Indianapolis, IN 46240 USA

Reader Services

Visit our website at www.informit.com/title/9780133846478 and register this book for convenient access to any updates, downloads, or errata that might be available for this book.

Introduction

What is DevOps? Is it a product you can buy from a vendor that will cure all your IT woes? Is it an industry buzzword that analysts and marketers spawned to captivate the attention of CIOs everywhere? Although the IT community's coverage of DevOps may border on the edge of sensationalism, that is more a function of the benefits that DevOps can provide rather than mere industry hype.

DevOps is a term given to a set of practices, ideals, and tools that are helping organizations of various sizes deliver value on their IT investments at quicker rate. What exactly does this mean?

Think of the amount of time and the number of processes in your organization that are required to take a software project from the concept phase through software development and on to production deployment. The longer this process takes, the longer your IT organization takes to demonstrate value to the overall company. Thanks to the ubiquitous availability of technology, customers are expecting IT services to be delivered with the ease of a mobile application store. They will not wait years for a feature to be implemented, and a company that responds slowly to customer demands may find it hard to be successful long term.

How can DevOps solve the customer delivery speed issue? Configuration management technology, for example, can prevent server configuration drift and increase the speed at which new servers can be brought online to handle rapid growth in customer requests. Continuous integration can ensure that automated testing is performed on your software's source code as developers make their commits. These are just a couple examples of technologies and techniques that we discuss in this book.

Web-scale IT organizations like Etsy, Netflix, and Amazon Web Services are seen as the poster children for DevOps. However, the number of attendees at Gene Kim's DevOps Enterprise Summit attests to the value that DevOps can bring to traditional IT organizations as well.

So, brace yourself, DevOps is coming. The good news is that you can be empowered to contribute to the success of DevOps initiatives in your IT organization. This book aims to cover not just the high-level ideas of DevOps, but it also provides hands-on examples of DevOps tools and techniques in action.

About This Book

In our experience, DevOps concepts and tools can provide significant improvements in IT operations. While large IT organizations like Amazon and Rackspace are reaping the benefits of implementing DevOps in their environments, Enterprise IT organizations are still getting acquainted with DevOps practices.

This book aims to give the reader hands-on examples of the DevOps tools that IT organizations are using to achieve success.

You the Reader

This book is intended for system administrators with experience using VMware's vSphere hypervisor as well as Linux operating systems. We will provide step-by-step introductions to the use of software solutions used by DevOps practitioners with additional resources indicated in each chapter for follow-up study.

What This Book Covers

The topics this book covers begin with a high-level overview of what you, the virtualization specialist, can do to become knowledgeable on DevOps practices. Then, the book proceeds to discuss various tools that are used by DevOps practitioners.

Chapter 1 covers a discussion of DevOps concepts, including defining what this term means and why practices associated with DevOps can help your IT organization be more successful.

Chapter 2 introduces some of the popular tools for DevOps practitioners. Chapter 3 prepares us for setting up test environments to use with the sample code in this book.

Chapters 4–6 cover the Puppet configuration management solution, including a basic introduction, a multitier application deployment, and coverage of Puppet's integrations with managing VMware vSphere servers and virtual machines.

Chapter 2 introduces some of the popular tools for DevOps practitioners. Chapter 3 prepares us for setting up test environments to use with the sample code in this book.

Chapters 4–6 cover the Puppet configuration management solution, including a basic introduction, a multitier application deployment, and coverage of Puppet's integrations with managing VMware vSphere servers and virtual machines.

Chapters 7–9 cover the Chef configuration management solution, including a basic introduction, common system management tasks, and coverage of Chef's integrations with managing VMware vSphere environments.

Chapters 10 and 11 introduce you to the Ansible configuration management and orchestration solution. These chapters cover the foundational knowledge of this technology and various application deployments.

Chapter 12 covers the foundations of PowerShell Desired State Configuration (DSC), including architecture and primary use cases for this new feature of Microsoft Windows PowerShell. Sample code is provided to demonstrate the basic functionality of DSC as well as explanations of the various components that make up the feature.

Chapter 13 explores ways that VMware administrators may look to implement PowerShell DSC in their environment. This chapter targets specifically use cases where a VMware administrator, who may not be the Windows system administrator as well, can provide additional value and capabilities using DSC. Various methods are discussed in this chapter, with recommendations and limitations of each method highlighted and discussed where appropriate.

Chapter 14 discusses an application deployment paradigm that is relatively new to enterprise IT organizations: the use of Linux containers. The chapter discusses the basics of the Docker container management system, with hands-on examples.

Chapter 15 takes the Linux container discussion further with coverage of Google Kubernetes, an open source tool for managing containers at scale in your data center.

Chapter 16 describes how to set up, configure, and use Razor, a full lifecycle automated provisioning tool that combines install and server management with configuration tools. Chapter 16 walks you through all the key concepts and components of Razor. It starts out by describing how Razor works and how to best get started using it. Once you know what Razor is and how to use it for automated provisioning combined with DevOps tools, you will learn what the different functional components of Razor are. Finally, the chapter covers how best to install and configure Razor.

Chapter 17 gives an introduction to the Elasticsearch, Logstash, and Kibana, also known as ELK, stack. Each of these tools can be used standalone, but the use of all of them together makes a perfect combination for managing logs. This chapter covers each tool individually and how best to combine them and to harness their power for increased productivity while managing the logs.

Chapter 18 features Jenkins for continuous integration. It discusses how to automate delivery of code once it is committed to the source code repository.

Chapter 19 discusses VMware's own DevOps initiatives, including integrations with VMware vRealize Automation with DevOps tools and the new VMware vRealize Code Stream solution.

Chapter 1

Introduction to DevOps

DevOps is a system deployment methodology that organizations can use to improve the speed and quality of their project deployments. It is not just another buzzword, and the proof of this is that traditional IT organizations are seriously investigating how DevOps practices and tools can help them achieve their objectives. Are the benefits just for cloud-scale organizations like Netflix and PayPal? Of course not; DevOps practices can benefit organizations of any size.

Topics covered in this chapter include the following:

- An overview of DevOps principles
- Practical implementations of DevOps principles in your organization
- The importance of honing your DevOps knowledge and skills

An Overview of DevOps Principles

DevOps involves changes in organization interactions and in deployment tools and practices. The main emphasis is on identifying and mitigating bottlenecks to productivity. Some of you may have read *The Phoenix Project*, by Gene Kim, in which he boiled down the important tenets of DevOps into what Gene refers to as the three ways of DevOps:

- **First Way:** Optimize the flow of work from development to IT operations.
- **Second Way:** Shorten and amplify your feedback loops.
- **Third Way:** Encourage experimentation and learn rapidly from failures.

These principles are in line with a popular concept known as CAMS (culture, automation, measurement, and sharing) discussed by John Willis and other DevOps thought leaders:

- **Culture:** Failures should not prompt blame assignment. Change the ways your team members think about deployment practices and how to respond to failures.
- **Automation:** Manual methods contribute to failures. Use tools that repeatedly and quickly deploy environments in a reliable manner.
- **Measurement:** Monitoring and analysis are essential to success. Otherwise, root cause analysis of failures will be next to impossible.
- **Sharing:** "Rock star" mentality, where individuals/teams hoard information as a means of maintaining elevated status or team dependency, has no place in IT culture. It slows down production instead of accelerating it.

Some of these ideas may be more within the power of management to effect a change. So what do they mean for you, the reader, as a virtualization expert in the IT department? How can you help lead this change?

Virtualization experts are in a unique position to help improve alignment between the development team and the operations team. In a converged infrastructure world, we are already familiar with coordinating with multiple disciplines (compute, network, storage, security, and so on) as we plan and deploy our virtualization infrastructures. This expertise will be critical in helping to align the development and IT operations teams in your organizations.

No matter how quickly we deploy virtual infrastructures, the success of your business's projects will depend on the efficiency of the transition from development to production.

Think of a relay race: If the team does not prepare *in advance* (review old film, practice baton transfer, strength workouts, and so forth), there are bound to be mistakes on the field (dropped baton, runners trip over each other, and so on). IT operations will be blamed for missed deadlines, and the use of "shadow IT" will become more prevalent.

I stressed "in advance" in the preceding paragraph because when the development team finishes their agile releases, it is often too late in the deployment timeline to get involved. What if one or more of your team members become consultants to the development organization and engage with them throughout their sprints and not just at the end of the release? We will illustrate what that means in the context of a fictitious deployment scenario discussed below.

Suppose, for example, that your company, DevWidgets, Inc., has decided to release a software-as-a-service (SaaS) offering of its integrated development environment (IDE) and source code management (SCM) software solution (Project Taao). The goal is to leverage the Internet to foster interactions between geographically dispersed team members through online peer programming, web conference code reviews, and so on.

Project Taao is a huge undertaking that senior leadership is sure will be the company's flagship product going forward. Some of the executives have read *The Phoenix Project*, and they want to implement this "DevOps thing" for the project because they are not happy with previous release schedules. The CEO is even considering building a specialized DevOps team staffed with all new hires to help make this happen (because more people always make a project move faster, right?).

The managers of the development and IT organizations manage to calm down the senior leadership a bit and ask for time to formulate a plan that will be presented at the end of the month. What can you do to help make this happen? We explore some possible steps you can take in the sections that follow.

Implement Systems Thinking

Systems thinking means considering all the teams involved in deploying a software release to be a cohesive unit rather than disparate teams with conflicting agendas. These teams include information security, operations, development, quality assurance (QA), product management, and so on.

> **NOTE**
>
> For our discussions, we consider a *system* to mean any project that goes through the entire software development lifecycle (that is, planning, development, QA, deployment, and maintenance), whether for internal or external consumption.

Change the Approach to Team Interactions

Let's focus on the first thing that you should do: become a consultant to the development team. Speak with the development team leads who are responsible for the regular planning sessions (in agile terminology, the products owners and scrum masters) and ask to join some of their meetings. Actively listen for any team goals or deliverables that might require infrastructure procurement/deployment. The next few paragraphs highlight sample needs/specifications from the development team and illustrate the feedback/expertise that you can provide during one such meeting:

- **"We need long-term data storage for the customers' source code."**

  The development team might not necessarily outright say that they need a new disk array. They may not even realize that storage procurement needs to take place. However, your knowledge of the storage systems clues you in to the need to do some capacity planning with the storage subject matter experts (SMEs). You also need to consider different tiers of storage as the developers discuss lifecycle management of the user data.

- **"We need to have our own instance of Project Taao running in production separate from the instance used by customers."**

  This immediately calls to mind the need for additional virtual networks and for virtual firewalls to keep the production and customer data traffic separate from the internal traffic. You will also need to consult with the information security team about audit procedures to provide customer assurances of data separation.

- **"During our last release cycle, code compiled and ran successfully on my local laptop, but it breaks when deployed to production."**

  A developer may bring up the problems that she had with previous code deployments where the committed code works fine on her laptop, but during the production deployment, failures occurred. Her local development environment, an Ubuntu virtual machine (VM) running locally, does not match the security patches or firewall rules implemented on the CentOS servers in the demilitarized zone (DMZ). So, immediate patchwork needed to be done to meet the deadline (a long night for both the development team and the operations team). Your knowledge of environment build tools such as Vagrant and Packer and configuration management tools like Puppet, Chef, and Ansible will allow you to build a standard test environment that can be used on developer laptops and that matches the specifications of the production servers.

  With the development team leaders seeing the effort expended by the operations team to mitigate development environment issues early in the release cycle, you'll have an easier time negotiating a reciprocation of some of that effort. For one thing, this means that the development team needs to ensure that none of their team members are using the catapult method of task handoffs between teams. (That is, "It's 5 p.m. on Friday, and I have no idea whether my code will work in production, but I will commit it to the repository anyway!")

  One organization spoke at a recent PuppetConf and shared its code deployment strategy: When code is deployed into production, the developers who wrote that code take part in the on-call rotation during that change window. That way, if any complications happen with their code specifically, they can immediately assist the operations team with troubleshooting and resolution. Let's be honest; it also is good motivation for the developers to write better code so that they do not have to deal with that 3 a.m. call to fix bugs.

Before moving on, here is a strong recommendation from Jez Humble for any managers who may be reading this book: Don't build a new DevOps team! It *is* a good idea to hire developers, QA engineers, operations staff, and so on who have expertise in DevOps methodology. However, creating a whole new DevOps team distinct from the rest of the teams in your organization will just add another silo to the mix. This may actually be counterproductive to your goals. Rather, continue to align the teams better so that they think and act as a single unit instead of looking out for each team's own best interests, as previously mentioned.

Change the Approach to Infrastructure Deployment

A few disturbing, yet common, phenomena in the data center can impede system progress: handcrafted gold images, snowflake servers, and the fragile box.

The common approach to server deployment, whether physical or virtual, has been to maintain a set of operating system configurations with necessary updates, patches, settings, and so on that are manually applied to make systems immediately ready for use upon deployment. These configurations are known as *gold images*, and they traditionally took the form of ISOs that have patches applied manually based on a runbook. Recently, gold images have become preserved in the form of template VMs. However, let's be honest: *Gold images can rust*!

Gold images are not bad in and of themselves. However, the manner in which they are built can cause problems. If they are built manually, the process can be a full-time job to keep up with module updates, security patches, and so forth and then reprovisioning ISOs/template VMs for later use. There has to be a more efficient way to do this, and there is!

The images can be automatically built using configuration management technologies covered in Chapters 4–13. As changes are made to the server configuration and checked into a repository like Git (covered in Chapter 3), a continuous integration (CI) system like Jenkins (Chapter 18) can output an updated gold image for use. Tools such as Packer can be used by the CI system to generate a template VM for Vagrant, for hypervisors, and for cloud providers.

Martin Fowler introduced the idea of a *snowflake server*, which is a physical machine, or VM, that started out with the best of intentions to remain standardized. However, whether due to quick fixes to close a trouble ticket, special projects mandated by a senior executive, or any other reason, the server becomes highly customized. These special changes solve a short-term problem but institute a long-term headache. What happens when it is time to upgrade packages on these servers? What about security patches or even operating system upgrades?

How do we resolve snowflake servers? First, we prevent them in the first place by mandating that no changes are made by logging in to server command-line interfaces; no one-off yum or apt-get executions or configuration file changes allowed. All server changes must be made by using configuration management technologies only.

For the existing snowflake server, a bit of "yak shaving" (tedious but necessary work) will need to be done. First, examine the server configuration so that you know exactly which configuration files need to be altered, which packages need to be installed, and any other critical settings that need to be included in a configuration management script. Build and test multiple iterations of the server, each time making adjustments to the configuration management scripts until the test environment runs exactly like your snowflake server. Commit the changes to a source code repository, and you will now have a repeatable build process in case that production server cannot be recovered.

The *fragile box* is a term derived from Nassim Nicholas Taleb's book *Antifragile*. It is a term to describe a physical or virtual server that runs a critical software stack, but everyone is afraid to touch it because the business might suffer a significant outage. Through many tech support calls/professional services engagements, the server has gotten to a point of stability, and, to make matters worse, the SME who managed the server left the company.

If stability is truly a concern, it is a good idea to do a physical-to-virtual conversion or virtual-to-virtual migration to the VMware vSphere platform. That way you can utilize VMware's infrastructure reliability mechanisms like Distributed Resource Scheduler (DRS), Storage DRS, High Availability (HA), and so on. After the server is converted, and you have a successful business continuity workflow in place (backups, snapshots), it is time to see whether this server can be replicated using the remediation steps described for the snowflake server earlier. Your development and QA engineers can then easily build a test environment without touching the fragile box.

Change the Approach to Software Development and Deployment

Now that we've addressed the speed and quality of infrastructure deployment, what are some ways that teams can decrease some of the bugs associated with moving code from development to staging to production? It is well known that the earlier that you catch a bug in the development cycle the less costly it is to fix. That is why we have QA teams in the first place.

What if we can catch bugs before code is even turned over to the QA engineers, though? This is where continuous integration systems, mentioned earlier, come into play. We discuss CI in a bit more detail later on. However, the basic gist is that when you commit your source code to the repository, the CI system can be alerted and set to automatically execute a battery of unit tests against the committed code. At the end of the process, a package can be built and automatically distributed for the QA team to implement and begin their thorough testing.

Collect and Respond to Useful Systems Feedback Often and Adjust Accordingly

Your transformation to systems thinking will only be as successful as your capability to monitor and analyze system performance. The pace of business is moving at a seemingly exponential rate, with consumers having greater expectations about system responsiveness and uptime. Reactive problem resolution is no longer an option; instead, your teams need to anticipate problems before they happen to maintain system stability.

Log analysis can be one of your most vital tools, especially if you have debug options enabled on your binaries. If your environment consists of more than a few servers, it is time to adopt some form of automated log analysis. You have a variety of options available, including VMware vRealize Log Insight, Splunk, and even open source tools like Logstash, Elasticsearch, and Kibana (covered in Chapter 17). These solutions enable system administrators to examine repeated events for correlations with unfavorable performance. As the team becomes more comfortable with these tools and becomes more adept at identifying issues, the usefulness of the systems will grow.

Furthering Your DevOps Knowledge and Skills

Once a strong foundation is built on systems thinking and improved system verification, teams can feel more confident in experimenting with new features on a regular basis. DevOps practices allow the developers to stage incremental features in production. One benefit is that developers can beta test new features in limited release with select users and collect metrics on infrastructure impact and on user acceptance. Your effective log analysis practices will allow you to catch significant issues before they become widespread.

The continual learning and improvement do not just apply to the deployment of new product features: It is vital that you continue to develop your own skills and expand your knowledge set. In addition to keeping up with the latest and greatest developments in VMware technologies, take an active interest in learning new skills that will facilitate more meaningful interactions with developers. Learn the basics of programming languages that are used by your company. Take an interest in the agile process. The more you can effectively communicate with the company's developers, the smoother the transitions of projects from the development to production.

Take an active interest in improving your understanding of fast flow, a term used by Gene Kim to describe streamlined product development and deployment. Often, the best way to do this is to attend meetups, conferences, user groups, and so on about DevOps practices and tools (for example, DevOpsDays, DevOps Enterprise Summit, PuppetConf, and Chef Conf). Read books/blog posts/tweets on the subject from thought leaders and engage them at industry events and on social media.

Summary

Now that we have established what DevOps is and the benefits to organizations, let's take a closer look at some of the tools that help teams achieve success.

References

[1] *The Phoenix Project*, by Gene Kim, Kevin Behr, and George Spafford

[2] "What Devops Means to Me," by John Willis: https://www.getchef.com/blog/2010/07/16/what-devops-means-to-me/

Chapter 2

DevOps Tools

There are a number of tools to help teams employ DevOps techniques. This chapter introduces them. Later in the book, they are covered in greater detail with hands-on examples.

Topics covered in this chapter include the following:

- Organizing for success
- Server deployment
- Configuration management
- Continuous integration
- Log analysis

Organizing for Success: Kanban

Traditional task management for operations teams usually involves some sort of ticket system. Trouble tickets are great for keeping track of problems and for historical analysis after the problem is resolved. The problem with trouble ticket systems is that they can present a challenge to correlate tasks that should be related. Another challenge is to identify root cause of bottlenecks in production delivery. Further, workers may not have visibility into what trouble tickets are being handled by others to whom they can lend their expertise. Last, what is the best way to manage work-in-progress so that operations team members are not overallocated? That is to say, if the operations team is constantly focused on assigned tasks that keep piling up, when will they have time to make improvements to systems and pay down technical debt? How do we prioritize work properly and account for dependencies between tasks?

The Kanban (translated literally "signal card") system can help address these and other concerns. The practice was developed by Taiichi Ohno during his work with Toyota Production Systems to help achieve just-in-time (JIT) production goals. This methodology examines flows of work through different steps of a manufacturing process and identifies bottlenecks that need to be remedied for the entire system to be more efficient. The idea is that as bottlenecks are mitigated, this will pull work tasks from a work-in-progress state to completion. Work-in-progress is limited to allow for slack time for workers to make improvements to the manufacturing process (for example, identify and eliminate new bottlenecks as old ones are mitigated). Figure 2-1 shows an example of a manufacturing process where estimated times to completion are not being met.

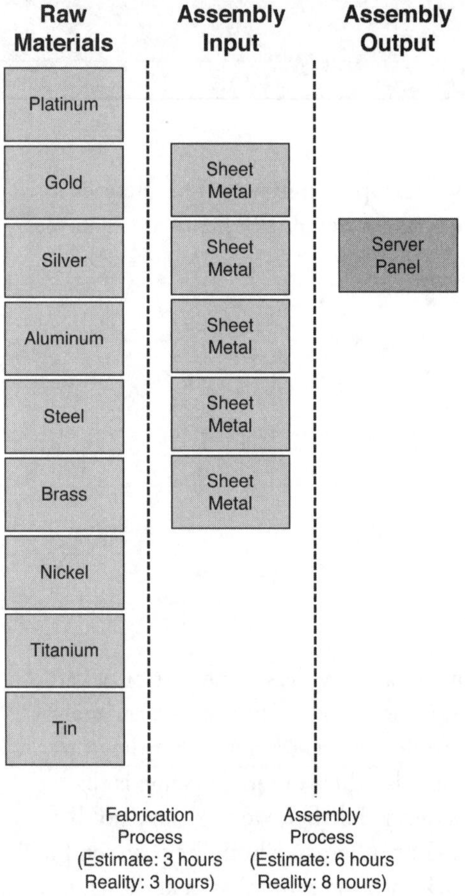

Figure 2-1 Manufacturing process

As the workflow proceeds from the raw material inputs through to the fabrication process and finally to the assembly process, we can see that the estimated times to completion are not matching the reality. There seems to be a problem with the assembly process. On further investigation, factory workers may see that the process to apply a special coating to the sheet metal may not be efficient. For example, the inputs for the server panel manufacturing process could show signs of not having the coating applied properly. So, rework is done, and the whole process is less efficient. Perhaps if the tray that holds the sheet metal for the coating process isn't overloaded, the outputs can be produced properly the first time, and there is little to no need for any rework to be done.

In the previous example, if the workers are heads down and obsessed with just fixing the incorrectly coated sheet metal instead of identifying the true root cause of the problem, wasted effort will continue. We've never seen this kind of problem in our IT operations workflows, right?

You may be wondering why we're talking about a manufacturing workflow organization methodology in a chapter about DevOps tools. However, before we can have a successful change in the way we work, we need to have an organized way of assigning tasks and identifying trouble in the system.

Even though Kanban is a manufacturing discipline, it has become popular in IT through the work of David J. Anderson and others who combined the concepts of lean with Toyota's Kanban methods. We will not cover the entirety of Kanban, but we will discuss the key points that can be helpful to IT operations teams.

The most important aspect of the Kanban system is the management of work-in-progress. It may seem counterintuitive that keeping IT operations staff 100% allocated on new work requests can lead to inefficiencies. However, operations teams face similar issues to manufacturing teams. For example, if a team is using gold images from prebuilt ISOs to build servers, there are opportunities for missteps when manual updates and patch applications are required if the gold images have not been updated in a while. If the team's manager's focus is primarily on satisfying server requests to the point that workers are 100% engaged in doing those workflows instead of finding ways to make the process more efficient, the work may continue. However, human error can contribute to setbacks. Important security updates may be missed or vulnerable ports left open, and remediation will be necessary to make sure that servers are not vulnerable. The teams may be so used to these inefficiencies that management is pleased with the amount of output. However, a lot of time and effort is wasted with this rework, a condition known as *technical debt*.

Technical debt is any unplanned work that arises due to mistakes or inefficiencies during planned work. Operations teams need to be given sufficient time to make system improvements even if this work is not tied to a specific deliverable. I am not advocating that operations teams be given "goof off" time. (Managers may think otherwise.) The operations team may seem to be efficiently servicing the current customer demands. However, what happens when the company wants to increase the scale of operations at a rapid pace? Existing workflows just won't cut it. Make the improvements to your systems now before you encounter scale problems that you're not equipped to address. If you're encountering some of those scale problems now, actively investigating and mitigating bottlenecks can help yield efficiencies.

Another important aspect of Kanban is the visualization of the workflows from start to completion. The most popular manifestation of this is the Kanban board. It can either be physical or digital. Figure 2-2 shows a Kanban board example that might be used by the DevWidgets, Inc. company introduced in Chapter 1.

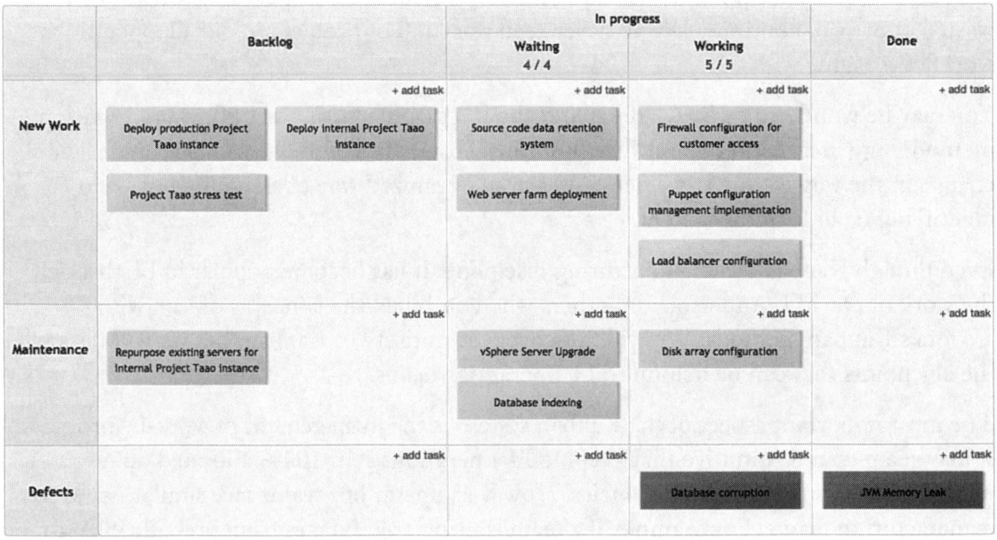

Figure 2-2 Online Kanban board

The idea is that each task is represented by an index card or Post-it note (also referred to as a *kanban*) and is queued on the left side of the board under the Backlog category. The columns that exist between Backlog and Done represent work-in-progress. Work-in-progress (WIP) limits (for example, 4/4 and 5/5) are placed on the work tasks as they are moved out of the Backlog. The Working column represents tasks that are actively being worked on, and the Waiting column represents tasks that are assigned but have dependencies on tasks in the Working column. Until one of the kanban moves on to the next column in the workflow, no additional work can be placed in the WIP columns.

Figure 2-2 shows different rows of tasks, also known as *swim lanes*. These swim lanes correspond to different types of work (for example, New Work, Maintenance, and Defects). Classifying the work correctly will help with prioritization.

When a team first starts working with Kanban, the WIP limits may be set based on past experiences. Afterward, as bottlenecks are mitigated and team efficiency improves, these limits may change so that the team is constantly seeking to improve the flow of work over time. Remember, the goal is to continuously improve while managing to keep the team from being 100% engaged on new tasks. If you are interested in introducing Kanban to your team, it would be worthwhile to have a consulting engagement with a lead practitioner in the discipline like Dominica DeGrandis or Lean Kanban University–accredited practitioners. Your Kanban board may not necessarily look like what is shown in Figure 2-2, and that is okay. The goal is to develop a clear and useful system that makes sense to your team.

Server Deployment

It is a given that system administrators do not have the luxury of manually deploying operating systems in the server farms. Tools such as Ghost and other image backup tools emerged in the 1990s that kind of got us closer to rapid deployment, but using these solutions required some kind of initialization process (for example, Sysprep for Windows) for the new system to become useful. PXE boot utilities like Red Hat Satellite emerged in later years to speed up the deployment process.

Today's workflows require a bit more personalization after the OS deployments are complete to make the systems ready for use. Of course, VMware released Auto Deploy, which helps greatly with deployments of vSphere servers. Red Hat took another look at their approach to systems deployment and developed CloudForms, which encompasses server deployment, configuration management (with Chef and Puppet integrations), server lifecycle management, and so forth on multiple platforms. On the open source front, Michael DeHaan developed Cobbler, and Nick Weaver introduced us to Razor (covered in Chapter 16). Other popular tools include Crowbar and Foreman.

Razor has become increasingly popular, and the latest release of Puppet Enterprise even bundles it with its installation media. Razor is not limited to working with Puppet. Razor's broker component can also support Chef, and plugins for other configuration management technologies can be written for it as well.

Configuration Management

As discussed in the first chapter, solely relying on handcrafted gold images for your server deployments can lead to inefficiencies during server deployment. Configuration management (CM) technologies can significantly improve the speed and reliability of building your gold images and deploying production system deployments. When you treat the server configurations like software, you can leverage source code management systems like Git (covered in Chapter 3) to keep track of environment changes.

CM technologies can also be used to provision consistent development environments that match production server configurations exactly. This can eliminate the "but it works fine on my development workstation" arguments that can go back and forth between the development and operations teams. CM technologies are designed to be flexible so that the same sets of instructions can be used across different platforms by dynamically adjusting to server characteristics (for example, OS flavor and location). The CM technologies covered in this book—Puppet (Chapters 4–6), Chef (Chapters 7–9), and PowerShell DSC (Chapters 12–13)—are declarative languages where you describe the desired state of the provisioned resources with less concern about how the work is done.

The benefits of configuration management can be realized at scale by using orchestration systems like Ansible (Chapters 10–11), Fabric, or MCollective that use an imperative style of describing environment state. Orchestration frameworks allow parallel execution of configuration management across multiple systems in a controlled manner.

Ansible can also be thought of as a CM technology because it does allow for descriptions of desired state. Some companies may choose to use Ansible only, whereas others may use a combination of Puppet/Chef as the CM technology, with Ansible to perform orchestration of the CM execution.

Continuous Integration

Jenkins (covered in Chapter 18), and solutions like it, can be a significant timesaver for development and operations teams. For development teams, it can help identify bugs early, provided that good unit tests are written, before code is turned over to QA. For operations teams, there is added assurance that they will not encounter code that has not been validated before entering staging.

Jenkins can integrate with Git and Gerrit, which allow code to be submitted automatically to Jenkins for compilation and test execution as soon as the development team commits their code to the software repository. Further, Jenkins job histories and console output allow all team members to examine various stages of the automated test and build cycles.

Log Analysis

Your system success needs to be measurable. What's one of the best ways to verify system stability? Look at the logs! You might need a human army to peer through logs manually. Also, the logs usually require privileged access that may not be available to the whole team. Thankfully, the entire operations team can benefit from a number of open source and commercially available solutions on the market that are useful for log collection and for data visualization.

Familiar names such as VMware vRealize Log Insight and Splunk come to mind. There are also open source solutions such as Logstash combined with Elasticsearch and Kibana (covered in Chapter 17), Graphite, and other tools that are popular in the DevOps community. Because they are available as packages for your Linux operating systems, these open source tools can be deployed with your favorite package manager such as yum or apt.

Summary

Now that you've had a brief overview of the tools available to DevOps practitioners, Chapter 3 will focus on how to build a test environment so that you can follow along with the workflows presented throughout the rest of this book.

References

[1] *Kanban*, by David Anderson

[2] *Toyota Kata*, by Mike Rother

[3] *The Phoenix Project*, by Gene Kim, Kevin Behr, and George Spafford

Chapter 3

Setting Up a DevOps Configuration Management Test Environment

Before we dive headfirst into implementing DevOps tools, let's examine how we can set up our test environments to adequately prepare ourselves. We'll also take a look at how we can start treating our infrastructure instructions just like a developer's source code.

Topics covered in this chapter include the following:

- Environment provisioning with AutoLab
- Environment provisioning with Vagrant
- Creating images with Packer
- Managing source code
- Git source code control

Environment Provisioning with AutoLab

AutoLab is a vSphere test lab provisioning system developed by Alastair Cooke and Nick Marshall, with contributions from others in the VMware community. AutoLab has grown so popular that at least one cloud provider (Bare Metal Cloud) allows you to provision AutoLab installations on its servers. As of this writing, AutoLab supports the latest release of vSphere, which will enable you to run a virtual lab that includes VSAN support. If you're unfamiliar with the tool, head over to http://www.labguides.com/ to check out the AutoLab link on the home page. After filling out the registration form, you will have access to the template virtual machines (VMs) to get your own AutoLab setup started. The team has a helpful selection of how-to videos on the AutoLab YouTube channel for anyone needing extra assistance.

Environment Provisioning with Vagrant

Vagrant is an environment provisioning system created by Mitchell Hashimoto and supported by his company, HashiCorp. Vagrant can help you quickly bring up VMs according to a pattern defined in a template file known as a Vagrantfile. Vagrant can run on Windows, Linux, and OS X (Mac) operating systems and supports popular desktop hypervisors such as VMware Workstation Professional, VMware Fusion Professional, and VirtualBox. Cloud providers such as Rackspace and Amazon Web Services can be used as well for your test environment. The Vagrant examples in this book are based on the VMware Fusion plugin, but the examples we provide can, with a few modifications, be used for other hypervisors and for cloud platforms. If you will be following along with the examples in this chapter, make sure to create a new directory for each Vagrantfile that you create.

NOTE

The VMware Fusion and Workstation providers require the purchase of a license for the plugin. See http://www.vagrantup.com/vmware for more details.

After installing Vagrant and the VMware Fusion or Workstation plugin, you need to find a Vagrant box to use with the system. A Vagrant box can be thought of as a VM template: a preinstalled operating system instance that can be modified according to the settings that you specify in your Vagrantfile. Vagrant boxes are minimal installations of your desired operating system with some boxes not being more than 300 MB. The idea is to present a bare-bones operating system that is completely configured by your automation tool of choice.

Some box creators opt to include the binaries for popular Vagrant-supported provisioners like Puppet, Chef, and so on, but other box creators do not, and users need to use the shell provisioner to deploy their favorite configuration management solution before it can be used. The box creation process is beyond the scope of this book. However, if you would like to develop your own boxes, there are tools like veewee and Packer (discussed later in this chapter) available that you can try out.

In previous versions of Vagrant, you had to specify the URL of the box file that you want to use when you initialized your vagrant environment:

```
vagrant init http://files.vagrantup.com/precise64_vmware.box
```

If the box file is located on your computer, you can specify the full path to the file instead of a URL.

Starting with Vagrant version 1.5, HashiCorp introduced the Atlas system (formerly known as Vagrant Cloud), an online repository that Vagrant will search for boxes if you use the account and box name of an image stored on its site:

```
vagrant init hashicorp/precise64
```

It is good to know both types of syntax because it will be necessary to use the old method for any boxes not hosted on Atlas. The online site is a great place to search for boxes for various operating systems instead of building your own.

The `vagrant init` command will automatically create a simple Vagrantfile that will reference the box that you specify. Listing 3-1 shows the default Vagrantfile that is generated with the command listed above.

Listing 3-1 Default Vagrantfile

```
# -*- mode: ruby -*-
# vi: set ft=ruby :

# Vagrantfile API/syntax version. Don't touch unless you know what you're
doing!
VAGRANTFILE_API_VERSION = "2"

Vagrant.configure(VAGRANTFILE_API_VERSION) do |config|
  config.vm.box = "hashicorp/precise64"
end
```

You'll notice that to save space I remove the comments that automatically get generated when you initialize your Vagrantfile. However, if you look in the comments, you'll see some helpful tips for using configuration management technology to make automated changes to your VM when it boots. As of today, the available options for provisioning your VM include basic shell scripts and configuration management tools such as Puppet, Chef, and Ansible. This is an immense value because your development and test environment can be stood up with the exact same settings that are used in your production deployments. This should cut down on the "well, it worked on my laptop" discussions that may go back and forth during a deployment mishap. Docker support was also added so that the provisioner could install the Docker daemon automatically and download the containers that you specify for use.

With your Vagrantfile in place, you can now boot your first test environment by using the following command:

```
vagrant up --provider=vmware_fusion
```

NOTE

If you're using VMware Workstation on the Windows or Linux platform, you would use a different provider: vmware_workstation.

You can now log in to the VM using the following command:

```
vagrant ssh
```

Take a look at a folder in your VM called /vagrant. You'll see that it contains your Vagrantfile! It's a shared folder that is automatically created for the VM so that you can easily transfer files to and from your desktop without having to use SCP, FTP, and so on.

If you examine the operating system resources, you'll notice that you have one vCPU and 512 MB of RAM. This may not be sufficient for the application that you want to run. So, we will take a look at how to modify the resources allocated to your Vagrant VM.

First, let's destroy this VM so that we can move on with the other configuration options. You can do this exiting the VM and then using the following command:

```
vagrant destroy
```

Vagrant will ask you to confirm that you really want to destroy this VM. Alternatively, you can use the `-f` option to skip that confirmation.

Listing 3-2 shows that Vagrant can modify the VM's VMX file to make the changes that we need. We use the `config.vm.provider` block of code to achieve this. By the way, the `memsize` attribute's units are megabytes. Notice that we are creating an object named v enclosed in vertical lines to change settings just for this VM. This object name has local scope only to this `config.vm.provider` statement, and it can be used again when defining other VMs, as you'll see in later examples. After executing `vagrant up`, the VM will be created with the desired attributes. At the time of this writing, the size and number of virtual disks cannot be controlled, but your Vagrant VMs will start with 40 GB of thin-provisioned storage.

Listing 3-2 Changing Default Vagrantfile

```
# -*- mode: ruby -*-
# vi: set ft=ruby :


# Vagrantfile API/syntax version. Don't touch unless you know what you're
doing!
VAGRANTFILE_API_VERSION = "2"
```

```
Vagrant.configure(VAGRANTFILE_API_VERSION) do |config|
  config.vm.box = "hashicorp/precise64"
  config.vm.provider :vmware_fusion do |v|
    v.vmx["memsize"] = 1024
    v.vmx["numvcpus"] = 2
  end
end
```

It is great that we can modify the VM's resources. What about a more complex setup, like multiple VMs? Vagrant supports such a topology as well. Of course, make sure that you have sufficient CPU cores and RAM to support the topology that you want to use! Multi-VM setups would be useful for testing realistic deployments with a separate database server and front-end server, for example. Listing 3-3 shows an example of a multi-VM Vagrantfile setup.

Listing 3-3 Multimachine Vagrantfile

```
# -*- mode: ruby -*-
# vi: set ft=ruby :

# Vagrantfile API/syntax version. Don't touch unless you know what you're
doing!
VAGRANTFILE_API_VERSION = "2"

Vagrant.configure(VAGRANTFILE_API_VERSION) do |config|
  config.vm.define :first do |vm1|
    vm1.vm.box = "hashicorp/precise64"
    vm1.vm.hostname = "devops"
    vm1.vm.provider :vmware_fusion do |v|
      v.vmx["memsize"] = 1024
      v.vmx["numvcpus"] = 2
    end
  end

  config.vm.define :second do |vm2|
    vm2.vm.box = "hashicorp/precise64"
```

```
    vm2.vm.hostname = "vmware"
    vm2.vm.provider :vmware_fusion do |v|
      v.vmx["memsize"] = 1024
      v.vmx["numvcpus"] = 2
    end
  end
end
```

The deployment utilizes multiple `config.vm.define` blocks of code: one for each VM that we are creating. `:first` and `:second` are labels that Vagrant will use to identify the two VMs when you run commands like `vagrant status`. These labels will also be used to connect to the VMs via Secure Shell (SSH)—for example, `vagrant ssh first`. If you're familiar with Ruby, you'll notice that these labels are Ruby symbols. The names in the enclosed pipe symbols (for example, `|vm1|`) denote the object whose information that vagrant is using to build and define your VM. The object name can be the same as the symbol (for example, `first.vm.box...`), but it doesn't have to be.

Using this syntax can be a bit tedious when you want to deploy more than two VMs. Thankfully, because Vagrant is written in Ruby, you can use the language's features such as lists, loops, and variables to optimize your Vagrantfile code. Listing 3-4 shows some optimization tips that I learned from Cody Bunch and Kevin Jackson in their *OpenStack Cloud Computing* book

Listing 3-4 Optimized Multimachine Vagrantfile

```
# -*- mode: ruby -*-
# vi: set ft=ruby :
servers = ['first','second']

Vagrant.configure("2") do |config|
  config.vm.box = "hashicorp/precise64"
  servers.each do |hostname|
    config.vm.define "#{hostname}" do |box|
      box.vm.hostname = "#{hostname}.devops.vmware.com"
      box.vm.provider :vmware_fusion do |v|
        v.vmx["memsize"] = 1024
        v.vmx["numvcpus"] = 2
      end
    end
  end
end
```

At the top of the file, I create a Ruby list called `servers` whose elements are the names of the VMs that I want to create. Then I use the Ruby list iterator called `each` to loop the execution of the VM definition for each element in the servers list. If we ever want to increase the number of VMs that are deployed, we just add more entries to the list. Not every VM needs to have the same set of resources, and we can use `if` statements within the `box.vm.provider` code block to be selective:

```
if hostname == "first"
  v.vmx["memsize"] = 3128
  v.vmx["numvcpus"] = 4
elsif hostname == "second"
  v.vmx["memsize"] = 1024
end
```

There are many more features in Vagrant that we will not be covering in this book, but with just these simple commands, you can build the test environment setups that we will be using in this book. If you'd like to learn more about Vagrant, be sure to check out the Vagrant website (http://www.vagrantup.com) and Mitchell's book, *Vagrant: Up and Running*.

Creating Images with Packer

Packer is another HashiCorp product that helps you to develop your own boxes for multiple platforms. Let's say you wanted to develop a VM image for Workstation/Fusion and ESXi from the same base box. Packer makes that possible.

Packer uses a JavaScript Object Notation (JSON) file format for you to specify how your Vagrant box will be configured (disk size, memory, and so on), and it will perform the initial OS deployment on your behalf once you specify the relevant automation parameters (for example, Ubuntu preseed files).

Packer is not just useful for creating Vagrant boxes; its main purpose is to produce image files that are compatible with popular cloud provider formats (OpenStack, AWS, and so forth). However, Packer includes a builder capability to automatically output Vagrant boxes that are compatible with VMware Fusion/Workstation and VirtualBox. Just like with Vagrant, popular configuration management technologies like Puppet and Chef can be used to customize the image that is produced.

Although we will not be discussing Packer in depth, we wanted you to be aware of it if you would like to experiment on your own with building custom Vagrant boxes. You can find more information about Packer at http://www.packer.io. If you would like to see examples of Packer definition files that you can use to develop your own VMs, the Chef team maintains a repository called *bento* on their Github account. https://github.com/chef/bento

Managing Source Code

Source code management (SCM) is an essential element in a DevOps environment. Think about it: If you will be turning your infrastructure into code, it is important that there is a way to review any changes and go back to different versions of a file in case new changes introduce problems (for instance, periodic instabilities in the best case, outages in the worst case). Some might think the "easy" way would be to make multiple copies of a file each with a unique name (Vagrantfile1, Vagrantfile2, Vagrantfile01012015, and so on), but then you have to deal with the hassle of renaming the file when you want to use it and trying to remember what was different about all the files.

The various teams in the development organization are most likely using some SCM system already to manage their work (for example, software developers storing their source code, QA teams managing their test scripts). As you begin using SCM technologies, it would be worthwhile discussing best practices with these other groups.

There are many SCM solutions, including SVN, Mercurial, and so on. Git happens to be one of the more popular SCM systems in the DevOps community. So, for this book, we use Git.

Using Git

Git is a distributed version control system, which means that you make a local copy of the central repository instead of just checking out individual files. Local commits can be synchronized back to the central server so that there is consistency in the environment, and users can always pull the latest version of the source from the central repository. This architecture differs from traditional source code management systems, in which only the central server ever has a complete copy of the repository.

As you work through the examples in this book, we recommend using one of the freely available online Git repositories, such as Bitbucket, GitHub, and Gitorious, as your central location for storing your code. Each site has its own unique features. For example, BitBucket allows unlimited free private repositories. GitHub is the online repository system that this book's authors used for their code. However, feel free to use whichever system meets your needs, as the methods by which you obtain code (clone/pull) and store code (push) are universal across any Git system.

NOTE

For projects in your production environment, consult with your legal department before considering using a public repository site. Although many offer private repository capabilities, your company leadership may prefer to use an internal central Git server.

Creating Your First Git Repository

First, install Git using your favorite package manager (for example, homebrew or macports on Mac OS X, apt-get on Ubuntu/Debian, yum on Red Hat/CentOS/Fedora). For Windows users, the popular online repositories like GitHub and BitBucket offer software clients that make it easy to interact with their online repository system. Alternatively, the http://git-scm.com site maintains a standalone install of the Git binary for Windows.

If you are using Linux or Mac OS X, you can open a terminal window to work with the following examples. Windows users must use the special shell that gets installed with whichever Git client that you use. The example syntax will be Linux/Mac-based, but the commands should be equivalent for the Windows platform.

Before we start writing any code, we need to set a couple global variables so that Git knows who we are. It's not as critical for local copies of the repository, but when we start pushing our code to a remote server, it will be very critical. The two global variables are your email address and username:

```
git config --global user.email "you@example.com"
git config --global user.name "Your Name"
```

As a matter of fact, if you try using Git and making your first commit without setting these variables, Git will prompt you to set them before you can continue.

If you followed along with the earlier Vagrant examples, you already have a directory of content that we can work with. Otherwise, create a new directory and create a text file in it. From here on out, make sure that you are in that directory on your command-line prompt.

First, let's initialize this directory to have a Git repository:

```
git init
```

If you do a listing of your directory with the option to show hidden files (`ls -a` on Linux/Mac or `dir /A:H` on Windows), you'll see that there is a hidden directory called .git. This directory contains your repository's files and settings specific to this repository. These local settings are combined with the global settings that we set earlier, and we can confirm this by using the following command:

```
git config -l
```

If you want to see the state of the files in your directory (has the file been added to the repository? Are there any changes since the last command? and so on), you can type **`git status`** and see output similar to what is shown in Listing 3-5.

Listing 3-5 Git Repository Status

```
git-test $ git status
On branch master

Initial commit

Untracked files:
  (use "git add <file>..." to include in what will be committed)

        .vagrant/
        Vagrantfile

nothing added to commit but untracked files present (use "git add" to track)
```

The last line is most important; it tells us that our files need to be tracked for the repository to manage it. This is important to take note of as putting files into the directory does not automatically get it tracked by the SCM tool. This feature prevents us from tracking junk files in the repository and wasting space.

Let's tell Git to track our Vagrantfile:

```
git add Vagrantfile
```

However, the .vagrant/ directory is not essential to be tracked because it only contains temporary files that Vagrant uses to set up your VM. We can explicitly tell Git to ignore this directory by creating a .gitignore file. Use your favorite text editor and create your .gitignore file with a single entry:

```
.vagrant/
```

Alternatively, you could use a simple `echo` command to accomplish the same thing. (Windows users will need to use the special Git Shell binary that is included with their Git install for this to work properly.)

```
echo '.vagrant/' > .gitignore
```

If you run the `git status` command again, you'll see that Git informs us about the .gitignore file as well. What gives? Remember that Git needs to be told what to do with any files or directories that the repository can see including the .gitignore file. Well, there are two ways to deal with your .gitignore file:

- Add the .gitignore file itself to the list of files and directories to ignore.
- Tell Git to track the .gitignore file as well.

I will use the second option so that anyone else who may use my repository will be able to ignore the appropriate files as well:

```
git add .gitignore
```

Now, if we check the status of the repository again, we should see output similar to what is shown in Listing 3-6.

Listing 3-6 Updated Repository Status

```
git-test $ git status
On branch master

Initial commit

Changes to be committed:
  (use "git rm --cached <file>..." to unstage)

        new file:   .gitignore
        new file:   Vagrantfile
```

All the files in our directory are either ready to be committed or added to the .gitignore list of nonessential files and directories. So, all that's left to do is to commit the repository changes:

```
git commit
```

A file editor will automatically be opened so that you can enter details about the files that you are committing. (By default, vi is used.) See Listing 3-7.

Listing 3-7 Your Commit Message

```
git-test $ git commit
This is my first commit.
# Please enter the commit message for your changes. Lines starting
# with '#' will be ignored, and an empty message aborts the commit.
# On branch master
#
# Initial commit
#
# Changes to be committed:
#       new file:   .gitignore
#       new file:   Vagrantfile
#
```

You must enter a message; otherwise, the commit will be canceled. If you are not familiar with vi, press I, type some text, press the Escape key, and then type **:wq** and press Enter. If you don't want to deal with the text editor, you can use the short form of the `git commit` command with the `-m` option to enter your commit message on the same line:

```
git commit -m "This is my first commit."
```

If the commit is successful, you should see the following output:

```
[master (root-commit) d962cd6] This is my first commit.
 2 files changed, 119 insertions(+)
 create mode 100644 .gitignore
 create mode 100644 Vagrantfile
```

Working with a Central Git Server (a.k.a. A Remote)

If you have opened an account on either GitHub, BitBucket, or whatever public Git repository site that you prefer, you will need to provide your computer's SSH public key to the site so that it can verify who you are. Each site may have a different way of doing this. So, consult the documentation for the appropriate steps. For Windows users, this is typically handled for you automatically by installing the client software for the site. Mac and Linux users must generate an SSH public key by using the `ssh-keygen` command.

Once your SSH public key is properly configured on your remote, it's time to create the repository on the remote site that you will be storing your files into: a process known as *pushing*. When you create your remote repository on the website, you should skip the automatic generation of the README file. After the repository is created, the site will provide you with a link that you can use to tell your local repository what is the location of your remote server, often labeled as origin.

In my setup, I gave the same name to my repository as I did to my local repository. This is optional, and the names can differ. I can use the `git remote` command with the link that GitHub gave me to update my local repository settings:

```
git remote add origin git@github.com:DevOpsForVMwareAdministrators/git
```

If I use the `git config -l` command, I will see new data about the location of my remote server:

```
remote.origin.url=git@github.com:DevOpsForVMwareAdministrators/git-test.git
remote.origin.fetch=+refs/heads/*:refs/remotes/origin/*
```

I can now push the files from my local repository to my remote repository:

```
git push origin master
```

I should see output similar to what is shown in Listing 3-8.

Listing 3-8 Git Remote Push Results

```
git-test $ git push origin master
Warning: Permanently added the RSA host key for IP address '196.30.252.129'
to the list of known hosts.
Counting objects: 4, done.
Delta compression using up to 8 threads.
Compressing objects: 100% (3/3), done.
Writing objects: 100% (4/4), 2.13 KiB | 0 bytes/s, done.
Total 4 (delta 0), reused 0 (delta 0)
To git@github.com:DevOpsForVMwareAdministrators/git-test.git
 * [new branch]      master -> master
```

Figure 3-1 shows what the repository looks like on GitHub after I push the first commit to the remote server.

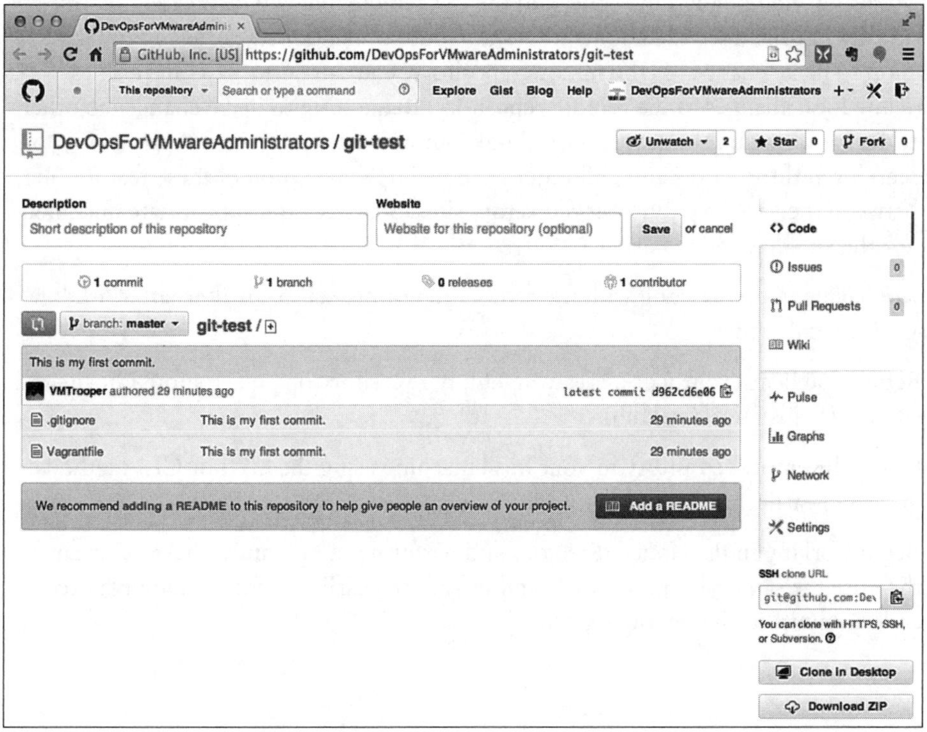

Figure 3-1 Remote Git repository

If there is a remote repository that you want to use, like the samples we're providing for this book, you can either use CLI-based methods or GUI-based methods to clone the remote repository to your local machine. Your remote repository system should have options similar to what is pictured on the lower-right corner of Figure 3-1.

The GUI-based methods will differ according to the site you are using. However, on GitHub, you can either use the Clone in Desktop button if you are using its Mac or Windows client, or you can use the Download Zip button, which will be a simple zip file that contains all the source code of the repository. If you are using the Windows or Mac platform, the Clone in Desktop option is recommended because it will create your Git remote link to the remote repository automatically.

The CLI-based method involves taking the SSH or HTTP clone URL and using the `git clone` command, similar to the following:

```
git clone https://github.com/DevOpsForVMwareAdministrators/git-test.git
```

After executing this command, Git will create a directory with the name of the repository (in this case, git-test) and copy the contents of the repository into that directory. You can begin using and updating the code, and the Git remote link will be created for you automatically just like with the Clone in Desktop button mentioned earlier. If you have permission to make changes to the remote repository, you can perform a Git push to forward any local changes to the remote repository. Requesting to make changes to others' repositories is not within the scope of this book; but if you are interested in the topic, you can research repository forks and pull requests. The implementation of these features may differ between the various public Git repository sites. So, check the appropriate documentation for the site that you are using.

If you are having issues working with the remote repository setup, an alternate workflow consists of the following:

1. Before you begin your work, create an empty repository on your remote Git site of choice (for instance, GitHub).
2. Clone the empty repository to your local machine using the GUI or CLI methods discussed earlier.
3. Begin working in the cloned directory and perform your commits there. You can then use the same `git push` command introduced earlier to forward your source code commits to the remote repository.

Summary

We discussed the foundational tools that we will use throughout the book to build our test environments, namely Vagrant and Git. Vagrant is useful for building your test environments quickly, and Git will help you keep track of changes that you make to your environment definitions in case you need to undo a change. In the next chapter, we begin discussing the Puppet configuration management technology with hands-on examples.

References

[1] http://docs.vagrantup.com/v2/

[2] https://help.github.com/

Chapter 4

Introduction to Puppet

Puppet is the configuration management solution developed by Puppet Labs, Inc. Puppet is available in two distributions: open source and Puppet Enterprise, which is commercially supported. Because Puppet Enterprise is required for the VMware provisioning capabilities, we focus on that particular distribution of Puppet. However, the majority of the functionality discussed in this chapter applies to the open source distribution as well.

Topics covered in this chapter include the following:

- Puppet architecture
- Puppet resources
- Puppet manifests
- Puppet modules

Puppet Architecture

Every item that can be managed by Puppet is referred to as a *Puppet resource*. Server packages, configuration files, and services are all examples of resources that can be managed by Puppet. Resource instructions are grouped into files that are known as *Puppet manifests*. If you want to deploy the Apache web server, as discussed later in this chapter, you would group together resources for the Apache web server package, configuration file, and service into the same manifest file. If you want to group your manifests with supplemental files such as your configuration files, your web content files, and so on into an easily distributable package, Puppet provides a construct known as a *Puppet module* just for that purpose. A module may have multiple manifests and other files. We discuss resources, manifests, and modules more in depth later in this chapter.

For now, we focus on popular Puppet deployment options for your environment. Puppet has two deployment topologies: standalone and master-agent.

Standalone Deployment

In the standalone configuration, each host is managed individually using the Puppet agent software installed locally. The manifest files are stored locally, and the agent compiles the configuration management instructions into a catalog of instructions for the agent to execute. See Figure 4-1 for an illustration.

By default, the Puppet agent compiles and executes the catalog every 30 minutes if it is running in daemon mode. Alternatively, if the agent is not running in daemon mode, it can be executed using some other scheduling mechanism, such as cron, or by using an orchestration system like MCollective. System administrators can keep the manifests updated using a synchronization technology, such as rsync, to distribute the files from a central repository.

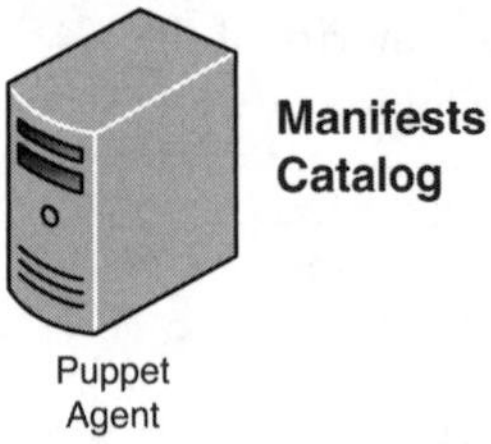

Figure 4-1 Puppet standalone topology

Master-Agent Deployment

The master-agent topology consists of one or more Puppet agent servers designated to become master servers. These Puppet masters run additional binaries to centrally manage all of the agent nodes, as illustrated in Figure 4-2.

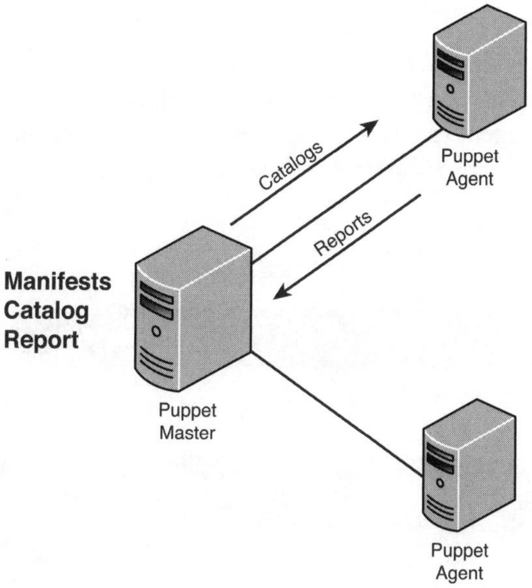

Figure 4-2 Puppet master agent topology

One significant difference in this topology is that the master centrally stores all manifests. The master will determine which Puppet code is executed by each agent by entries found in the site.pp file that it stores locally (/etc/puppetlabs/puppet/environments/production/manifests for Enterprise and /etc/puppet/manifests for open source). The master compiles the manifests into catalogs and transmits them to the agents to execute. The agent then reports the status of the Puppet run back to the master.

Puppet Master Components

In addition to the Puppet Master binaries, the master server will run the following components:

- Console
- PuppetDB
- MCollective orchestration
- Cloud provisioning

Console

The Console is the web interface that aggregates reports of Puppet agents' activities. From here, the system administrator can perform such tasks as creating/assigning/removing groups and classes, ad hoc Puppet agent run executions, and so on. The Console component is only available with Puppet Enterprise. Figure 4-3 shows the Puppet Enterprise Console.

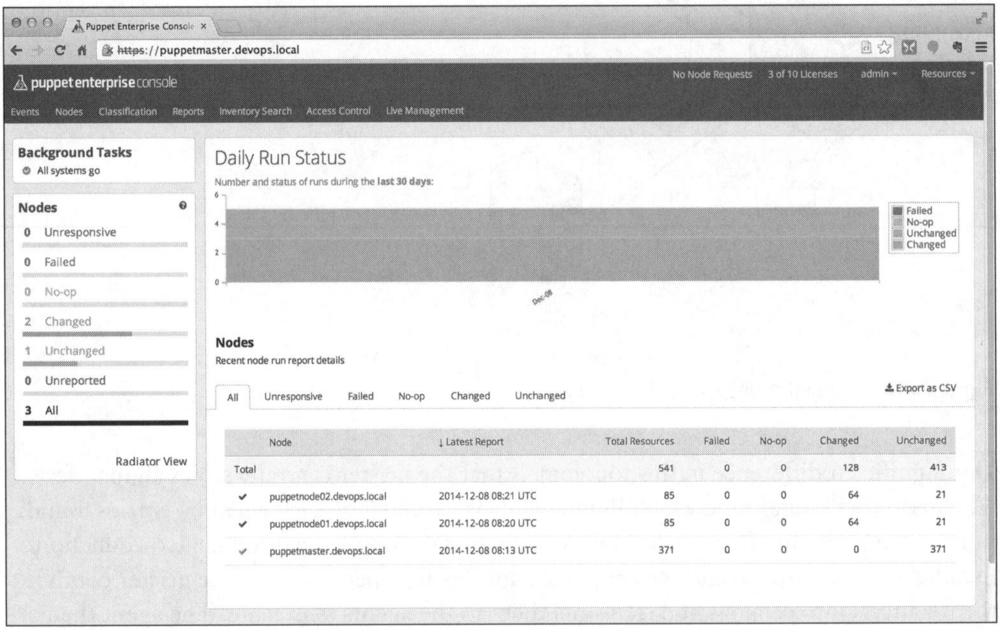

Figure 4-3 Puppet Enterprise Console home page

The Console home page allows the system administrator to see a list of the nodes currently managed by the Puppet master. The menu items on the top left of the page enable the user to perform the various administrative tasks listed earlier.

PuppetDB

PuppetDB stores catalogs, facts, and reports in an indexed, persistent format in a PostgreSQL database for reporting purposes. It was introduced in 2012 as a separate module, but it is now a required component of the Puppet master architecture. For a production deployment, it is advisable to install the PuppetDB component on a dedicated server.

MCollective (Marionette Collective)

MCollective is orchestration software for executing tasks on multiple nodes. The MCollective components communicate via a message bus system (ActiveMQ by default) for asynchronous management of the nodes in your environment. MCollective is included with Puppet Enterprise to enable the "live management" capabilities such as triggering ad hoc Puppet runs. However, MCollective can be used with open source Puppet as well.

Cloud Provisioning

This capability enables provisioning of cloud workloads to VMware vSphere, Amazon EC2, and Google Compute Engine environments. Administrative tasks include creating new virtual machines (VMs), automatic deployment of the Puppet agent on the VMs, and adding VMs to classes so that they can have Puppet code automatically executed on them. VMware vSphere provisioning is only possible with Puppet Enterprise.

Preparing Your Puppet Test Lab

The examples in Chapters 4–6 use Puppet Enterprise in the master-agent topology. The environment should consist of three virtual machines:

- **Puppet master:** Ubuntu (12.04 or later)
- **Puppet agent 1:** Ubuntu (12.04 or later)
- **Puppet agent 2:** CentOS (6.5 or later)

The fully-qualified domain names for my virtual machines are puppetmaster.devops.local, puppetnode01.devops.local, and puppetnode02.devops.local, respectively. The quickest way to set up the environment is to use Vagrant (discussed in Chapter 3). Make sure to provide at least 4 GB of RAM to the Puppet master VM. Puppet agent RAM allocations can be a bit more modest at 512 MB. This book's GitHub page has a sample Vagrantfile that you can use as a base to start building your test lab.

Download the Puppet Enterprise software from the Puppet Labs website, and follow its instructions to deploy the software. Make sure to select the Puppet Master, Console, PuppetDB, and Cloud Provisioning options when installing to your lab's master server. Your Puppet agent nodes only require the Puppet Agent option when installing, but they will need to have DNS, or /etc/hosts, entries that will point them to the Puppet master. By default, the agent nodes will look for the master using a hostname/alias called *puppet*. This book's GitHub page also includes sample answer files that you can use to automate your Puppet Enterprise installs.

When installation is complete, the Puppet agent nodes will be waiting for the Puppet master to sign their cert requests and begin communication. You can do so by logging in to the master server and executing the following command:

```
puppet cert sign --all
```

This will automatically kick off a Puppet run on the agents. Because we do not have any Puppet manifests defined yet, the agents will just report their facts back to the master. Your environment is now ready for the examples that follow.

Puppet Resources

Resources are the building blocks of Puppet's configuration management scripts (that is, manifests). See Figure 4-4 for a sample Puppet resource.

Figure 4-4 A Puppet resource of type file

A number of elements make up a resource:

- **Type:** The kind of resource that will be configured (package, file, and so on). There are many resource types, and you can see a more complete listing of types on the Puppet Labs website (http://docs.puppetlabs.com/learning/ral.html).
- **Title:** How the configuration management script will refer to the resource.
- **Attributes:** The settings that you specify for the resource. Different resource types will have different attributes.
- **Providers:** The utilities associated with how the configuration management script will refer to the resource.

Providers are not usually explicitly declared in the resource statement. Puppet utilizes the correct provider automatically according to the resource type (for example, yum for installing packages on Red Hat–based operating systems). If you ever define your own Puppet type, you may also need to specify which provider to use. Developing custom types is beyond the scope of this book, but it is great to know that Puppet Labs allows that kind of flexibility.

Before we move on from resources, there is a special resource attribute to be aware of: namevar. It is the value that Puppet uses to identify the resource you are declaring, and it must be unique. If you declare the name attribute, the namevar attribute takes this value. If you do not declare a name variable, the namevar is set to the title of the resource. Why is this important to know? Puppet resources must have unique namevar values. Otherwise, you will get errors when it is time to execute the Puppet manifest. It is a good idea to explicitly name your resources.

Puppet Manifests

Manifests are collections of resources. They are the configuration scripts that administrators use to manage the servers in their environments. The system administrator can define special attributes to relate various resources together. This gives the administrator flexibility with how the manifest is structured.

Puppet does not necessarily process your manifest in the order that it is written. So, if there is a preferred order in which your resources should be handled, Puppet has special attributes, known as *metaparameters*, to define relationships between the resources in your manifests. These attributes are `before`, `require`, `notify`, and `subscribe`. The use of metaparameters is unique to Puppet, and it is important that you keep them in mind if there is a preferred order of execution for your manifests. Listing 4-1 shows an example of the use of `require` and `subscribe` statements.

Listing 4-1 Puppet Manifest for an Apache Web Server

```
package { 'apache':
        name    => 'httpd',
        ensure => installed,
}

file {'apacheconf':
        name     => '/etc/httpd/conf/httpd.conf',
        ensure   => file,
        mode     => 600,
        source   => '/etc/puppet/files/httpd.conf',
        require => Package['apache'],
}
```

```
service {'apache':
        name      => 'httpd',
        ensure    => running,
        enable    => true,
        subscribe => File['apacheconf'],
}
```

The manifest in Listing 4-1 will work on a CentOS server (that is, Puppet agent 2). You will need to type the code into a manifest file on the agent server, and be sure to use the pp extension in the filename. The manifest requires an Apache configuration file (see the file resource) that is compatible with the CentOS version that you are running. Be sure to change the file resource's source attribute to reflect where you store the Apache configuration file. Even if the configuration file is in the same directory as your manifest, provide the explicit path.

Let's pause here to give you a chance to execute the code on your test machine. Remember, the command to execute your manifest is as follows:

```
puppet apply filename.pp
```

If you would like to observe what the puppet code is doing, you can use the `-d` option with the `apply` command.

Now, getting back to the sample code: The `require` metaparameter in the file resource will ensure that the specified resource (`Package["apache"]`) exists before its own resource (`file('apacheconf')`) is deployed. This makes sense because there is no point in trying to deploy a configuration file for a service that does not exist!

The `subscribe` metaparameter behaves similarly to `require`, with an extra functionality: Puppet will monitor the target resource for any changes and perform an appropriate action in response. For a service resource, this would mean restarting the service after detecting a change in the configuration file.

> **NOTE**
>
> You might have noticed that I am capitalizing the Puppet type name when indicating the order relationship to an existing resource (for example, `subscribe => File['apacheconf']`). This is a Puppet convention. When you initially declare a resource, the type name is lowercase, and when you refer to it later on in the manifest, the first letter of the type name is uppercase.

The `before` and `notify` metaparameters are the opposite of `require` and `subscribe`, respectively. If we used `before` and `notify` in our manifest, it would look similar to Listing 4-2.

Listing 4-2 Alternative Puppet Manifest for an Apache Web Server

```
package { 'apache':
        name   => 'httpd',
        ensure => installed,
        before => File['apacheconf'],
}

file {'apacheconf':
        name    => '/etc/httpd/conf/httpd.conf',
        ensure  => file,
        mode    => 600,
        source  => '/etc/puppet/files/httpd.conf',
        notify => Service['apache'],
}

service {'apache':
        name      => 'httpd',
        ensure    => running,
        enable    => true,
}
```

There is another way to define relationships, and that's with *chaining arrows* (`->` for `before/require` relationships and `~>` for `notify\subscribe` relationships). In lieu of the metaparameter statements, the arrows can be placed between the resource declarations, as shown in Listing 4-3.

Listing 4-3 Puppet Manifest Written with Chaining Arrows

```
package { 'apache':
        name   => 'httpd',
        ensure => installed,
}
->
file {'apacheconf':
```

```
        name    => '/etc/httpd/conf/httpd.conf',
        ensure  => file,
        mode    => 600,
        source  => '/etc/puppet/files/httpd.conf',
}
~>
service {'apache':
        name      => 'httpd',
        ensure    => running,
        enable    => true,
}
```

As an alternative to placing the relationship arrows between the resources, you can just declare the resources and at the end of your manifest include the resource titles with the arrows drawn between them as follows:

```
Package['apache'] ->

File['apacheconf'] ~>

Service['apache']
```

There isn't a preferred method for defining the resource ordering. However, it is advised that your team decides on a convention that will be easiest for everyone to understand.

You can get creative with the placement of your resources in the manifest, but we recommend adopting a logical progression when writing your Puppet code. (For instance, if resource B depends on resource A, list resource A before B in the manifest.) This will make it easier for other team members to understand the intentions of your workflow. Also, in a year's time, you might not even remember what your thought processes were when you wrote the manifest. As much as is possible, keep things simple.

NOTE

You may be wondering, "Why not just execute the Puppet code in the order that we write it?"

Even long-time Puppet users have given similar feedback, and Puppet has implemented manifest order analysis of resources (MOAR) starting with Puppet 3.3.0. MOAR will eventually become the default behavior in future releases of open source Puppet and Puppet Enterprise. However, users who prefer the current behavior (a.k.a. title hash) will be able to enable it.

The preceding examples show the quintessential approach to writing Puppet manifests: package-file-system. You specify which package should be deployed, the related configuration or content files for that package, and the service state (running, stopped, and so forth) of the package. It's a great model to follow when you begin writing Puppet code regularly.

Conditional Expressions and Variables

Basic manifests such as the one shown earlier are powerful. However, you may want to make modifications to the way the manifest executes according to the properties of the system that is executing the manifest. Also, if the name of the package ever changes, editing your code can become a bit tedious because the package name change will most likely affect other resources (configuration file path, service state commands, and so forth).

For these and other reasons, Puppet allows the use of variables and conditional expressions. In addition, a binary called *facter* is included when Puppet is installed, and it automatically generates a list of variables that describe server characteristics that are referred to as facts (Is this a physical machine or virtual machine? What is the IP address? What is the operating system? and so on). Facts can be accessed from the command line by running the `facter` command. You explore individual facts by specifying them when you run the `facter` command (`facter is_virtual`, `facter ipaddress`, `facter operatingsystem`, and so on). All facts are available at runtime to your Puppet manifest.

All variable labels are prefixed with a $ sign in your manifest file, including the automatically generated facts (`$is_virtual` and so forth). Your variables do not need to have a type declared such as string or int. Just like with Ruby, Puppet understands which type of variable you are declaring by the value that you initialize it with.

When using variables in your code with string values, it is necessary to use double quotation marks instead of single quotation marks. The inclusion of a variable's data in a string is known as *interpolation*, as illustrated by the use of the `$webserver` variable in the following code example:

```
$webserver='httpd'
file {'apacheconf':
        name    => "/etc/$webserver/conf/$webserver.conf",
        ensure  => file,
        mode    => 600,
        source  => "/etc/puppet/files/$webserver.conf",
        require => Package['apache'],

}
```

If you are concerned with making mistakes with single quotes versus double quotes or other Puppet syntax items, there are helpful integrated development environment (IDE) and text editor plugins such as Geppetto and Sublime Text's Puppet bundle that support Puppet syntax highlighting. These tools can prove helpful for avoiding mistakes with quotes and other Puppet conventions.

Conditional statements allow you to fully take advantage of the power of puppet variables. The conditional statements supported in Puppet are `if` and `case`. Going back to my Apache deployment example from earlier, the name of the Apache package varies based on the operating system flavor that you deploy. For example, on Red Hat-based systems, the Apache binary is known as httpd. On Debian-based systems, the package is known as apache2. I will be using the `operatingsystem` fact to determine the appropriate settings to use in my manifest.

Here is an example using an `if` conditional:

```
if $operatingsystem == 'centos' {
      $webserver= 'httpd'
      $confpath = "/etc/$webserver/conf/$webserver.conf"
  }
elsif $operatingsystem == 'ubuntu': {
      $webserver= 'apache2'
      $confpath = "/etc/$webserver/$webserver.conf"
  }
else {
  fail("Unsupported OS")
}
```

Here is an example using a `case` conditional:

```
case $operatingsystem {
  centos: {
      $webserver= 'httpd'
      $confpath = "/etc/$webserver/conf/$webserver.conf"
  }
  ubuntu: {
      $webserver= 'apache2'
      $confpath = "/etc/$webserver/$webserver.conf"
  }
  default: {
      fail("Unsupported OS")
  }
}
```

In the preceding examples, I use the `operatingsystem` fact to make decisions about the values for the two variables that I declare. If the server that I'm running this script on is neither a Red Hat–based nor a Debian-based operating system, I generate a failure notification for the manifest execution because it is an unexpected environment.

For conditional checks that decide between one or two values, `if` statements may be preferable. However, if you need to select from a long list of value options, you may want to use `case` statements instead.

After I add my `case` statement and variables, the earlier Apache manifest would look something like Listing 4-4.

Listing 4-4 Puppet Manifest Using Conditional Statements to Support Multiple Platforms

```
case $operatingsystem {
  centos: {
      $webserver= 'httpd'
      $confpath = "/etc/$webserver/conf/$webserver.conf"
  }
  ubuntu: {
      $webserver= 'apache2'
      $confpath = "/etc/$webserver/$webserver.conf"
  }
  default: {
      fail("Unsupported OS")
  }
}

package { 'apache':
       name    => $webserver,
       ensure => installed,
}

file {'apacheconf':
       name     => $confpath,
       ensure   => file,
       mode     => 600,
       source   => "/etc/puppet/files/$webserver.conf",
       require => Package['apache'],
}

service {'apache':
```

```
        name       => $webserver,
        ensure     => running,
        enable     => true,
        subscribe => File['apacheconf'],
}
```

Puppet Modules

Puppet modules allow system administrators to group useful puppet code for reuse in future manifests. Let's consider the Apache deployment example. Every time that I want to deploy a new Apache host, I would need to copy and paste that code over and over again into new manifests. The problem with this approach is if I want to change the way I deploy Apache, I will edit multiple puppet manifests to make the desired changes.

To promote efficient code reuse, Puppet Labs designed the Puppet class functionality. The concept is similar to the classes in object-oriented programming languages. Don't worry though; we won't be going too deep into computer science theory.

Classes can be used within a manifest, but they are more useful when they are packaged into a module that can be used by other manifests.

Let's first take a look at how to set up a Puppet class. We'll start by modifying our Apache deployment manifest, as shown in Listing 4-5.

Listing 4-5 Creating a Puppet Class from an Existing Manifest

```
class apache {
  case $operatingsystem {
    centos: {
        $webserver= 'httpd'
        $confpath = "/etc/$webserver/conf/$webserver.conf"
    }
    ubuntu: {
        $webserver= 'apache2'
        $confpath = "/etc/$webserver/$webserver.conf"
    }
    default: {
        fail("Unsupported OS")
    }

  }
```

```
    package { 'apache':
         name   => $webserver,
         ensure => installed,
    }

    file {'apacheconf':
         name    => $confpath,
         ensure  => file,
         mode    => 600,
         source  => "/etc/puppet/files/$webserver.conf",
         require => Package['apache'],
    }

    service {'apache':
         name      => $webserver,
         ensure    => running,
         enable    => true,
         subscribe => File['apacheconf'],
    }
}
include apache
```

Whew! That was hard. We added a whole three lines. In all seriousness, all that is required to change your manifest into a class is to prepend `class` *`name`* `{` to the manifest and append `}`. Then, you tell the manifest to include the class.

If you would like to specify parameters for your class, that is possible as well. For example, if you want to instruct Puppet to deploy a particular landing page, you could define your class as follows:

```
class apache($landingpage = "/etc/puppet/files/index.html") {
<your manifest code>
}
include apache
```

We define a single parameter (`$landingpage`), and set a default value with the assignment operator. If the manifest author doesn't specify any parameters, as I did earlier, the default value is used.

Again, classes are great, but if you want to easily reuse them, you need to turn them into Puppet modules. Modules need to be placed in a location specified by the `modulepath`

Puppet setting, which is user configurable. If you are using Puppet Enterprise, your modules can be placed in either /etc/puppetlabs/puppet/environments/production/modules, /etc/puppetlabs/puppet/modules, or /opt/puppet/share/puppet/modules. If you are using open source Puppet, your modules can be placed in /etc/puppet/modules or /usr/share/puppet/modules. You can verify your system's module path setting using the `puppet config print modulepath` command on the master server.

Puppet Forge

Before we delve deeper into module creation, I want to introduce Puppet Labs' online repository for sharing modules: the Puppet Forge (accessible at http://forge.puppetlabs.com). You can think of it almost as a GitHub for Puppet modules. On the Forge website, you can find modules contributed and supported by the Puppet user community as well as by Puppet Labs.

Open a free account on the Forge site so that you can reserve your username. I recommend using the same username as your GitHub account. We will be using your Puppet Forge username during the module creation. So, keep it handy.

Now that you have a Puppet Forge account, create a repository on Github. Since we are creating a web server module, go ahead and name the repository "apache." For now, the repository will be a placeholder until you set it up as the remote for your local repository later.

Creating Your First Puppet Module

Modules require a specific tree structure for Puppet manifests to properly access them. The good news is that you do not have to create the directory structure manually. Puppet includes a command to generate the module directory folders correctly.

First, change to a directory that you have selected for working with the examples in this book. Then, use the following command to begin the module directory path creation:

```
puppet module generate username-modulename
```

It is safe to accept the default values or leave values blank for which you do not have input. When the utility asks you for the source code repository, you can specify the HTTP link for the GitHub repository that I asked you to create before. If you make a mistake with any of the responses, you can edit the metadata.json file that gets produced.

Before we move on, we need to make a few changes to the generated directory structure so that we can use it properly with our examples. The `puppet module generate` command assumes that you are building a module to be shared on the Puppet Forge website, and the directory's naming convention reflects that with the username-module format. This will prevent our code from working properly locally. Also, we are missing two important subdirectories: *files* and *templates*. Let's fix these items.

First, change the name of the directory from username-modulename to just modulename. For example, I would change my directory name from vmtrooper-apache to apache. Next, create the subdirectories called templates and files under the apache directory. Figure 4-5 shows an example of the corrected directory structure. Without these corrections, you will encounter challenges with the sample code in this chapter.

```
apache
├── checksums.json
├── files
├── Gemfile
├── manifests
│   ├── init.pp
├── metadata.json
├── Rakefile
├── README.md
├── spec
│   ├── classes
│   │   └── init_spec.rb
│   └── spec_helper.rb
├── templates
└── tests
    └── init.pp
```

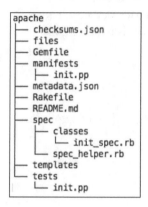

Figure 4-5 A Puppet module directory structure

The critical folder is manifests, which will contain any Puppet code that is relevant to the module. Standard module convention is to have a special manifest file called init.pp that defines the class. You can place code in other manifest files. However, at a minimum, the init.pp file must exist in the manifests directory. We'll show an example of that, but first, let's describe the other important components that make up a module:

- **files:** All the files that you want to distribute during the manifest execution (for example, the apache configuration file) need to be placed here. As you'll see in the init.pp example that follows, this will allow us to use a new method of accessing the files, which is a bit cleaner and helps us avoid path problems.
- **lib:** If you write any custom facts or types, place that code here.
- **spec:** This folder contains any tests for the custom code in the lib folder.
- **templates:** If you would like to deploy configuration or content files with your package that change based on runtime information, you place them here with some Embedded RuBy (ERB) code included.
- **tests:** This folder contains any examples that you want to include to show people how to use your module.

- **metadata.json:** This file contains the module version number in the semver format as well as the rest of the data that you provided with the `puppet module generate` command.

Now is a good time to initialize the Git repository for your module, specify your GitHub repository as the module's remote repository, and perform your first commit and push back to origin. Your virtual machine (VM) might not already have Git installed. So, use the operating system's package manager to install it. As you progress throughout this chapter, make sure to commit your work regularly so that you can back out any changes that cause issues. If you need a refresher on the relevant Git commands to accomplish these tasks, flip back to Chapter 3.

Puppet Module Initialization Manifest (init.pp)

As shown in Listing 4-6, the manifest code that we've been working with would go into the init.pp file with a minor change.

Listing 4-6 The init.pp File for Our Apache Web Server Module

```
class apache {
  case $operatingsystem {
    centos: {
        $webserver= 'httpd'
        $confpath = "/etc/$webserver/conf/$webserver.conf"
    }
    ubuntu: {
        $webserver= 'apache2'
        $confpath = "/etc/$webserver/$webserver.conf"
    }
    default: {
        fail("Unsupported OS")
    }

  }

  package { 'apache':
       name   => $webserver,
       ensure => installed,
  }

  file {'apacheconf':
```

```
        name     => $confpath,
        ensure   => file,
        mode     => 600,
        source   => "puppet:///modules/apache/$webserver.conf",
        require => Package['apache'],
    }

    service {'apache':
        name       => $webserver,
        ensure     => running,
        enable     => true,
        subscribe => File['apacheconf'],
    }
}
```

The entire class definition will go into the init.pp file, which, in my default installation, will be placed in the /etc/puppetlabs/puppet/modules/apache/manifests/ directory.

Before we move on, let's focus on the file resource. If you look at the source attribute, you'll see a different path than we used previously. The path utilizes a special puppet URL format.

An additional benefit of using a module is that puppet treats your module path almost like a file server. The prefix `puppet:///modules/apache/` tells puppet to look for the source file in the files subdirectory of the apache module found in your Puppet master's `modulepath` (that is, /etc/puppetlabs/puppet/modules/apache/files). If you create a directory within the files directory, you just insert it in front of the filename, such as `puppet:///modules/apache/subdirectory/$webserver.conf`.

So, regardless of the system your manifest is running from, you do not need to worry about the full path of where you place files. Just place them in /etc/puppetlabs/puppet/modules/apache/files/.

Templates

Before we wrap up our module discussion, let's examine how to use templates to make our deployments a bit more flexible. We could use a single configuration file template instead of having different files for CentOS and for Debian. However, a discussion of the various options and Apache configuration file is beyond the scope of this book. Instead, we will work with a simpler example for our discussion, such as the content of an index.html file. The default web page will tell our user what kind of operating system is running the web server. In practice, this is not the kind of information we would want publicized to malicious users. However, this simple example shows you how templates can prove useful.

First, we create a file called index.html.erb in our apache module's templates directory, and it will contain the following content:

```
<html><body><h1>Puppet Rocks!</h1>
<p>This is the default web page for
<%# Print the correct Operating System name with the right article i.e. "a"
  vs "an"%>
<% if @operatingsystem[0].chr =~/[AEIOU]/ %>
  <%= "an" %>
<% else %>
  <%= "a" %>
<% end %>
<b><%= @operatingsystem %></b> server.</p>
<p>The web server software is running and content has been added by your
  <b>Puppet</b> code.</p>
</body></html>
```

Note that there are different prefixes to the blocks of Ruby code:

- `<%=` is for any values that you want output into the file that you are generating from the template (for example, the operating system name and the *a* or *an* article).
- `<%#` is for comments to explain what the template code is supposed to be doing for anyone editing the file.
- `<%` is for Ruby code such as conditional statements or loops. This proves useful if you want to output multiple lines of values based on entries in an array, list, hash, and so forth. The conditional statement that we are including in index.html.erb utilizes Ruby's regular expression capabilities to verify whether the operating system's name begins with a vowel or a consonant.

Next, we modify our apache class to have an additional file resource for the default web page. We will add a relationship metaparameter so that the HTML file isn't deployed before the Apache web server is fully up and running. Also, we need to be aware of the path where the index.html file will be deployed because the default path differs for CentOS and Ubuntu. We will add a new variable called `htmlpath` to account for this, and our Puppet code will now look like the code sample in Listing 4-7.

Listing 4-7 Updated Apache Class with the index.html ERB Template

```
class apache {
  case $operatingsystem {
    centos: {
        $webserver= 'httpd'
        $confpath = "/etc/$webserver/conf/$webserver.conf"
```

```
        $htmlpath = "/var/www/html/index.html"
    }
    ubuntu: {
        $webserver= 'apache2'
        $confpath = "/etc/$webserver/$webserver.conf"
        $htmlpath = "/var/www/index.html"
    }
    default: {
        fail("Unsupported OS")
    }

  }

  package { 'apache':
      name   => $webserver,
      ensure => installed,
  }

  file {'apacheconf':
      name    => $confpath,
      ensure  => file,
      mode    => 600,
      source  => "puppet:///modules/apache/$webserver.conf",
      require => Package['apache'],
  }

  service {'apache':
      name      => $webserver,
      ensure    => running,
      enable    => true,
      subscribe => File['apacheconf'],
  }
  file {'apachecontent':
      name    => $htmlpath,
      ensure  => file,
      mode    => 644,
      content => template('apache/index.html.erb'),
      require => Service['apache'],
  }
}
```

There are a couple differences between using a static file and a template with a file resource. With templates, we use the `content` attribute in the file resource instead of the `source` attribute. The `content` attribute is normally used to specify the actual content of the file. If we use the `template` keyword with the `content` attribute, Puppet will insert the content of the template file, as it processes the ERB code, into the target file.

The `content` attribute isn't the only difference; the path that you specify with the `template` keyword differs as compared to the path used with the source attribute. The format is as follows:

```
<module name>/<template filename>
```

In our sample code, the module's name is apache, and the template filename is index.html.erb. The template file must be placed in the templates directory of the module's path (/etc/puppetlabs/puppet/modules/apache/templates/).

Using a Puppet Module

In your original manifest, the only code needed to deploy the Apache web server is simply the following:

```
include apache
```

If you define an additional class as part of your module (for example, `vhost`), it could be used in the manifest by making the following call:

```
include apache::vhost
```

Final Step: Version Control Commit

We've done a lot of work for our Apache web server module. Before we close out the chapter, do not forget to commit your changes and push the commit to your remote repository. We will use this module again by cloning it from the remote repository in Chapter 5.

Summary

This chapter covered quite a number of Puppet features and concepts. We started out with a discussion of Puppet architecture. Then we moved on to the Puppet resources, which are the objects to be managed by Puppet (for example, packages, configuration files, and services). Next, we discussed how those resources are combined into an instruction file known as Puppet manifest. The chapter also explained how Puppet modules, which are collections of related manifests, can be used to deploy applications according to user specifications. In the next chapter, you will work through a potential Linux-Apache-MySQL-PHP (LAMP) stack deployment. Before you move on, though, if you would like to practice some more Puppet technology basics, check out the Learning Puppet VM available from the Puppet Labs website.

Reference

[1] "Puppet 3 Reference Manual": http://docs.puppetlabs.com/puppet/3/reference/

Chapter 5

Systems Management Tasks with Puppet

Puppet is useful for quickly deploying and configuring your critical applications. In this chapter, we investigate a multitier deployment that includes a web server, an application server, and a database server tier. Such combinations of applications are often referred to as *LAMP* (Linux-Apache-MySQL-PHP) *deployments*. The various letters in the acronym may change based on actual modules installed (for example, LEMP when nginx [pronounced "engine X"] is used instead of Apache).

We will build on the work that we have done so far with deploying the Apache web server in the preceding chapter to flesh out the entire LAMP stack. For the examples in this chapter, we use the three-node setup introduced in Chapter 4: one Puppet master server (puppetmaster.devops.local), and two Puppet agent servers (puppetnode01.devops.local and puppetnode02.devops.local). Your module code needs to be stored on the Puppet master's `modulepath`. Refer to Chapter 4 if you want a refresher on how to figure out the correct path.

Topics covered in this chapter include the following:

- Web tier
- Optimizing the web tier with data separation
- Application tier
- Database tier

Optimizing the Web Tier with Data Separation

Before we discuss the components of our multitier application, let's introduce a recommended practice for writing better Puppet modules: data separation. This practice involves separating the instructions we are executing in our manifests from the data used by those instructions. The data would be stored in a central location so that multiple manifests in the module can reuse the values, instead of having multiple definitions of those values across multiple files. This will help you employ the "don't repeat yourself" (DRY) practice with your Puppet code so that you have less source code to manage in case your data changes. If you examine the Puppet Forge modules, you will notice that they employ this practice.

In Listing 5-1, we take another look at our Apache class from Chapter 4 to see how we can implement data separation.

Listing 5-1 Original Apache Module

```
class apache {
  case $operatingsystem {
    centos: {
        $webserver= 'httpd'
        $confpath = "/etc/$webserver/conf/$webserver.conf"
    }
    ubuntu: {
        $webserver= 'apache2'
        $confpath = "/etc/$webserver/$webserver.conf"
    }
  }

  package { 'apache':
       name   => $webserver,
       ensure => installed,
  }

  file {'apacheconf':
       name    => $confpath,
       ensure  => file,
       mode    => 600,
       source  => "puppet:///modules/apache/$webserver.conf",
       require => Package['apache'],
  }
```

```
  service {'apache':
       name      => $webserver,
       ensure    => running,
       enable    => true,
       subscribe => File['apacheconf'],
  }
}
```

In its current state, our Puppet code is fairly portable and easy to maintain. However, your real-world modules may feature multiple classes, each with its own manifest file. If you want those classes to make decisions based on the operating system type, you must copy your conditional logic from init.pp to each of the other manifest files.

Maintenance for the data selection logic across multiple manifest files can become a bit of a headache for you as well as for your coworkers. For this and other good reasons, it is advisable to separate your Puppet manifest code from the data that it uses.

Parameters Class (params.pp)

One approach to data separation that module authors utilize is to create a special class called `params`. This `params` class (see Listing 5-2) contains the conditional logic and data that your manifests use as input for their operations. The `params` class is stored in a file called params.pp, and it resides in the manifests directory of your module along with the init.pp file.

Listing 5-2 Parameter Class

```
#/etc/puppetlabs/puppet/module/apache/manifests/params.pp
class apache::params {
  case $::operatingsystem {
    'CentOS': {
        $webserver= 'httpd'
        $confpath = "/etc/$webserver/conf/$webserver.conf"
        $htmlpath = '/var/www/html/index.html'
    }
    'Ubuntu': {
        $webserver= 'apache2'
        $confpath = "/etc/$webserver/$webserver.conf"
        $htmlpath = '/var/www/index.html'
    }
    default: {
```

```
            fail("The ${module_name} does not support this Operating System")
        }
    }
}
```

The name of the class is prefixed by the name of the module to indicate the scope of our data. When referenced by other files, all the variables in the `params` file will be prefixed by `apache::params`. You'll notice that I am explicitly defining the scope of the operating system fact (`$::operatingsystem`). This will help other administrators who are modifying our code to understand that we intentionally want to use the system facts instead of a variable with the same name that may be declared somewhere else in the params.pp file. Even if you do not declare another `$operatingsystem` variable in your class, it is a good practice to explicitly indicate variable scope when you are using facts within a class. The last change that I have made to help make the code more portable is that I updated the default action for my `case` statement to have a more meaningful error message for the user. So, how does our init.pp manifest use the data in the params.pp file? Let's take a look at the updated file (see Listing 5-3) to find out.

Listing 5-3 Updated Apache Module

```
#/etc/puppetlabs/puppet/module/apache/manifests/init.pp
class apache (
  $webserver= $apache::params::webserver,
  $confpath = $apache::params::confpath,
  $htmlpath = $apache::params::htmlpath,
) inherits apache::params

{
  package { 'apache':
         name    => $webserver,
         ensure => installed,
  }

  file {'apacheconf':
       name     => $confpath,
       ensure   => file,
       mode     => 600,
       source   => "puppet:///modules/apache/$webserver.conf",
       require => Package['apache'],
  }
```

```
    service {'apache':
          name       => $webserver,
          ensure     => running,
          enable     => true,
          subscribe => File['apacheconf'],
    }
    file {'apachecontent':
            name     => $htmlpath,
          ensure   => file,
          mode     => 644,
          content => template('apache/index.html.erb'),
          require => Service['apache'],
    }
}
```

In continuing to borrow from object-oriented programming principles, Puppet uses the `inherits` keyword to indicate the relationship between our main manifest (init.pp) and our `params` class (`class apache {…} inherits apache::params`). An optional change that I recommend is to have our class definition become a parameterized class with default values that correspond to the data in params.pp. I say "optional" because it is sufficient to declare the class without parameters. The `inherits` statement would allow us to call the names of the variables in the `params` file without explicitly specifying the scope. Again, for the sake of facilitating easier code maintenance, it is highly recommended that you do things such as explicitly defining scope. Other than these changes, the rest of the manifest remains the same.

Before we move on, let's take this opportunity to try applying the new version of our apache module in prototypical master-agent fashion.

This is a two- or three-step process:

1. Clone your Apache web server module from your remote repository to the correct path on your Puppet master. (Confirm with `puppet config print modulepath`.)
2. Edit the Puppet master site.pp file, and specify which host should run our module.
3. (Optional) Tell the Puppet agent node to apply the Puppet code that we have defined. Alternatively, you could just wait for the next automated Puppet agent execution, but where's the fun in that?

Step 1 should be fairly easy to figure out. Commit the changes we have made so far, and push them to your remote repository. On the Puppet master server, use Git to clone the remote repository to your modulepath. You should then have the tree structure shown in Figure 5-1 under your Puppet Master's modules directory.

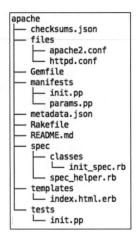

```
apache
├── checksums.json
├── files
│   ├── apache2.conf
│   └── httpd.conf
├── Gemfile
├── manifests
│   ├── init.pp
│   └── params.pp
├── metadata.json
├── Rakefile
├── README.md
├── spec
│   ├── classes
│   │   └── init_spec.rb
│   └── spec_helper.rb
├── templates
│   └── index.html.erb
└── tests
    └── init.pp
```

Figure 5-1 The apache module's directory structure

Step 2 requires editing the site.pp file found in the /etc/puppetlabs/puppet/environments/production/manifests directory on your Puppet master. You will notice that there is a default entry that we can use as a template for defining our nodes. Let's make two copies of the default entry and name them after our two puppet nodes: If you're following my naming convention, the fully qualified domain names (FQDN) will be puppetnode01.devops.local and puppetnode02.devops.local. Decide which of your Puppet agent servers will be the web server and include the apache module that we've created. (In my example, puppetnode01 will be the web server.) Your site.pp settings should look similar to Listing 5-4.

Listing 5-4 site.pp Entries for Your Puppet Agent Servers

```
node default {
  # This is where you can declare classes for all nodes.
  # Example:
  #   class { 'my_class': }
}

node 'puppetnode01.devops.local' {
  class { 'apache': }
}

node 'puppetnode02.devops.local' {
   # We'll fill this in later
}
```

Step 3: Let's run the following command on our Puppet agent server:

```
puppet agent -td
```

Wait a minute. Why is the command `puppet agent` and not `puppet apply`? The `agent` tells the agent to execute the instructions that the Puppet master has for it. The `apply` command is for ad hoc executions of local puppet manifests.

The first time that you run the `puppet agent` command, you will get a certificate error, and no instructions will be executed on the agent. This is because the Puppet master has to authorize the Puppet agent servers. On the Puppet master server, you can see the list of Puppet agent servers with a certificate signing request (CSR) by using the command `puppet cert list`. In production, you want to be selective of which requests you authorize. However, because this is just a test environment, you will go ahead and sign all the requests using the command `puppet cert sign --all`.

After the Puppet master confirms that the requests were processed, go ahead and rerun the `puppet agent -td` command on the Puppet agent server. Try accessing your new web server from a browser to verify that Apache was installed and configured properly.

> **NOTE**
>
> Puppet enables you to preview the changes that your `puppet agent` and `puppet apply` executions will make by using the `--noop` option with these commands (that is, `puppet agent --noop -td`). The noop command tells Puppet that you want to see only the changes that it will make, instead of actually implementing them.

Hiera

Params.pp is great. However, what happens when we want to consider additional operating systems besides just CentOS and Ubuntu? We must update the conditional statement in params.pp. Even though params.pp is fairly short, consider a larger list of values with multiple conditional statements based on various system facts. Wouldn't it be great if we could let Puppet determine which data to apply at the appropriate time instead of having to write more conditional statements ourselves? Enter Hiera.

Hiera is an open source utility that ships with Puppet 3.x versions. (To use Hiera with older Puppet versions, a separate manual installed is required.) Hiera is a popular alternative for separating code from data. Hiera allows you to store key:value data in a variety of data stores including YAML (YAML Ain't Markup Language) files, JSON (JavaScript Object Notation) files, and MySQL databases. For the Hiera examples in this book, we use YAML.

When we want to reference the values that are stored in Hiera, we would use the command, `hiera('value')`. If we implement Hiera in our apache module, our init.pp manifest could look like Listing 5-5.

Listing 5-5 Apache Module init.pp with Hiera

```
class apache {
  $webserver= hiera('webserver')
  $confpath = hiera('confpath')
  $htmlpath = hiera('htmlpath')

  package { 'apache':
        name   => $webserver,
        ensure => installed,
  }

  file {'apacheconf':
        name    => $confpath,
        ensure  => file,
        mode    => 600,
        source  => "puppet:///modules/apache/$webserver.conf",
        require => Package['apache'],
  }

  service {'apache':
        name      => $webserver,
        ensure    => running,
        enable    => true,
        subscribe => File['apacheconf'],
  }
  file {'apachecontent':
     name    => $htmlpath,
     ensure  => file,
     mode    => 644,
     content => template('apache/index.html.erb'),
     require => Service['apache'],
  }
}
```

Let's take a look at how to get our system ready to use Hiera. First, we need to configure Hiera to work properly with our data.

The Hiera configuration file is found at /etc/puppetlabs/puppet/hiera.yaml in Puppet Enterprise (/etc/puppet/hiera.yaml with open source Puppet). Hiera's settings are defined in the YAML format, as you may have guessed from the configuration file's extension.

Listing 5-6 displays a sample Hiera configuration file. Make a backup copy of your hiera.yaml file (ex: hiera.yaml.old). Then, change the contents of your hiera.yaml file to match the settings in Listing 5-6. Be careful with spacing.

Listing 5-6 hiera.yaml

```
---
:backends:
  - yaml
:hierarchy:
  - defaults
  - "%{::osfamily}"
  - "%{::fqdn}"
  - global

:yaml:
# datadir is empty here, so hiera uses its defaults:
# - /var/lib/hiera on *nix
# - %CommonAppData%\PuppetLabs\hiera\var on Windows
# When specifying a datadir, make sure the directory exists.
  :datadir: '/etc/puppetlabs/puppet/hieradata'
```

The `:backends:` section tells Hiera how the key:value pairs will be stored. Again, we are using YAML in our lab.

The `:hierarchy:` section tells Hiera in which files to find your key:value pair data. This section can use system information from `facter` (introduced in the previous chapter) in case you wanted to make YAML files according to the operating system family, for example. So, if we want to have specific settings for Debian-based operating systems, like Ubuntu, we would place them in a file called Debian.yaml. (You'll see an example of this little bit later.) Hiera will search for values based on the order that is listed in this section of the configuration file.

Based on the sample hiera.yaml file in Listing 5-6, if you ask Hiera to look up a variable named `$webserver`, it will first look for it in a file called defaults.yaml. If defaults.yaml does not have a value for `$webserver`, or if the file doesn't exist, it will look for a

YAML file whose name matches the `osfamily` value for the agent server currently being evaluated (for example, Debian.yaml). The process will continue on until Hiera finds the value it is looking for or until it exhausts searching in global.yaml. If the value doesn't exist in global.yaml, Hiera will return a `nil` value to the manifest compilation process that called it.

The `:yaml:` section tells Hiera where we will be storing all of the YAML data files that we specified in the `:hierarchy:` section. For our apache module, I would create two data files to match the value returned by the `"%{osfamily}"` fact (RedHat for Red Hat, Fedora, and CentOS systems; and Debian for Debian and Ubuntu systems): Debian.yaml and RedHat.yaml. Remember to place these files in the `:datadir:` path that you specified (/etc/puppetlabs/puppet/hieradata in my example) (see Listing 5-7).

Listing 5-7 Operating System-Specific YAML Files

Debian.yaml

```
---
webserver:
  - 'apache2'
confpath:
  - '/etc/apache2/apache2.conf'
htmlpath:
  - '/var/www/index.html'
```

RedHat.yaml

```
---
webserver:
  - 'httpd'
confpath:
  - '/etc/httpd/conf/httpd.conf'
htmlpath:
  - '/var/www/html/index.html'
```

Data separation solely for the purpose of writing clean code may seem trivial, but consider another use case: management of sensitive data such as passwords. If you will be storing your manifests in a repository for others to access, you might not necessarily want the entire team to have access to passwords for critical resources. At some point, that manifest may be viewed by folks who do not have sufficient authorization to have root access to critical resources like database or DNS servers. Even when you have secure access control for the Hiera files, you may want to encrypt any sensitive data using a plugin like hiera-gpg to keep important data safe.

Node Classification

Hiera can also be used to specify what kinds of classes that our server should be deployed with.

Remember the following entry from site.pp on the Puppet master:

```
node 'puppetnode01.devops.local' {
  include apache
}
```

We can update the entry to look like the following:

```
node 'puppetnode01.devops.local' {
  hiera_include ('classes')
}
```

The `hiera_include` command informs Puppet to look for class definitions inside one of the YAML files. We will now create a YAML file specifically for this host in the /etc/puppetlabs/puppet/hieradata directory and call it puppetnode01.devops.local.yaml with the following entry:

```
---
classes:
  - apache
```

NOTE

You might have noticed that all of our YAML files reside outside of our module's path. This would make it a bit challenging for other members of the community to use our module. R. I. Pienaar, the original author of Hiera, has developed a solution for this problem: an open source project called ripienaar/module_data. By implementing this capability with your module, it will be possible to develop portable modules that rely on Hiera. However, this topic coverage is beyond the scope of this book.

Application Tier

The application tier in our deployment will be a simple PHP server. For our setup, we will include the PHP binary, the PHP component for communicating with MySQL databases, and a sample index.php file to verify that PHP is running successfully. PHP needs to be installed on the same system as the Apache web server. So, in my setup, I will be deploying PHP to puppetnode01.devops.local. First we will take a look at how to deploy the PHP components, and then we will examine the changes that we need to make to the configuration files.

As you might have guessed, the names of the modules will vary according to the operating systems on which we are deploying PHP. For Debian-based systems, the module names are php5 and php5-mysql. For Red Hat–based systems, the module names are php and php-mysql. The path for our sample index.php file is the same as for the HTML content for the Apache web server. We will be using Hiera for the PHP module. So, we will add the appropriate values to the Debian.yaml and RedHat.yaml files (see Listing 5-8).

Listing 5-8 PHP Values Added to the Operating System Family Hiera Files

Debian.yaml

```
---
webserver:
  - 'apache2'
confpath:
  - '/etc/apache2/apache2.conf'
htmlpath:
  - '/var/www/index.html'
phpserver:
  - 'php5'
phpmysql:
  - 'php5-mysql'
phppath:
  - '/var/www/index.php'
```

RedHat.yaml

```
---
webserver:
  - 'httpd'
confpath:
  - '/etc/httpd/conf/httpd.conf'
```

```
htmlpath:
  - '/var/www/html/index.html'
phpserver:
  - 'php'
phpmysql:
  - 'php-mysql'
phppath:
  - '/var/www/html/index.php'
```

The last piece of the PHP module is to create the module directory under your Puppet master's module path (see Chapter 4 for a refresher on module directory structure) with the appropriate init.pp file (see Listing 5-9).

Listing 5-9 Sample init.pp File for a PHP Module

```
class php {
  $webserver = hiera('webserver')
  package { 'php':
    name => hiera('phpserver'),
    ensure => installed,
  }
  package { 'phpmysql':
    name => hiera('phpmysql'),
    ensure => installed,
    require => Package['php'],
  }
  file { 'phpsample':
    name => hiera('phppath'),
    ensure => file,
    mode => 644,
    source => 'puppet:///modules/php/index.php',
    require => Package['phpmysql'],
  }
}
```

Database Tier

The final component of our multitier application is the database. In our deployment, we will use the MySQL database. Although we can build our own module, let's take advantage of the Puppet Forge and use the MySQL module built by Puppet Labs.

On the Puppet master, execute the following command to download the MySQL module:

```
puppet module install puppetlabs/mysql
```

Now, let's edit the site.pp to have an entry for the database server node. In my lab environment, the database server is puppetnode02.devops.local:

```
node 'puppetnode02.devops.local' {
  hiera_include ('classes')
}
```

As with my web server, I'll create a YAML file (puppetnode02.devops.local.yaml) specifically for the classes I want to deploy on the database server, and I will set the root password for the MySQL database:

```
---
classes:
  - mysql::server

mysql::server::root_password: 'Puppetize1234'
```

The preceding instructions tell our database server to deploy the `mysql::server` class and to set the root password of the database according to the value that we specified.

Implementing a Production Recommended Practice

Network Time Protocol (NTP) is critical for production workloads, especially for virtual machines (VMs) whose system clocks can vary widely over time. Even though this is just a test lab, let's apply good system administrator principles and deploy NTP in the environment. Besides, because time synchronization is essential in VMware single sign-on (SSO) deployments, all VMware administrators are knowledgeable about NTP by now, right?

There are numerous NTP modules on the Puppet Forge, just like there are for MySQL, but again, we'll go with the module developed by Puppet Labs:

```
puppet module install puppetlabs/ntp
```

For your test environment, it is fine to stick with the default NTP server values that point to pool.ntp.org. However, in your production environment, you will want to edit the params.pp file for this module so that it uses the correct NTP servers for your environment.

Because it is appropriate for NTP to run on all servers in your environment, you can place it in the defaults section of the site.pp file on your Puppet master (`class {'ntp':}`). Alternatively, you could add the NTP class to the YAML files.

Deploying the Application Environment

After deciding which data separation method you like best (the `params` class versus Hiera), update your modules accordingly, and modify your site.pp file so that puppetnode01 includes the php and apache modules and puppetnode02 includes the mysql module. After rerunning the `puppet agent` command on both puppetnode01 and puppetnode02, your modules will be installed and ready for you to work on building your application.

Summary

The LAMP (Linux-Apache-MySQL-PHP) stack deployment is made simpler by using Puppet modules. Puppet modules can be made portable by employing data separation so that you have a single location to change the data used by the Puppet code. When creating your modules, you have two options for data separation: the `params` class and Hiera. Either method is valid (although the `params` class method seems to be popular with Puppet Forge contributors). In the next chapter, we take a look at how Puppet integrates with VMware vSphere.

Reference

[1] "Puppet 3 Reference Manual": http://docs.puppetlabs.com/puppet/3/reference/

Deploying the Application Environment

Chapter 6

VMware vSphere Management with Puppet

Puppet can be used to manage resources in the VMware vCloud Suite. Puppet Enterprise has a cloud provisioner component that can deploy new virtual machines (VMs) on VMware vSphere. In addition, the VMware vCloud Air Team has open-sourced a few of the modules that they use internally for managing vSphere components. For the examples in this chapter, we will need to have at least one Linux VM template created in our vSphere deployment, and we will need a Puppet Enterprise master server that has network connectivity to a vSphere cluster that is attached to a vCenter server instance.

Topics covered in this chapter include the following:

- Puppet's cloud provisioner for VMware vSphere
- VMware's management modules

Puppet's Cloud Provisioner for VMware vSphere

The Puppet Enterprise cloud provisioner enables system administrators to deploy VMs from templates in their environment. The cloud provisioner is an optional component. So, you have to deliberately select it during installation of the Puppet Enterprise master server.

Preparing VM Templates

Make sure that VMware Tools is installed on the Linux VM that will become your template. Verify that the Domain Name System (DNS) entries for your Puppet master are correct on the Linux VM. Alternatively, if you are working in a test lab that does not have a DNS server, edit your template VM's /etc/hosts file to include an entry for the Puppet master. Last but not least, add your Secure Shell (SSH) public key to one of the users on your Linux template, preferably one with sudo permissions (for ease of management).

Preparing Puppet Master

After you confirm that the cloud provisioner is installed on the Puppet Enterprise master, you must configure the credentials on the Puppet master that it should use to perform management tasks in vCenter. Those credentials are stored in a file called .fog that will be stored in the home directory of whichever user that you normally log in to the master server with. The user does not have to be root. However, for the sake of simplicity, you can use the root user on the master server. The data structure used in the .fog file should look familiar because it utilizes YAML syntax (see Listing 6-1).

Listing 6-1 Sample .fog File

```
:default:
  vsphere_username: administrator
  vsphere_password: Puppetize1234
  vsphere_server: vCenter.devops.local
  vsphere_expected_pubkey_hash: 118d38f5267ca92948b9a8c9fdb8c64decf67530d4a
```

You may be wondering, "Where do we get the hash value for the .fog file?" Well, that is something that we cannot generate ahead of time. After we have our .fog file configured, we need to attempt to execute one of the commands (for example, `puppet node_vmware list`) against vCenter, and the first time that we do this, the hash will be generated and displayed for us to add to our .fog file.

Now, we are ready to execute the various commands available in the cloud provisioner. Before we can deploy a VM, we need to know which templates are available for us to deploy from. The `puppet node_vmware list` command achieves this for us. In a test environment, it may be fine to list all of your VMs. However, in production, you may want to filter your search results. In that case, you can pipe the output of the `list` command to grep to get the list of just the templates: `puppet node_vmware list | grep true -B 7`. In my example, I search for the keyword `true` because there is a Boolean value (`template`) that indicates whether the VM in the list is a template, as shown in Listing 6-2.

Listing 6-2 Puppet Listing Your VMs

```
/Datacenters/VMTrooperHQ/vm/centos-6-x64-template
  powerstate: poweredOff
  name:       centos-6-x64-template
  hostname:   --------
  instanceid: 5005ed33-f57e-6106-36a7-b2ee1626bc4c
  ipaddress:  ---.---.---.---
  template:   true
--

/Datacenters/VMTrooperHQ/vm/precise-template
  powerstate: poweredOff
  name:       precise-template
  hostname:   --------
  instanceid: 50055b0a-b56b-6790-3295-fbc31e9608ca
  ipaddress:  ---.---.---.---
  template:   true
```

Take note of the first line in each VM listing, which is essentially the path that Puppet will follow to access your template:

```
/Datacenters/VMTrooperHQ/vm/precise-template
```

- `Datacenters`: The object that Puppet will search for your vCenter data center object.
- `VMTrooperHQ`: This value corresponds to the name of your data center object in vCenter Server.
- `vm`: This is the root folder, in the vCenter VMs and Templates view, that your VM is stored in. If your VM is placed in a folder, the path reflects that (for example, .../vm/Discovered virtual machine/...).
- `precise-template`: This is the name of the VM template.

Next, we will use the path of the template that we would like to deploy the VM from with the `create` command. Two important inputs for this command are the full path of the VM template from the `list` output and the name that you will give the VM in vCenter. One optional input that you may want to add to this command if it is part of a shell script is the `wait` option. Your scripts can either wait for the VM to finish cloning, or they can wait for the VM to finish booting and obtain an IP address successfully. Here is an example of a VM creation:

```
puppet node_vmware create--vmname=devops --
template=/Datacenters/VMTrooperHQ/vm/precise-template -i
```

The `--vmname` specifies the VM's name. The `--template` specifies the VM template path. The last option (`-i`) specifies to wait for the VM to boot and then obtain the IP address. If you want your script to just wait for the VM clone operation to finish, change the `i` to a `w`.

After the VM is up and running with an IP address (192.168.1.100 in my example), the Puppet Master can deploy an agent on the VM using the `install` command:

```
puppet node install --keyfile=devops_rsa --login=root --installer-
payload=pe-precise.tar.gz --installer-
answers=answers.lastrun.puppetnode01.devops.local 192.168.1.100
```

Notice that the Puppet deployment is performed by the generic node command instead of `node_vmware` that we've been using. Other items to note include the following:

- `--keyfile`: The private key that we will use to log in to the VM. If you have not done this already, you can run `ssh-keygen` on the deployed VM to generate a new public and private key pair.
- `--login`: The user with sufficient authority to install the Puppet agent.
- `--installer-payload`: The Puppet Enterprise installation files in a gzip tarball that you downloaded for your installs in Chapter 4.
- `--installer-answers` : The automated input that will allow the Puppet Enterprise installer to deploy the agent without prompting for various options. In case you do not have an answer file, the Puppet Enterprise installation media has an answers directory with examples. For further documentation on creating answer files, consult the Puppet Labs website: https://docs.puppetlabs.com/pe/latest/install_answer_file_reference.html.

When you want to get rid of a VM, use the `terminate` command:

```
puppet node_vmware terminate /Datacenters/VMTrooperHQ/vm/devops
```

Other `puppet node_vmware` commands that can prove useful include the `start` and `stop` commands. If you have VMware Tools installed on the template VM, the `stop` command will attempt to shut down the VM's operating system gracefully. Otherwise, you can use the `stop` command with the `force` option to power off the VM without waiting.

VMware's Management Modules

In addition to the cloud provisioner, Puppet users can take advantage of the modules that the VMware vCloud Air Automation Team shared with the community.

- vmware/vcenter
- vmware/vcsa
- vmware/vshield
- vmware/vmware_lib

The first three modules actually perform actions on VMware resources, and the fourth module contains supporting code for the other modules. As a matter of fact, vmware/vmware_lib gets imported whenever you import one of the other three modules. These modules leverage the open source rbvmomi Ruby application programming interfaces (APIs) to communicate with VMware components

Using the vmware/vcenter Module

For this chapter's discussion, we focus in on the vmware/vcenter module. As with the other modules that we used in Chapters 4 and 5, make sure to put the vmware/vcenter module directory into your master server's module path (verify with `puppet config print modulepath`). Listing 6-3 shows a sample manifest that uses the vcenter module.

Listing 6-3 vCenterTest.pp Puppet Manifest

```
vcenter::host { 'vsphere01.vmtrooper.com':
  path => "/VMTrooperHQ",
  username => "root",
  password => "Puppetize1234",
  transport => Transport['vcenter'],
}
transport { 'vcenter':
  username => 'administrator',
  password => 'Puppetize1234',
  server   => 'vcenter.vmtrooper.com',
  options  => { 'insecure' => true }
}
```

My manifest uses the `vcenter::host` defined type in the vmware/vcenter module to add an ESXi host to vCenter. Puppet defined types are a new concept for us, and this book does not cover them in depth. However, let's take a few moments to discuss what they are.

When you look at the instance of the `vcenter::host` defined type in my manifest, the syntax should look familiar: It's the same syntax as declaring a Puppet resource. So, a Puppet defined type is a way for users to define their own resource types.

You may be thinking, "What is the difference between a defined type and a class?" Well, the two concepts are similar except for one key difference: Puppet classes are meant to be used once in a manifest, whereas Puppet defined types are meant to be used multiple times within a manifest.

For example, in our LAMP deployment, we only needed to deploy one instance of PHP and one instance of Apache on our puppetnode01 server. So, the class structure is appropriate for the modules that we created. When we are adding ESXi hosts to vCenter, our manifest may have multiple ESXi host definitions, and the defined type is more appropriate for this kind of object.

The `vcenter::host` defined type has a few required parameters. (We discuss the optional parameters a little later.)

- `path`: The location in vCenter where the host will be placed, usually the root of your vCenter data center object (for example, VMTrooperHQ in my environment)
- `username`: The login name for the ESXi host
- `password`: The password of your ESXi host
- `transport`: The vCenter connection

Before moving on, let's focus briefly on the transport resource. The `options` parameter allows us to tell Puppet to ignore any SSL errors it may encounter when connecting to vCenter. In production, of course, you will not use this option. However, for our test lab, we may not have correct SSL certificates in place. The `'insecure' => true` value enables the capability to ignore SSL errors. In the `vcenter::host` declaration, we make sure that Puppet establishes the relationship between the transport resource and the `vcenter::host` with the `transport` metaparameter.

The `vcenter::host` defined type is pretty flexible, and if there are additional options that you want to set, such as the NTP servers to use, enabling shell or SSH access, and so on, you can do so by setting the appropriate options in your own manifest. Listing 6-4 shows these options in detail.

Listing 6-4 `vcenter::host` Puppet Defined Type

```
# Copyright (C) 2013 VMware, Inc.
# Manage vcenter host resource
define vcenter::host (
  $path,
  $username,
  $password,
  $dateTimeConfig = {},
  $shells         = {},
  $servicesConfig = {},
  # transport is a metaparameter
) {

  $default_dt = {
    ntpConfig => {
      running => true,
      policy => 'automatic',
      server => [ '0.pool.ntp.org', '1.pool.ntp.org', ],
    },
    timeZone => {
      key => 'UTC',
    },
  }
  $config_dt = merge($default_dt, $dateTimeConfig)

  $default_shell = {
    esxi_shell => {
      running => false,
      policy => 'off',
    },
    ssh => {
      running => false,
      policy => 'off',
    },
    esxi_shell_time_out => 0,
    esxi_shell_interactive_time_out => 0,
    suppress_shell_warning => 0,
  }
  $config_shells = merge($default_shell, $shells)
```

```
$default_svcs = {
  dcui => {
    running => true,
    policy => 'on',
  },
}
$config_svcs = merge($default_svcs, $servicesConfig)

vc_host { $name:
  ensure    => present,
  path      => $path,
  username  => $username,
  password  => $password,
  transport => $transport,
}

# ntp
esx_ntpconfig { $name:
  server    => $config_dt['ntpConfig']['server'],
  transport => $transport,
}

esx_service { "${name}:ntpd":
  policy    => $config_dt['ntpConfig']['policy'],
  running   => $config_dt['ntpConfig']['running'],
  subscribe => Esx_ntpconfig[$name],
}

# shells
esx_shells { $name:
  # to disable cluster/host status warnings:
  #   http://kb.vmware.com/kb/2034841 ESXi 5.1 and related articles
  #   esxcli system settings advanced set -o /UserVars/
    SuppressShellWarning -i (0|1)
  #   vSphere API: advanced settings UserVars.SuppressShellWarning =
    (0|1) [type long]
  suppress_shell_warning => $config_shells['suppress_shell_warning'],
  # timeout means 'x minutes after enablement, disable new logins'
  #   vSphere API: advanced settings UserVars.ESXiShellTimeOut = [type
    long] (0 disables)
```

```
    #   http://kb.vmware.com/kb/2004746 ; timeout isn't 'log out user after
      x minutes inactivity'
    esxi_shell_time_out  => $config_shells['esxi_shell_time_out'],
    # interactiveTimeOut means 'log out user after x minutes inactivity'
    #   vSphere API: advanced settings UserVars.ESXiShellInteractiveTimeOut
      = [type long] (0 disables)
    esxi_shell_interactive_time_out  => $config_shells['esxi_shell_
      interactive_time_out'],
    transport => $transport,
  }

  esx_service { "${name}:TSM":
    policy    => $config_shells['esxi_shell']['policy'],
    running   => $config_shells['esxi_shell']['running'],
    subscribe => Esx_shells[$name],
  }
  esx_service { "${name}:TSM-SSH":
    policy    => $config_shells['ssh']['policy'],
    running   => $config_shells['ssh']['running'],
    subscribe => Esx_shells[$name],
  }

  # simple services
  # - fully managed by HostServiceSystem
  # - behaviors are boot-time enablement and running/stopped
  # - vSphere API provides no additional configuration
  esx_service { "${name}:DCUI":
    policy  => $config_svcs['dcui']['policy'],
    running => $config_svcs['dcui']['running'],
  }
}
```

Starting at the beginning of the `vcenter::host` defined type definition, we'll see that there are three optional parameters denoted by the empty value assignments (`"= {}"`):

- `dateTimeConfig`: The NTP servers
- `shells`: The options regarding enabling\disabling shell\SSH access
- `servicesConfig`: The options regarding which services on the ESXi host to enable/disable

The default values for the NTP servers, the shells options, and the services options can be seen at the `$default_dt`, `$default_shell`, and `$default_svcs` entries, respectively. You'll notice there are a few defined type instances of the `esx_ntpconfig` and `esx_service` types defined elsewhere to perform the required time server and service configurations.

Setting these options in your manifest is a fairly simple task. Listing 6-5 displays the sample manifest again with ESXi shell and SSH enabled, and the vCenter warnings suppressed.

Listing 6-5 vCenterTest.pp Puppet Manifest with ESXi Shell and SSH Enabled

```
vcenter::host { 'vsphere01.vmtrooper.com':
  path => "/VMTrooperHQ",
  username => "root",
  password => "Puppetize1234",
  shells => {
    esxi_shell => {
      running => true,
      policy => 'on',
    },
    ssh => {
      running => true,
      policy => 'on',
    },
    esxi_shell_time_out => 0,
    esxi_shell_interactive_time_out => 0,
    suppress_shell_warning => 1,
  },
  servicesConfig => {
    dcui => {
      running => true,
      policy => 'on',
    },
    esxi_shell => {
      running => true,
      policy => 'on',
    },
    ssh => {
      running => true,
      policy => 'on',
    },
```

```
  },
  transport => Transport['vcenter'],
}

transport { 'vcenter':
  username => 'administrator',
  password => 'Puppetize1234',
  server   => 'vcenter.vmtrooper.com',
  options  => { 'insecure' => true }
 # options   => $vcenter['options'],
}
```

I highlighted in bold the new `shells` and `servicesConfig` sections added to the `venter::host` resource definition for my custom values. Now it may look like we're declaring Puppet resources within each other (Puppet inception!), but we are not. The shells and `servicesConfig` parameters actually take in Ruby hashes as their input.

Feel free to experiment with other services and maybe even extending the code to support new functionality when you feel confident enough. Remember, though, that you have the other two VMware modules to experiment with as well.

Summary

Puppet's support for VMware facilitates adding the management of vSphere components from within our Puppet workflows. Now that we've covered a fairly thorough introduction to Puppet and how it can be used with VMware technologies, let's take a look at the Chef configuration management system in the upcoming chapters.

References

[1] "Puppet 3 Reference Manual": http://docs.puppetlabs.com/puppet/3/reference/

[2] VMware Puppet Module documentation: https://forge.puppetlabs.com/vmware

Chapter 7

Introduction to Chef

This chapter covers what Chef is, some of Chef's core philosophies, some terminology and getting down into business with what ChefDK is, and writing your own first (simple) recipe. In some materials out there, this is covered in multiple chapters; but with the leaps Chef has made with ChefDK, it fits fantastically in an "Intro to Chef" chapter.

Topics covered in this chapter include the following:

- An introduction to Chef
- The core philosophies behind Chef
- Chef terminology
- Hosted Chef or Chef Server
- ChefDK
- Knife
- How to create your first Hello World Chef recipe

What Is Chef?

Chef is an infrastructure automation platform written by Adam Jacob. The server portion is written in Erlang, and the client is written in Ruby and uses a domain-specific language (a.k.a. a DSL). Having a DSL allows new users to Chef to quickly pick up on how to write recipes. Chef's goal is to automate your infrastructure, whether it is private cloud, public cloud, or bare metal.

The user writes a recipe, which is part of a cookbook that describes the desired state of the machine. Whether you're simply managing a server's Network Time Protocol (NTP) configuration or deploying an application, both can be achieved easily with Chef. A recipe writer declares the package, configuration, and any service associated with the recipe. To keep things data driven, attributes are used by cookbooks. This allows for specifics to be abstracted away from cookbook recipes, making them highly portable and reusable by others.

Chef at one point was simply an open source client with a server, but in recent years a hosted version (software-as-a-service [SaaS]) offering allows users to ramp up quickly on Chef without having to maintain the Chef Server installation. In 2014, Chef (formally known as Opscode) combined its Enterprise Chef product with its open source product and renamed it Chef Server.

Chef can be used to manage Linux, UNIX (Solaris, AIX, or the BSD family), and Windows.

Core Philosophies Behind Chef

Chef was developed to address a need (or lack of a solution) in the configuration management space. Other tools and platforms existed when Chef was released, but each tool had a different approach (or philosophy) to solve a problem. The areas that Adam Jacob, on behalf of HJK Solutions, wanted to focus on with Chef were order of recipe, idempotence, an API interface (to allow for things like search), endpoint processing (as opposed to a central server doing the compiling of a run), and a test-driven infrastructure.

Order of Recipe

The order of how you write a recipe is important. For example, when setting up Tomcat, the Tomcat package must be installed before laying down the server.xml or web.xml configuration. In addition a Java virtual machine (JVM), such as Oracle Java or OpenJDK, must be present for Tomcat to properly start. Resources, within a recipe, are applied in the order in which the resource is listed. You can also add in (or "include") other recipes. This allows the user to create a recipe that describes the entire application by referencing other recipes (or cookbooks) that would make the application function.

Idempotence

The idea is that a recipe can run on the machine over and over again and the results should always be the same. The Chef client checks the system to ensure that resources are not performed if the resource defined in the recipe has not changed. For example if a "package" resource is used to define the installation of Apache, rerunning the recipe a second time does not reinstall Apache.

API-Based Server

Chef Server is built from the ground up to be a RESTful application programming interface (API) server accessible over HTTPS protocols. The REST API provides access to objects on the Chef Server, including nodes, environments, roles, cookbooks (and its version), recipes, and run lists, and is managed via public/private key exchange between either the node or the user. The idea behind the Chef Server (SaaS or self-hosted) is that it serves as a repository of data (for example, recipes, cookbooks, attributes) and the data stored on the Chef Server can be utilized by writing in search functionality within your recipes.

The Client Does All the Legwork

Often, the most process-intense portion about an infrastructure automation platform is when you are "compiling" the run that needs to take place on the node where the Chef client is being executed. The Chef client only interacts with the Chef Server (over the API) when it needs to, but it downloads a copy of all cookbooks, recipes, templates, and so forth needed on that server. The Chef client then executes its *run list* in the order specified (Remember: Order matters!), and upon a successful client run, it saves all the state of the node back to the Chef Server.

Test-Driven Infrastructure

What makes Chef so powerful is the tools that are in the Chef ecosystem to validate and ensure that the state of the machine you are defining via recipes is well tested before it ever hits production. Rather than trying to fix issues after a code deployment to your production environment, you fix the issue early on in the recipe-creation portion. With tools such as Foodcritic, ChefSpec, and Test Kitchen gaining wide adoption, Chef released a ChefDK (Chef Development Kit) in 2014 to all its users that delivers a consistent development environment with all these tools integrated.

Chef Terminology

Chef has a lot of idioms that relate to modern-day cooking terms. With words such as *recipe*, *cookbook*, *food critic*, and *test kitchen* being thrown around, it might appear that Chef is a difficult product to use. This section breaks down these terms for you.

Recipe

A recipe is the most basic configuration element within Chef. A recipe is written using Chef's DSL, which sits on top of Ruby. A recipe is a collection of resources and needs to be stored in a cookbook. The idea behind writing a recipe is that your objective should be the *what* should be done and not the *how* it should be done.

Cookbook

A cookbook is a set of recipes that describe an application. A cookbook contains the recipes, templates, and a set of default attribute values that describe the state of an application. An example is a cookbook describing nginx. There may be recipes that describe how to install nginx and others to configure portions of nginx.

Attributes

Attributes are pieces of configuration data that can used in a recipe to provide a sane default setting or to override another setting. Attributes can be associated or redefined at the node, role, environment, or cookbook level.

Role

A role is a user-defined and -created collection of recipes and attribute values that describe a common configuration. An example is a base role that is required to be applied to all servers in Chef where system packages such as ntp, sudoers, and DNS resolver are held.

Run List

A run list is a list of recipes to be applied to a node in a defined order (order matters!). A run list can be made out of zero or more roles or recipes. Multiple roles and recipes (and roles within roles) can be specific, but remember that the order matters.

Resource

A resource defines a single configuration item on a node that is under management by Chef. During a Chef client run, each resource is evaluated. A recipe, for example, is a set of resources, each doing something specific to a node.

Environments

An environment is a group of systems with different configuration settings. Environments can be used to restrict which version of a cookbook should be used on that machine or different configuration items such as IP addresses, usernames, and firewall configurations that exist between different environments. Consider a Tomcat cookbook, for example. The cookbook logic is the same between a server that resides in Production and one that resides in QA, but it might have a different IP address within its JDBC configuration.

The Difference Between Hosted Chef and Chef Server

Chef's best capabilities are realized when using a Chef Server. There are two versions of the Chef Server: Hosted Chef, an SaaS offering by Chef Software; and Chef Server, an installable program to be managed and used by the user rather than by Chef Software. The following subsections explain both products.

Hosted Chef

When Chef was originally founded, it launched with an SaaS offering allowing users to forgo the need to set up a Chef Server within their own data center. In pure cloud situations, where the customer does not maintain any physical infrastructure but could be hosting it all on a public cloud (for example, EC2 or Azure), this is a great option. Chef, by default, allows all users of the hosted Chef platform to use five free nodes, and setting up a hosted Chef account takes minutes. (Plus, more important, no credit card number is required.)

Chef Server

Chef has always had an open source version of Chef Server as well. Later, it introduced Enterprise Chef (known also as Private Chef), which was very similar to its hosted product but could be run inside someone's data center as opposed to using Chef's hosted solution. In 2014, Chef combined the open source offering and Enterprise Chef offering and called it *Chef Server*. Chef Server allows an administrator to move between the open source and Enterprise offering at the click of a mouse (or press of a key).

Chef Server comes with a ton of features, including open source features such as a user interface (UI), role-based access control (RBAC), multitenancy, and Enterprise-type features such as analytics and reporting. Both add on to Chef's API, and the cookbooks you write (or clients you run) will work with either Chef Server or hosted Chef.

NOTE

In this book, we use the hosted Chef infrastructure because its setup is simpler.

Introduction to ChefDK

ChefDK is a software program released by Chef Software and includes the utilities and tools needed for the exercises in this book. The following subsections explain what ChefDK is, how to install it, and what ChefDK does for Chef.

What Is ChefDK?

Over the years, Chef has built quite a community on cookbooks, but also testing tools (like Kitchen CI) and cookbook dependency solvers (like Berkshelf). Most of these tools are written in the same language the Chef client is written in, Ruby. The biggest problem with Ruby is the version of Ruby you're running, or on a lot of Linux distributions, how your distribution compiled and bundled Ruby. This could cause an issue when it comes to the consistency of tools. Chef ships in a package called the *Omnibus* package, in which it ships its own compiled version of Ruby. This version can coexist with the operating system's version of Ruby, and it allows for a consistent Chef client behavior on all the platforms and versions that Chef supports.

ChefDK is an application package that bundles all the testing tools together and is Chef's answer to also providing a consistent environment for all the various testing tools such as Kitchen CI, ChefSpec, and Foodcritic. ChefDK bundles all the dependencies (Ruby and various Ruby gems) and ships the same version of these packages across different operating systems. It also includes a new tool to streamline the Chef workflow, in addition to all the usual tools that ship with Chef (Chef client, Knife, and Ohai). This way, the user can be assured that the version of Test Kitchen is consistent on its development environment or build server where automated jobs to verify your cookbook's contents are validated and tested.

Installing ChefDK

The installation of ChefDK is extremely easy. It supports all major Linux variants, Mac OS X 10.8+, and Windows 7 or later. In examples later in this book, we use ChefDK to install additional plug-ins that enhance the functionality of Chef with vSphere Center.

To get started, follow these steps:

1. Go to http://www.chef.io/downloads/chef-dk/ to obtain the most current package of ChefDK, as shown in Figure 7-1.

Figure 7-1 ChefDK download page

> **NOTE ON LINUX OR OS X**
>
> If you have installed the Chef client before installing the ChefDK, the ChefDK installer will replace the default symlinks in /usr/bin with the ChefDK installed versions of these tools (for example, /usr/bin/knife will point to /opt/chefdk/bin/knife).

2. Open a terminal/PowerShell window and run:

   ```
   chef verify
   ```

   This will verify the installation of ChefDK, and it should come showing "succeeded":

   ```
   $ chef verify
   Running verification for component 'berkshelf'
   Running verification for component 'test-kitchen'
   Running verification for component 'chef-client'
   Running verification for component 'chef-dk'
   ...
   ---------------------------------------------
   Verification of component 'berkshelf' succeeded.
   Verification of component 'chef-dk' succeeded.
   Verification of component 'chef-client' succeeded.
   Verification of component 'test-kitchen' succeeded.
   ```

That's it; the ChefDK is now ready for use.

Using Knife

Knife is a command-line tool that provides an interface between your local Chef repository and the Chef Server. Knife is there to help you manage the following:

- Node objects (your virtual machine [VM] instances, physical servers, cloud objects)
- Cookbooks and underlying recipes
- Roles
- Environments
- Installation of Chef client on new nodes (also called *bootstrapping*)
- Searching the indexed data on your Chef Server

In addition to providing that out-of-box functionality, Knife can be extended to also talk to third-party APIs (for example vSphere, EC2, Terremark, and many other sources).

Earlier we installed the ChefDK, and the ChefDK ships with Knife (but also an entire embedded Ruby installation). We can use the `chef` command to use the embedded Ruby rather than use the system Ruby.

Let's try to add an additional plug-in to Knife by adding knife-windows. Knife-windows is an optional Knife plug-in maintained by Chef that provides WinRM functionality to Knife.

Open a terminal/PowerShell window.

Let's first verify that knife-windows is not installed, as follows (see Figure 7-2):

```
chef gem list knife-windows
```

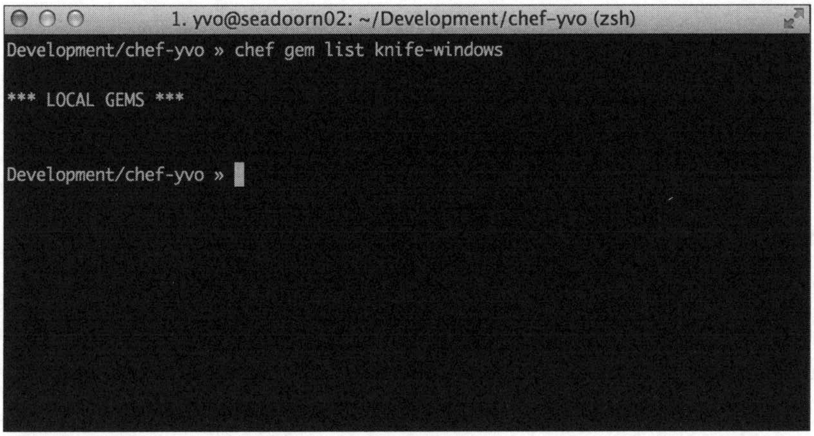
1. yvo@seadoorn02: ~/Development/chef-yvo (zsh)
Development/chef-yvo » chef gem list knife-windows
*** LOCAL GEMS ***
Development/chef-yvo »

Figure 7-2 Verifying whether Knife is installed

Then install knife-windows by running the following (see Figure 7-3):

```
chef gem install knife-windows
```

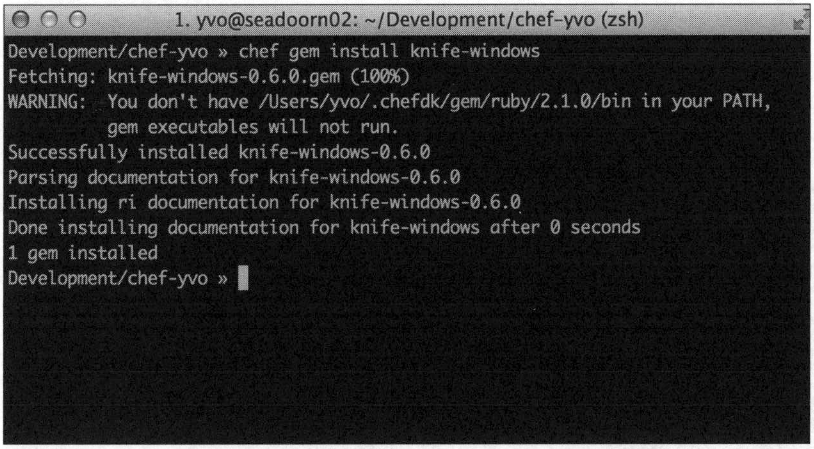
1. yvo@seadoorn02: ~/Development/chef-yvo (zsh)
Development/chef-yvo » chef gem install knife-windows
Fetching: knife-windows-0.6.0.gem (100%)
WARNING: You don't have /Users/yvo/.chefdk/gem/ruby/2.1.0/bin in your PATH,
gem executables will not run.
Successfully installed knife-windows-0.6.0
Parsing documentation for knife-windows-0.6.0
Installing ri documentation for knife-windows-0.6.0
Done installing documentation for knife-windows after 0 seconds
1 gem installed
Development/chef-yvo »

Figure 7-3 Installing Knife

NOTE

The output might differ slightly depending on your OS. What gem is doing is installing knife-windows and all dependencies.

NOTE

Chef maintains a list of current Knife plug-ins at http://docs.opscode.com/plugin_knife.html.

Creating Your First Hello World Chef Recipe

To create your first hello world Chef recipe, you need the following:

- A text editor such as Notepad ++, Sublime, VIM, Emacs, anything as long as it is not Notepad or WordPad
- ChefDK installed
- A blank development directory

In a text editor, put the following code in a file and save the file as **helloworld.rb**:

```
# helloworld.rb - Creates a helloworld.txt in your home directory
file "#{ENV['HOME']}/helloworld.txt" do
       content "Hello World and welcome to Chef!\n"
end
```

After you save your file, some text editors will recognize it for Ruby and style the syntax accordingly, as shown in Figure 7-4.

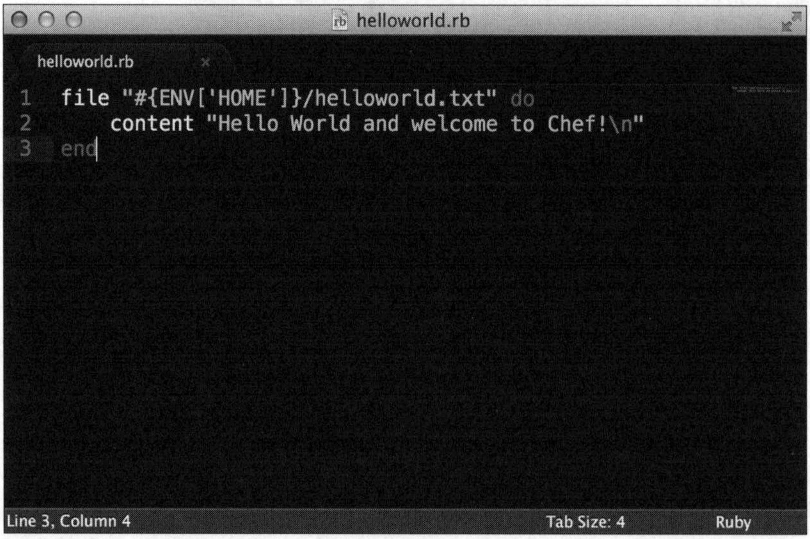

Figure 7-4 Hello World recognized for Ruby

Now open a terminal or PowerShell window and execute the following in the directory where you have saved helloworld.rb:

```
$ chef-client --local-mode helloworld.rb
Starting Chef Client, version 11.14.0
resolving cookbooks for run list: []
Synchronizing Cookbooks:
Compiling Cookbooks...
Converging 1 resources
Recipe: @recipe_files::/Users/yvo/Development/chef-yvo/helloworld.rb
  * file[/Users/yvo/helloworld.txt] action create
    - create new file /Users/yvo/helloworld.txt
    - update content in file /Users/yvo/helloworld.txt from none to 1c6683
        --- /Users/yvo/helloworld.txt      2014-05-27 15:56:47.000000000
-0700
        +++ /var/folders/qz/zggg8hjd61b43hz4rl2twbcr0000gq/T/.helloworld.
txt20140527-7046-1fjplsq    2014-05-27 15:56:47.000000000 -0700
        @@ -1 +1,2 @@
        +Hello World and welcome to Chef!


Running handlers:
Running handlers complete
Chef Client finished, 1/1 resources updated in 1.533804 seconds
```

Chef client should finish indicating that "1/1 resources updated." This is because the recipe ran a single resource, the file resource, to create a new file.

You verify that the recipe performed the correct action. Look inside of your home directory to see whether you see a file called helloworld.txt and that the content stored within the file is correct.

In an *NIX/OS X terminal window, enter the following:

```
$ cat $HOME/helloworld.txt
    Hello World and welcome to Chef!
```

In a Windows PowerShell window, enter the following:

```
    > type $env:userprofile\helloworld.txt
    Hello World and welcome to Chef!
```

Now let's rerun Chef client on your machine. The idea is that the output will reflect zero out of one resources updated:

```
$ chef-client --local-mode helloworld.rb
Starting Chef Client, version 11.14.0
resolving cookbooks for run list: []
Synchronizing Cookbooks:
Compiling Cookbooks...
Converging 1 resources
Recipe: @recipe_files::/Users/yvo/Development/chef-yvo/helloworld.rb
  * file[/Users/yvo/helloworld.txt] action create (up to date)

Running handlers:
Running handlers complete

Chef Client finished, 0/1 resources updated in 1.457341 seconds
```

This shows that your recipe is idempotent and that Chef did not need to make any changes because the desired state of your machine has not changed. So, let's make a change. Open the helloworld.txt file in your text editor and remove the "Hello World and" part, just leaving "welcome to Chef!" behind. Save the file and rerun Chef client:

```
$ chef-client --local-mode helloworld.rb
Starting Chef Client, version 11.14.0
resolving cookbooks for run list: []
Synchronizing Cookbooks:
Compiling Cookbooks...
Converging 1 resources
Recipe: @recipe_files::/Users/yvo/Development/chef-yvo/helloworld.rb
  * file[/Users/yvo/helloworld.txt] action create
    - update content in file /Users/yvo/helloworld.txt from 821447 to
1c6683
        --- /Users/yvo/helloworld.txt      2014-05-27 16:05:13.000000000
-0700
        +++ /var/folders/qz/zggg8hjd61b43hz4rl2twbcr0000gq/T/.helloworld.
txt20140527-7230-1yj8vmq     2014-05-27 16:05:24.000000000 -0700
        @@ -1,2 +1,2 @@
        -welcome to Chef!
        +Hello World and welcome to Chef!

Running handlers:
Running handlers complete
Chef Client finished, 1/1 resources updated in 1.512766 seconds
```

Chef client reran on the machine, and sure enough, it reverted the hellowworld file back to its desired state.

Let's reopen a text editor and create another recipe. This recipe is to clean up the mess we created with helloworld.

In a text editor, put in the following contents:

```
file "#{ENV['HOME']}/helloworld.txt" do
  action :delete
end
```

Save the file in the same directory as helloworld.rb and name it **cleanup.rb**, as shown in Figure 7-5.

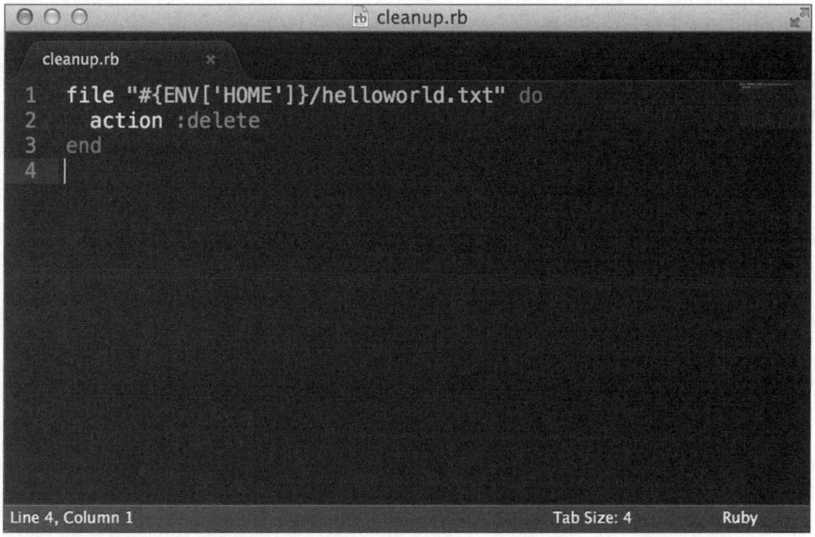

Figure 7-5 cleanup.rb

What the code is doing is reusing the file resource; but instead of using the default action of create, we are telling the recipe to delete the file when encountered. This proves useful if you are attempting to do an application deployment where you want to ensure previous versions are no longer maintained except for the version you're deploying.

Now run Chef client with your newly created recipe:

```
$ chef-client --local-mode cleanup.rb
Starting Chef Client, version 11.14.0
resolving cookbooks for run list: []
```

```
Synchronizing Cookbooks:
Compiling Cookbooks...
Converging 1 resources
Recipe: @recipe_files::/Users/yvo/Development/chef-yvo/cleanup.rb
  * file[/Users/yvo/helloworld.txt] action delete
    - delete file /Users/yvo/helloworld.txt
Running handlers:
Running handlers complete
Chef Client finished, 1/1 resources updated in 1.519316 seconds
Chef client
```

Summary

This chapter covered the history of Chef, core philosophies, terminology, and the various tools that make up the Chef ecosystem. In addition, the chapter covered the difference between Chef Server and hosted Chef.

You installed the ChefDK, installed a Knife plug-in via the ChefDK, created your first two recipes, and ran Chef client to see how Chef interacts with your machine. This book will barely scratch the surface of the Chef ecosystem, but you've just gone from learning terminology to writing your first very basic recipe. Awesome!

Chapter 8

Systems Management Tasks with Chef

So with that newfound Chef knowledge, let's put it to use by maintaining some of your virtual infrastructure with VMware. This chapter covers the signup process for hosted Chef, explains what community cookbooks are, and walks through at least two use cases using community cookbooks. This chapter also covers more Knife capabilities to help set you up for Chapter 9.

Topics covered in this chapter include the following:

- Signing up for hosted Chef
- Community cookbooks
- Setting up system management
- Configuring your virtual guests
- Enforcing the policy
- Managing the root password

Before we begin, you need the following:

- A workstation running ChefDK able to reach https://manage.chef.io
- Two Linux (RHEL/CentOS 6.5 recommended) virtual machines located in your VMware infrastructure with Secure Shell (SSH) enabled
- The ability to sudo to root when connecting the machine
- The ability to reach http://www.chef.io

- A program that can extract both zip files and tar.gz files (for example, 7zip or WinRAR)
- Hosted Chef account (which is covered in this chapter)
- A web browser (Firefox 20+, Google Chrome 20+, or IE 10+) capable of reaching https://manage.chef.io

Signing Up for Hosted Chef

Hosted Chef is easy to sign up for. Every hosted Chef account gets five free nodes, and in this book we will use just two of the five slots. All that is required is a valid email account:

1. Open your web browser and go to https://manage.chef.io. You will be presented the page shown in Figure 8-1.

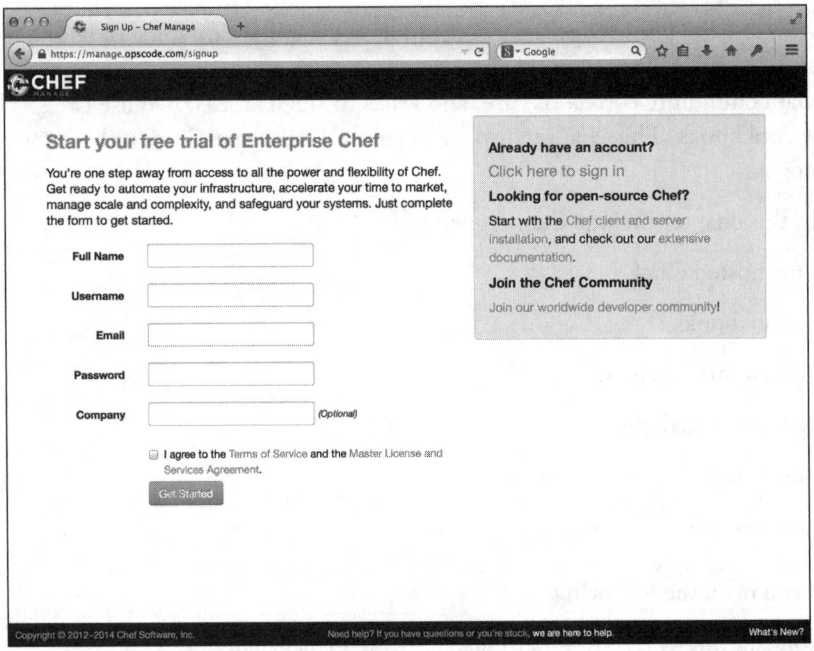

Figure 8-1 Hosted Chef home page

2. Fill out the text fields to sign up for an account, as shown in Figure 8-2.

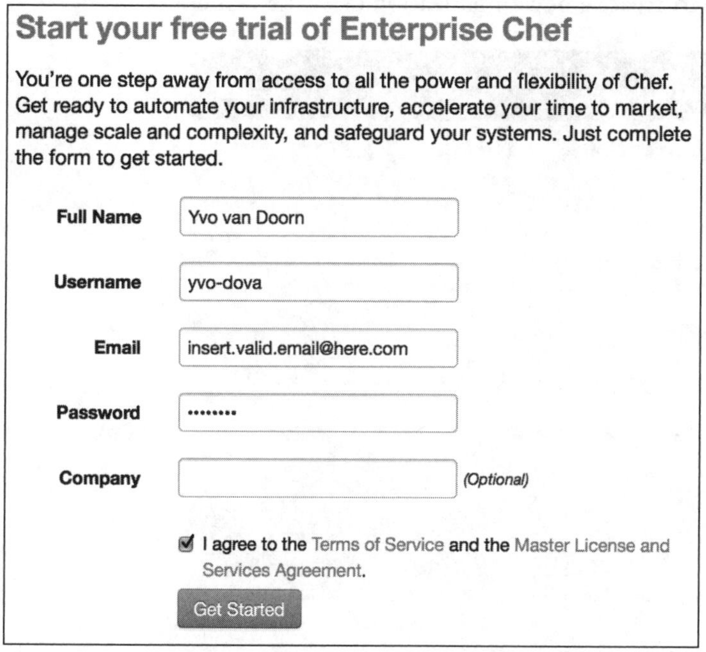
Start your free trial of Enterprise Chef
You're one step away from access to all the power and flexibility of Chef. Get ready to automate your infrastructure, accelerate your time to market, manage scale and complexity, and safeguard your systems. Just complete the form to get started.
Full Name
Yvo van Doorn
Username
yvo-dova
Email
insert.valid.email@here.com
Password
••••••••
Company
(Optional)
I agree to the Terms of Service and the Master License and Services Agreement.
Get Started

Figure 8-2 Signing up for a Chef account

3. Once you click on **Get Started**, you are prompted to either join an existing organization or create a new one, as shown in Figure 8-3. For this exercise, we create a new one. Optionally, you can enter your organization's name in dova (or DevOps for VMware administrators).

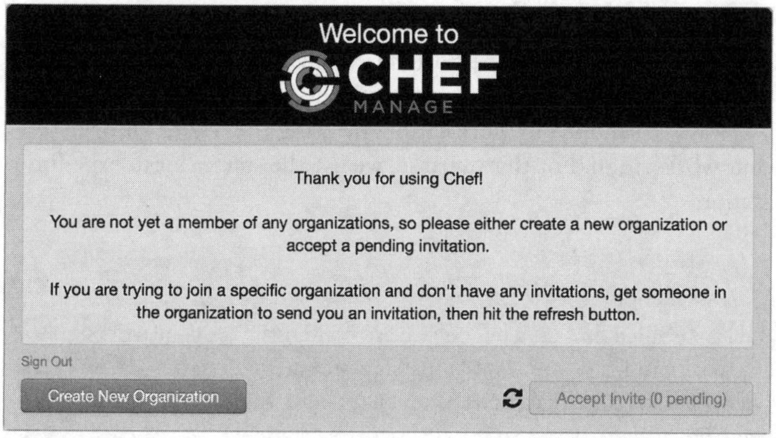
Welcome to
CHEF
MANAGE
Thank you for using Chef!
You are not yet a member of any organizations, so please either create a new organization or accept a pending invitation.
If you are trying to join a specific organization and don't have any invitations, get someone in the organization to send you an invitation, then hit the refresh button.
Sign Out
Create New Organization
Accept Invite (0 pending)

Figure 8-3 Joining/creating a Chef organization

Once you click **Create New Organization**, hosted Chef presents the screen shown in Figure 8-4 to create a new organization on hosted Chef.

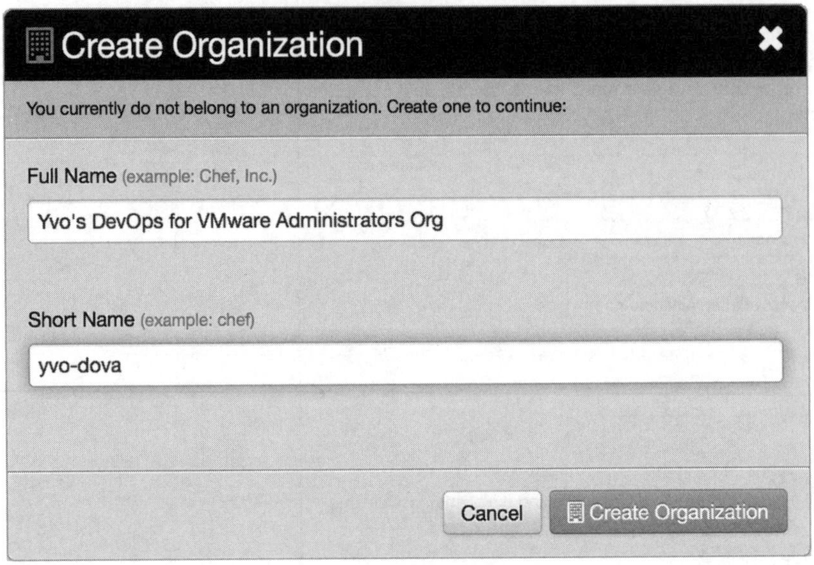

Figure 8-4 Creating a new organization on hosted Chef

After it is created, it takes a few moments to create your new organization on Chef's servers. Afterward, you will be logged in to the Getting Started section of Chef's website.

Setting Up Local Repo with the Starter Kit

After creating your user and organization on the hosted Chef platform, we will set up your workstation. Your workstation is used to communicate with the hosted Chef Server over HTTPS. There are two ways to set up your workstation: by using the starter kit or by manually setting up your workstation. For this exercise, we use the starter kit to expedite setting up your workstation.

> **NOTE**
>
> Make sure that ChefDK is installed on the machine you are configuring as your workstation. You can set up as many workstations as you want by passing around your starter kit zip file. Keep in mind that your starter kit contains a private key that allows someone to communicate with your hosted Chef account, so be sure to keep it stored safely.

1. Click **Download Starter Kit**.

> **NOTE**
>
> Chef never stores any of your private keys, so keep in mind that whenever you click Download Starter Kit, it will invalidate any previous public keys for your user and organization account.

2. Open the location where you've downloaded the starter kit in your operating system's file management program (for instance, Windows Explorer on Windows or Finder on Mac OS X), as shown in Figure 8-5.

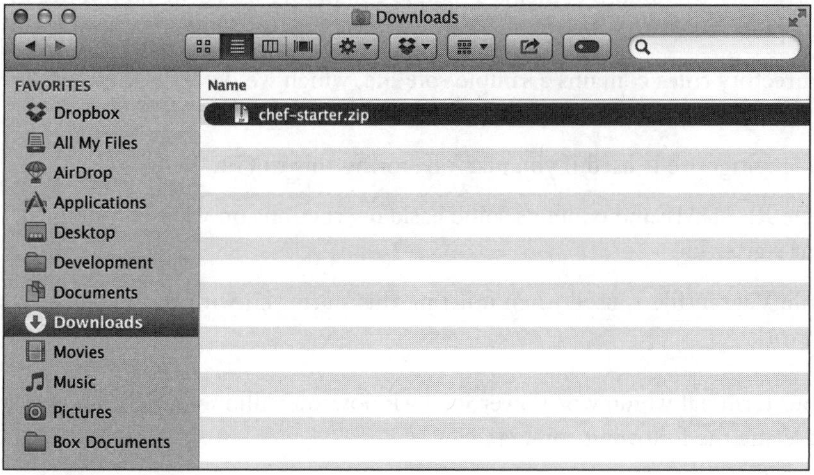

Figure 8-5 Opening the starter kit

3. Extract the chef-starter.zip to a location of your choice using a program capable of extracting zip files. Name the folder you are extracting it to **chef-repo**. In this book, I will be moving it to my Development location inside my user profile.

4. Open either a terminal window (Linux/OS X) or PowerShell window (Windows) and go to your new chef-repo folder (for instance, type **cd ~/Development/chef-repo** on OS X or **cd $env:userprofile\Development\chef-repo** on Windows). Perform a listing by executing `ls -al` (on OS X/Linux/UNIX) or `dir -Force -File` (on Windows). It should report at least three directories and three files:

```
$ ls -al
total 24
drwxr-xr-x@  8 yvo  staff   272 May 31 14:54 .
```

```
drwxr-xr-x  29 yvo  staff   986 May 31 14:54 ..
drwxr-xr-x@  5 yvo  staff   170 May 31 14:54 .chef
-rw-r--r--@  1 yvo  staff   495 May 31  2014 .gitignore
-rw-r--r--@  1 yvo  staff  2416 May 31  2014 README.md
-rw-r--r--@  1 yvo  staff  3649 May 31  2014 Vagrantfile
drwxr-xr-x@  4 yvo  staff   136 May 31  2014 cookbooks
drwxr-xr-x@  3 yvo  staff   102 May 31 14:54 roles
$ "
```

- The directory .chef is where your client configuration and private key are stored.
- The directory cookbooks contains a sample cookbook, which we do not use in this chapter.
- The directory roles contains a sample role file, which we do not use in this chapter.
- The file .gitignore is used if you plan on storing this to Git.
- The file README.md contains some basic instructions on what is contained in your starter kit.
- The file Vagrantfile is used when utilizing this starter kit with the Vagrant framework.

5. Inside of your terminal window or PowerShell window and still in your chef-repo directory, execute the following command:

   `knife user list`

   This should return a single username, more specifically the username used during the hosted Chef signup process, as shown in Figure 8-6.

   When Knife is executed, it always tries to locate a .chef directory where its configuration is stored inside of the knife.rb file. This is why the exercise had you change to your chef-repo directory. If you attempt to execute Knife outside of the chef-repo directory, it returns an error.

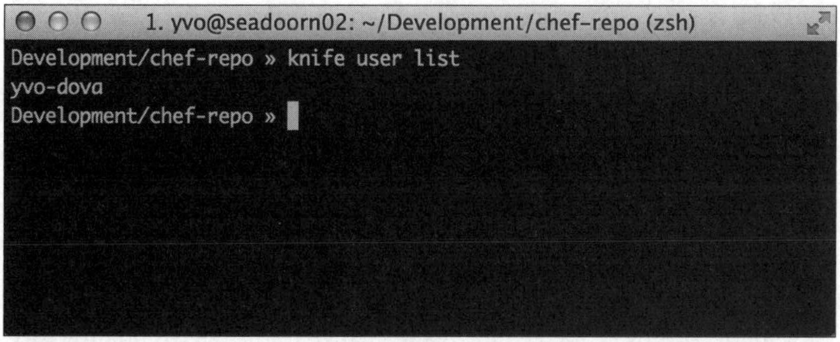
1. yvo@seadoorn02: ~/Development/chef-repo (zsh)
Development/chef-repo » knife user list
yvo-dova
Development/chef-repo »

Figure 8-6 Executing Knife to verify connectivity to hosted Chef

Community Cookbooks

Over the years, the Chef community has created more than 1,400 cookbooks (and growing) that can manage applications, databases, and configuration files. Some of these cookbooks are maintained by Chef; others are community maintained. Never blindly use a community cookbook without reviewing its recipe contents, similar to reviewing a recipe for what ingredients are required "in the real world" when you are attempting to make your creation in the kitchen.

Some community cookbooks have dependencies on other community cookbooks. (For example, the apache2 community cookbook depends on the logrotate cookbook to set up proper log file rotation.) You can use a program called Berkshelf (part of the ChefDK) as a dependency resolver for cookbooks.

Setting Up System Management

One of the early implementations around configuration management involved managing basic system services such as the Network Time Protocol (NTP) client and server configuration, password management, and other basic tasks (compared to automating application deliveries or performing schema updates to a database). In this section, we use the NTP community cookbook and apply the policy against VMware virtual machines (VMs).

Prep/Setup System Management Task 1: Managing Time

The first system management exercise covered in this chapter relates to time management. VMware ESXi offers the potential of managing time through VMware Tools, but VMware recommends NTP for maintaining time for your guests. The first portion of the system management task is to do some prep work, which will involve downloading the NTP cookbook and then uploading it to your hosted Chef organization.

The NTP cookbook published on the Chef community website offers a recipe to enable the NTP client. By default, the recipe sets up the NTP client configuration to talk to default NTP pool servers. We will be modifying the list of servers via an environment attribute.

Download the NTP Cookbook

Open your terminal window or PowerShell window and change to the chef-repo directory extracted earlier in the chapter.

Issue the following command:

```
knife cookbook site download ntp
```

This opens a connection to Chef's website and downloads the specified NTP cookbook. You will see output similar to this:

```
$ knife cookbook site download ntp
Downloading ntp from the cookbooks site at version 1.6.2 to /Users/yvo/
Development/chef-repo/ntp-1.6.2.tar.gz
Cookbook saved: /Users/yvo/Development/chef-repo/ntp-1.6.2.tar.gz
```

Open a file management window (for example, Windows Explorer or OS X's Finder) and go to the directory where the NTP cookbook was downloaded. Open the file in a program capable of extracting tar.gz files and extract the contents (which should be a single ntp folder) to the cookbooks directory located in your chef-repo directory.

> **NOTE**
>
> The cookbooks directory is where you will maintain all the cookbooks you plan on using with Chef.

After the contents have been extracted from the tar.gz file downloaded off of Chef's website, feel free to remove the tar.gz file from your chef-repo directory.

In your terminal or PowerShell window, in your chef-repo directory, issue the following command:

```
knife cookbook upload ntp
```

This command uploads the NTP cookbook to your hosted Chef repository on Chef's servers. You will see output similar to this:

```
$ knife cookbook upload ntp
Uploading ntp            [1.6.2]
Uploaded 1 cookbook.
```

You can confirm the upload two different ways:

1. Via the command line, issue the command `knife cookbook list ntp`, which will return the NTP cookbook with the versions uploaded.

   Your output will be something similar to this:

   ```
   $ knife cookbook list ntp
   ntp   1.6.2
   ```

2. Via the GUI, open a web browser and go to https://manage.chef.io and log in with your credentials created earlier in the chapter. Click **Policy** at the top of the interface. By default, this will bring you to the Cookbooks section, and you will see the NTP cookbook in the main area of the GUI, as shown in Figure 8-7.

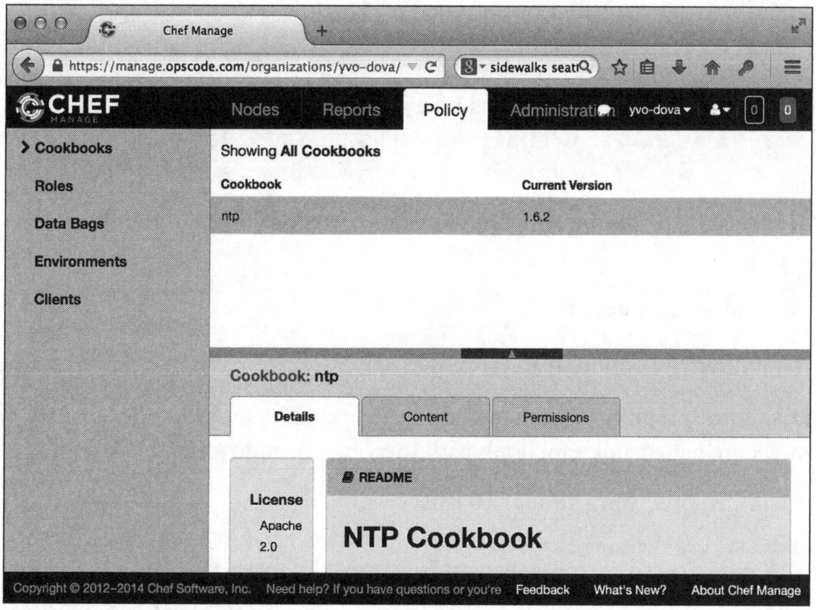

Figure 8-7 Confirming NTP cookbook upload

Prep/Setup System Management Task 2: Managing Root Password

The second system management task covered in this chapter is managing the root password across the two test VMs. The cookbook used is one specifically crafted for this book. Note that although the cookbook works as expected, Chef offers more secure ways to store the password hash other than an attribute.

We will use the attribute that manages the password hash and change it across different Chef environments to illustrate how attributes are set and handled by Chef.

Downloading the Manage Root Cookbook

The cookbook to manage the root password is being maintained in a repository on GitHub that was created specifically for this book. Open your web browser and enter the following URL: **http://bit.ly/1kwP34o**. The URL has been shortened because it is quite long otherwise.

From this website, you download a zip file to your browser's download folder. Open your operating system's file management utility and go to your browser's Download folder. Extract the downloaded file (yvovandoorn-managedroot.zip) to the cookbooks directory located inside of the chef-repo directory that we set up during the hosted Chef setup.

> **NOTE**
>
> Make sure that the directory from the extracted zip file is named managedroot and not yvovandoorn-managedroot. Rename it to managedroot if it isn't named that way.

In your terminal or PowerShell window, in your chef-repo directory, issue the following command:

```
knife cookbook upload managedroot
```

You can confirm the upload two different ways:

1. Via the command line, issue the command `knife cookbook list managedroot`, which returns the managedroot cookbook with the versions uploaded.

   Your output will be something similar to this:

   ```
   $ knife cookbook list managedroot
   managedroot   0.1.1
   ```

2. Via the GUI, open a web browser and go to https://manage.chef.io and log in with your credentials created earlier in the chapter. Click **Policy** at the top of the interface. By default, this brings you to the Cookbooks section, and you will see the managedroot cookbook in the main area of the GUI.

Configuring Your Virtual Guests

This is where the rubber meets the road. Your hosted Chef organization is now hosting at least two cookbooks, and all we need is some actual servers to apply the policy to. In the following steps, the first portion covers installing Chef client onto your virtual guests, followed by adding a run list (via the Chef Manage website) to your new nodes and rerunning the Chef client with the new policy list.

Installing Chef Client

Knife can bootstrap a node. With recent versions of Chef, Knife can now bootstrap nodes that accept either Secure Shell (SSH) connections or WinRM connections. We will use two virtual guests to bootstrap and configure Chef.

The server names used are virtualserver-01 and virtualserver-02. Let's begin with bootstrapping the first server (in this case, virtualserver-01 in the following example).

NOTE

Make sure that your virtual guests have the ability to connect to https://www.chef.io. While your VMs can be NAT'ed or on a private network, make sure that they have the ability to connect over the Internet.

NOTE

Although, paradoxically, we are going to be managing time with one of the system management tasks, make sure that before executing the bootstrap command your virtual guest's clock has not drifted more than 15 minutes. If it has, you can execute `sudo ntpdate 0.pool.ntp.org` on your virtual guest to set up the time properly.

Open a terminal or Windows PowerShell terminal and go to your chef-repo directory.

The commands executed here will differ slightly based on how your virtual guests are set up. If your user account on the virtual guest has sudo access without prompting for a password, your command will differ slightly from if you are required to enter a password. In the following example, virtualserver-01 does not require a password, but virtualserver-02 does require a password.

You can choose to omit the `--ssh-password` portion on the command line. When you do so, it will prompt when you press Enter for a password as opposed to passing it to the host.

Although a version of Chef isn't required to be specified on the command line, and can be omitted if you want, it was added here to ensure a smooth learning experience.

The `bootstrap` command when sudo does not prompt for a password is as follows:

```
knife bootstrap --ssh-user RemoteUser --ssh-password RemoteUserPassword

--sudo --bootstrap-version 11.12.4 VMguestHostname
```

Here is an example:

```
knife bootstrap --ssh-user yvo --ssh-password password --sudo --boot-
strap-version 11.12.4 virtualserver-01
```

The `bootstrap` command when sudo *does* prompt for a password is as follows:

```
knife bootstrap --ssh-user RemoteUser --ssh-password RemoteUserPassword
--sudo --use-sudo-password --bootstrap-version 11.12.4 VMguestHostname
```

For example:

```
knife bootstrap --ssh-user yvo --ssh-password password --sudo
--use-sudo-password --bootstrap-version 11.12.4 virtualserver-02
```

Here is the truncated output of a `bootstrap` command:

```
chef-repo/cookbooks " knife bootstrap --ssh-user yvo --ssh-password
password --sudo --bootstrap-version 11.12.4 virtualserver-01
Connecting to virtualserver-01
virtualserver-01 Installing Chef Client...
....
virtualserver-01 Installing Chef 11.12.4
virtualserver-01 installing with rpm...
virtualserver-01 warning: /tmp/install.sh.1295/chef-11.12.4-1.el6.x86_64.
rpm: Header V4 DSA/SHA1 Signature, key ID 83ef826a: NOKEY
virtualserver-01 Preparing...                ################################
############## [100%]
virtualserver-01    1:chef                   ################################
############## [100%]
virtualserver-01 Thank you for installing Chef!
virtualserver-01 Starting first Chef Client run...
....
virtualserver-01 Starting Chef Client, version 11.12.4
virtualserver-01 Creating a new client identity for virtualserver-01.chef-
demo.com using the validator key.
virtualserver-01 resolving cookbooks for run list: []
virtualserver-01 Synchronizing Cookbooks:
```

```
virtualserver-01 Compiling Cookbooks...
virtualserver-01 Converging 0 resources
virtualserver-01
virtualserver-01 Running handlers:
virtualserver-01 Running handlers complete
virtualserver-01
virtualserver-01 Chef Client finished, 0/0 resources updated in 6.202156227
seconds
```

The preceding output is from virtualserver-01. Because we did not assign any policy to your newly bootstrapped node (which can be done at the time of bootstrap), you should see "0/0 resources updated."

Rerun the `bootstrap` command, now pointing at the second virtual guest.

After you have bootstrapped (installed Chef client) on both virtual guests, run the following command, while in your chef-repo directory, in your terminal or Windows PowerShell window:

```
knife node list
```

It should return two servers now registered with your hosted Chef organization:

```
$ knife node list
virtualserver-01.chefdemo.com
virtualserver-02.chefdemo.com
$
```

Systems Management Tasks

Now that two servers (or in Chef speak, *nodes*) are configured, let's add the NTP cookbook to *one* of your server's run list so that the next time Chef client executes on your server it will run the necessary steps to bring your server into compliance.

> **NOTE**
>
> Only follow these steps for *one* of your two registered servers.

1. Open a web browser and go to https://manage.chef.io.
2. Click the **Nodes** text at the top of the interface; it should display your two registered servers with hosted Chef, as shown in Figure 8-8.

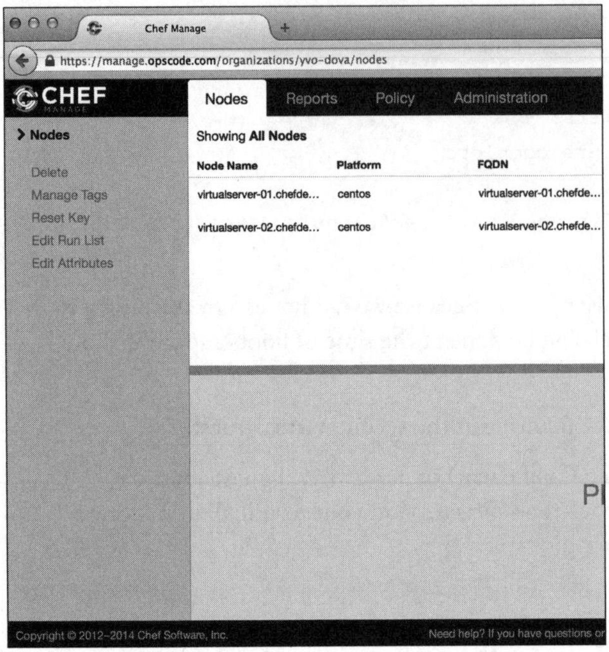

Figure 8-8 Displaying registered servers with hosted Chef

3. Click the first server, which will populate the lower interface with various options. Find the section called Run List, which should be empty. Proceed to click **Edit**, as shown in Figure 8-9.

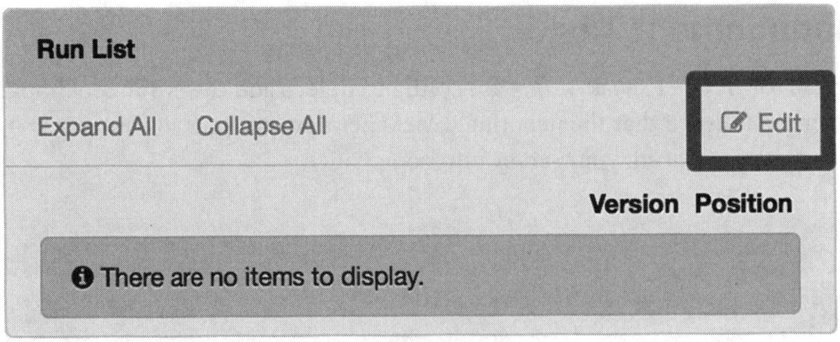

Figure 8-9 Modifying the run list

4. This will bring up a new interface in which you can edit the node's run list. It will display all available recipes that have been uploaded to the Chef organization. For now, only add NTP to the current run list. Do this by selecting **ntp** under Available Recipes and dragging it to Current Run List, as shown in Figure 8-10.

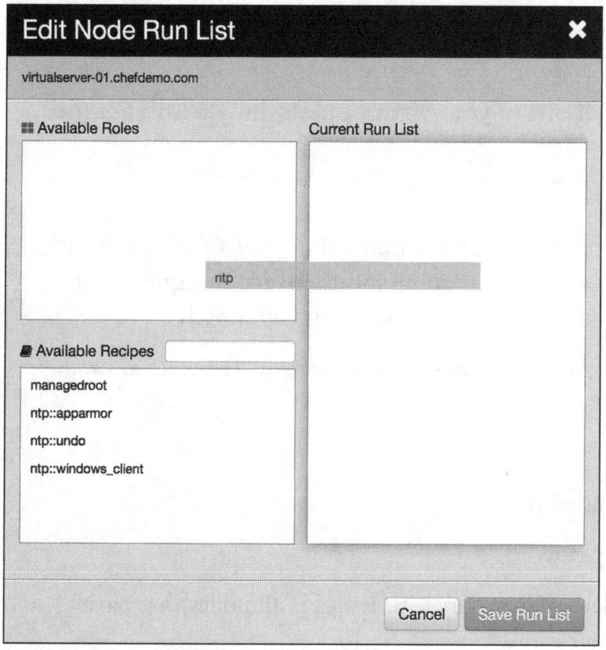

Figure 8-10 Creating a run list for the node

5. Click **Save Run List** to confirm your new run list.

In the next section, we rerun Chef client and enforce the new run list on one of your servers.

Running Chef Client

Chef is pretty powerful because the server also maintains a search index of all nodes, including the run list currently set on all your nodes in your environment. There are two ways we can execute chef client, via `knife ssh`, on your node:

1. The boring way:

   Open a terminal or Windows PowerShell window and confirm that you are in your chef-repo directory.

Execute the following:

```
knife ssh --ssh-user RemoteUser --ssh-password RemoteUserPassword -m
VMguestHostname "sudo chef-client"
```

For example:

```
knife ssh --ssh-user yvo --ssh-password password -m virtualserver-01
"sudo chef-client"
```

This will just specifically target one of your virtual guests, but doesn't use the search index.

2. The search way:

   Knife can be used to also search the index maintained in your Chef organization. We will list two ways where we can use search (and these are two queries of many different queries you can use to execute commands remotely):

   a. `knife ssh --ssh-user RemoteUser --ssh-password RemoteUserPassword "recipe:ntp" "sudo chef-client"`

      Breaking it down:

      - `ssh-user` is your username.
      - `password` is your password.
      - `"recipe:ntp"` queries Chef Server to look for all nodes that have recipe:ntp set in their run list.
      - `"sudo chef-client"` instructs Knife to execute Chef client, via sudo on all returned servers.

        For example:

        ```
        knife ssh --ssh-user yvo --ssh-password password "recipe:ntp"
        "sudo chef-client"
        ```

   b. Another way is to rerun Chef client on *all* nodes running Linux in your organization:

      ```
      knife ssh --ssh-user **RemoteUser** --ssh-password
      **RemoteUserPassword** "os:linux" "sudo chef-client"
      ```

      For example:

      ```
      knife ssh --ssh-user yvo --ssh-password password "os:linux" "sudo
      chef-client"
      ```

> **NOTE**
>
> You can add `--why-run` to Chef client (for example, `chef-client --why-run`) to run a simulation of the Chef client. The output would tell you what Chef *would* do, without actually making changes to your system.

Managing the Root Password

Now that we're managing one server's NTP configuration with the cookbook, let's do the same thing with the managedroot cookbook. In addition, let's change up the default NTP server configuration. This section introduces the *environments* feature from Chef. Environments can be used to set environment-specific attributes (such as password hashes or unique NTP servers); they are also a place where you can constrain which version of the cookbook should be installed. We focus on the unique environment-specific attributes and leave it to you as an additional exercise to explore cookbook version constraints.

> **NOTE**
>
> For this exercise, we go back to the terminal or PowerShell window. We also need a text editor such as Notepad++ on Windows or Sublime (Linux, Mac, Windows) because we will be creating a few new files.

A few sample password hashes (SHA-512, generated on CentOS 6.5) were created and stored in a GitHub gist:

> http://bit.ly/SnkO4H (or https://gist.github.com/yvovandoorn/083f44dff822c168b971)

We will be using the hash for Production and Test/QA stored in this gist.

We're about to do the following:

- Create two environments files
- Upload each environment file to your hosted Chef organization
- Log in to your hosted Chef organization and do the following:
  - Assign each server to an environment
  - Modify each server's run list to run the managedroot cookbook
- Rerun the Chef client from the command line, using `search`, to apply policy to your servers

- Validate, using `knife ssh`, that the /etc/shadow file shows the applied hash
- Validate, using `knife ssh`, that ntp.conf is configured

Creating Two Environment Files

Using your operating system's file management program, in your chef-repo directory create a new directory called **environments**.

The recommended route is as follows:

A GitHub gist exists with the two environment files, located here:

> http://bit.ly/U60JBu (or https://gist.github.com/yvovandoorn/dae2c1ecf71452bf8057)

You can download both files located at this gist and store them in a directory called environments, which is created at the root of your chef-repo directory.

The typey-typey route (use this if you're supplying your own password hashes) is as follows:

Open a text editor (such as Notepad++ or Sublime) and type out the following:

```
Content:
name "production"
description "Your production environment"
default_attributes ({
        "root" => {
                "password" => "$6$uLD5kuid$pvYSgFZMp5a.m8Q2fjVaIhcCIyhG-
FytWZYQXCkCW8oC.JvNWV5hmCptApdBOBZLA4DJc.rimnngPF9oZoZ6Ga1"
        },
        "ntp" => {
                "servers" => [ "0.vmware.pool.ntp.org", "1.vmware.pool.ntp.
org", "2.vmware.pool.ntp.org" ]
        }
})
```

Save this file in the environments directory under your chef-repo directory and name it **production.rb**.

Open a new text editor window and enter the following:

```
name "testqa"
description "Your testqa environment"
default_attributes ({
```

```
        "root" => {
                "password" => "$6$EYgMQC0o$vaFIm/f81YRTjihvIk5brpE4oJhSiPn4Y-
2Bw2hsxOkC4og4V7KfSCYEmkw40MriUHICZppkGwPpZ4r44tGCIF1"
        },
        "ntp" => {
                "servers" => [ "0.pool.ntp.org", "1.pool.ntp.org", "2.pool.
ntp.org" ]
        }
})
```

Save this file in the environments directory under your chef-repo directory and name it **testqa.rb**.

You will now have either created or downloaded two environment files and stored them in your environments directory located under your chef-repo directory.

Uploading Environment Files to your Hosted Chef Organization

In a terminal or Windows PowerShell window, change directories to your chef-repo directory.

Execute the following command:

```
knife environment from file production.rb testqa.rb
```

You will see output similar to this:

```
$ knife environment from file production.rb testqa.rb
Updated Environment production
Updated Environment testqa
```

Confirm the existence of your two new environments by entering the following:

```
knife environment show production
```

This command returns something similar to what Figure 8-11 shows.

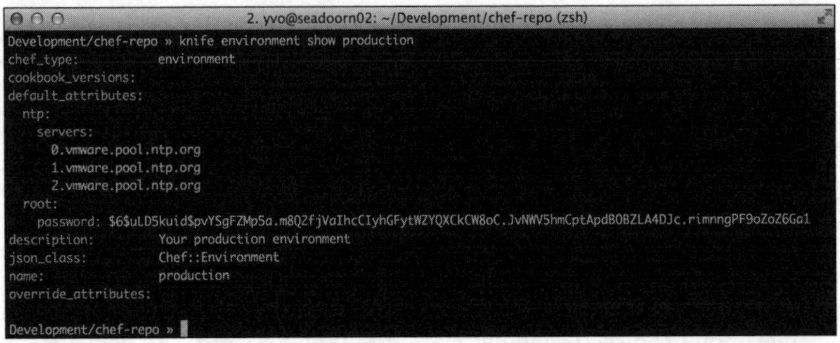

2. yvo@seadoorn02: ~/Development/chef-repo (zsh)
Development/chef-repo » knife environment show production
chef_type: environment
cookbook_versions:
default_attributes:
ntp:
servers:
0.vmware.pool.ntp.org
1.vmware.pool.ntp.org
2.vmware.pool.ntp.org
root:
password: 6uLD5kuid$pvYSgFZMp5a.m8Q2fjVaIhcCIyhGFytWZYQXCkCW8oC.JvNWV5hmCptApdBOBZLA4DJc.rimnngPF9oZoZ6Ga1
description: Your production environment
json_class: Chef::Environment
name: production
override_attributes:
Development/chef-repo »

Figure 8-11 Confirming the creation of your environment

You can replace `production` with `testqa` in the `knife environment` command to do the same for the testqa environment.

Assigning Each Server to an Environment

The next set of steps will go over how to change the environment your node belongs to. An environment might contain unique attribute information (for example, a database IP address). In this exercise, we will configure each of the virtual machines against two of the created environments from the last exercise.

Open your web browser and go to https://manage.chef.io. Log in with your credentials we set up at the beginning of the chapter.

Click **Nodes** at the top of the interface, and then click your first registered server (a.k.a. node). This will populate the lower portion of the screen with detailed information on your node.

1. Assign this node to one of the two created environments (production or testqa), as shown in Figure 8-12.

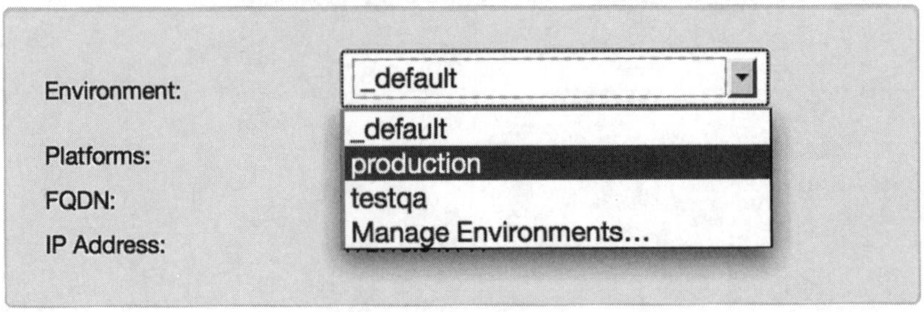

Figure 8-12 Assigning a node to a created environment

2. Once selected, it will confirm the environment change. Click **Save** to confirm the change.

3. Click the second node registered with your hosted Chef account and assign it to the other environment (opposite of the environment selected for the first node).

   The main node interface will show you the two registered nodes and the environment each node is assigned to.

Modifying Each Server's Run List to Run the Managedroot Cookbook

Open your web browser and go to https://manage.chef.io. Log in with your credentials we set up at the beginning of the chapter.

Click **Nodes** at the top of the interface, and then click your first registered server (a.k.a. node). This will populate the lower portion of the screen with detailed information on your node.

1. Scroll down to the Run List portion of your node's configuration. If this node was previously configured to run the NTP cookbook, that is okay.

   Click **Edit** in the Run List section. This will bring up a new screen where you will modify the run list, as shown in Figure 8-13.

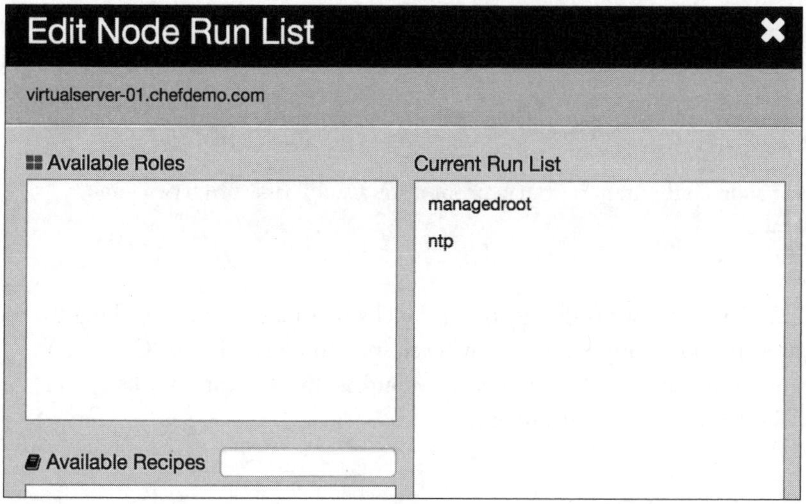

Figure 8-13 Editing the node run list

> **NOTE**
>
> Remember that order matters with Chef. The recipe specified first in your run list is executed first.

2. Click **Save Run List** for your first node.
3. Click the second registered server and repeat Step 1 and Step 2 on this server. Make sure both the ntp and managedroot recipes are in the run list.

Applying Your Changes to Your Nodes

With the environments and run lists altered for your two virtual guests, let's apply the changes to the nodes.

In a terminal or Windows PowerShell window, change directories to your chef-repo directory.

Execute the following command:

```
knife ssh --ssh-user RemoteUser --ssh-password RemoteUserPassword
"os:linux" "sudo chef-client"
```

For example:

```
knife ssh --ssh-user yvo --ssh-password password "os:linux" "sudo
chef-client"
```

> **NOTE**
>
> Depending on your sudo configuration, it may prompt for a sudo password when you execute this command.

Output will scroll in your window notifying you of the changes Chef client is making to your two virtual guests. Upon completion, you will see something similar to "Chef client finished, X/10 resources updated." The number of resources updated can vary based on which node was assigned to which environment.

Validating the Enforced Policy

Chef client may have run on the two servers, but are the changes actually in effect. Let's use `knife ssh` to determine some configuration files on each machine.

In a terminal or Windows PowerShell window, change directories to your chef-repo directory.

Let's first begin by determining whether the /etc/shadow for each node matches the desired state you set up through policy (cookbooks and environments), as shown in Figure 8-14.

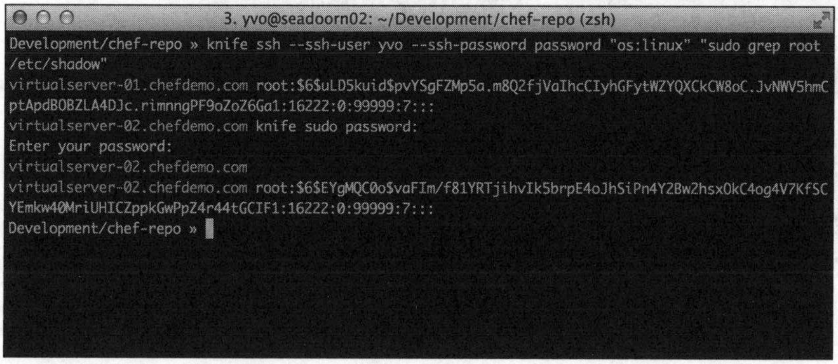
3. yvo@seadoorn02: ~/Development/chef-repo (zsh)
Development/chef-repo » knife ssh --ssh-user yvo --ssh-password password "os:linux" "sudo grep root /etc/shadow"
virtualserver-01.chefdemo.com root:6uLD5kuid$pvYSgFZMp5a.m8Q2fjVaIhcCIyhGFytWZYQXCkCW8oC.JvNWV5hmCptApdBOBZLA4DJc.rimnngPF9oZoZ6Ga1:16222:0:99999:7:::
virtualserver-02.chefdemo.com knife sudo password:
Enter your password:
virtualserver-02.chefdemo.com
virtualserver-02.chefdemo.com root:6EYgMQC0o$vaFIm/f81YRTjihvIk5brpE4oJhSiPn4Y2Bw2hsxOkC4og4V7KfSCYEmkw40MriUHICZppkGwPpZ4r44tGCIF1:16222:0:99999:7:::
Development/chef-repo »

Figure 8-14 Validate the changes to /etc/shadow via search

```
knife ssh --ssh-user RemoteUser --ssh-password RemoteUserPassword
"os:linux" "sudo grep root /etc/shadow"
```

For example:

```
knife ssh --ssh-user yvo --ssh-password password "os:linux" "sudo grep root
/etc/shadow"
```

Next let's determine whether ntpd is running and whether the HTP configuration is set to the servers described in each respective environment file. You can determine this by using `knife ssh`, as follows (see Figure 8-15):

Figure 8-15 Validate the installation and startup of ntpd via search

```
knife ssh --ssh-user RemoteUser --ssh-password RemoteUserPassword
"os:linux" "/etc/init.d/ntpd status && grep 'pool.ntp.org' /etc/ntp.conf"
```

Summary

This chapter built on the "Intro to Chef," quickly delving into setting up a hosted Chef account. It also covered community cookbooks, how to download a community cookbook, and more important, how to bring desired state configuration to two virtual guests.

One important thing to note is the best practice of not modifying cookbook code. In this chapter, and as a general practice, unique attributes should be set outside of the cookbook. Each cookbook may come with its set of "sane" defaults (in the case of the managedroot cookbook, there is no sane default for a root password hash), but attributes that are node or environment specific should not be directly made in the cookbook.

Various system management tasks can be done to nodes in your Chef organization. Challenge yourself by trying a few more Chef community cookbooks (like setting up a SQL Server instance, managing all users via a cookbook, and so forth).

The next chapter builds on features like bootstrap, assigning run lists, and combining them with a Knife plugin called knife-vsphere, which you can use to manage your vSphere infrastructure; you can also use it to bootstrap new servers, assign environments, run lists to servers that you're bootstrapping, or modify existing virtual guests.

References

[1] http://kb.vmware.com/selfservice/microsites/search.do?language=en_US&cmd=displayKC&externalId=1006427

[2] Full URL: http://github.com/yvovandoorn/managedroot/zipball/master/

Chapter 9

VMware vSphere Management with Chef

You will need a machine installed with ChefDK to understand and implement the topics covered in this chapter.

In this chapter, we go beyond Chef and find the various integration points that Chef has with various VMware management layers like ESXi or vSphere vCenter. Chef offers two great points of integration to VMware: Knife and Chef provisioning.

Topics covered in this chapter include the following:

- Knife plugins
- Chef provisioning

Knife, as you learned in earlier chapters, is a command-line utility that resides on a management server/workstation. Knife can be extended beyond the ability to talk to just the Chef Server (whether that Chef Server is located inside your data center or, as in this book, the hosted Chef service maintained by Chef). The ability to extend Knife is done through its plugin system, where users can issue commands such as `chef gem install knife-vsphere` or `chef gem install knife-esxi`.

Chef provisioning is a relatively new technology developed by Chef. Chef provisioning takes writing recipes to a whole new level. In Chapter 8, Chef was used to write a cookbook that managed a virtual machine (VM). The concept behind Chef provisioning is that it uses the same ideology, only applied to an entire machine. You can create recipes that describe entire application stacks by utilizing the *machine* resource. Just as Chef operates on a single node (or machine), the ordering on a recipe that describes machines *matters*. This is important if you consider the requirements/dependencies when orchestrating an entire application stack and ensuring that a database (with the proper contents) comes up before an application server that is hosting an application that requires the aforementioned database server.

The earlier chapters leveraged ChefDK, which is a program that this chapter continues to leverage. This chapter is intentionally less hands-on than Chapter 8 because it uses some of the exercises covered in that chapter to understand how it ties in with knife-vsphere or Chef provisioning.

- A workstation running ChefDK able to reach https://manage.chef.io
- A vSphere vCenter server with which you can
    - Clone a VM out of an RHEL6-based image
    - Create customization templates
- A chef-repo folder that we created in Chapter 8
- A web browser (Firefox 20+, Google Chrome 20+. or IE 10+) capable of reaching https://manage.chef.io
- A text editor such as Sublime Text, Notepad++, or Bluefish

Knife Plugins

One of the biggest advantages of Knife is its capability to extend itself through adding plugins. Knife utilizes Ruby gems to add capabilities to itself. With ChefDK, you can issue a `chef gem install plugin` command to utilize the Ruby interpreter shipped with ChefDK.

The two most popular Knife plugins for managing your VMware environment are knife-esxi and knife-vsphere. The knife-esxi plugin extends Knife to talk to individual ESXi hypervisors in your environment by using the documented VMware application programming interfaces (APIs) to handle both calls into VMware and into your Chef Server.

The knife-vsphere plugin is designed to extend Knife to talk to a vSphere vCenter server and your Chef Server. A common use case for knife-vsphere is to use it to clone a new image and use customization specifications right from the command line, whether it is Linux, Mac OS X, or Windows. There are no dependencies on VMware's PowerCLI tools because Knife talks directly via the API to vSphere.

Some of the features supported by knife-vsphere include the following:

- **Listings**
  - VMs
  - Folders
  - Templates
  - Datastores
  - VLANs (currently requires vSphere Distributed Switch)
  - Resource pools
  - Clusters
  - Customization specifications
  - Hosts in a pool or cluster
- **VM operations**
  - Power on/off
  - Clone (with optional Chef bootstrap and run list)
  - Delete
  - VMDK addition
  - Migrate
  - Connect/disconnect network
- **Clone-specific customization options (for Linux guests)**
  - Destination folder
  - CPU core count
  - Memory size
  - DNS settings
  - Hostname/Domain name
  - IP addresses/default gateway
  - VLANs (currently requires distributed vswitch)
  - Resource pools

Getting Started with knife-vsphere

To get started, we first need to install the knife plugin. With the release of ChefDK, this is an extremely easy process. In earlier chapters, ChefDK was installed, and that program is used again to perform an installation of the knife-vsphere plugin.

Open a terminal or Windows PowerShell window and change directories to your chef-repo directory. A quick example is to enter `cd ~/Development/chef-repo` on OS X or `cd $env:userprofile\Development\chef-repo` on Windows.

Now, as demonstrated in Figure 9-1, enter `chef gem install knife-vsphere`.

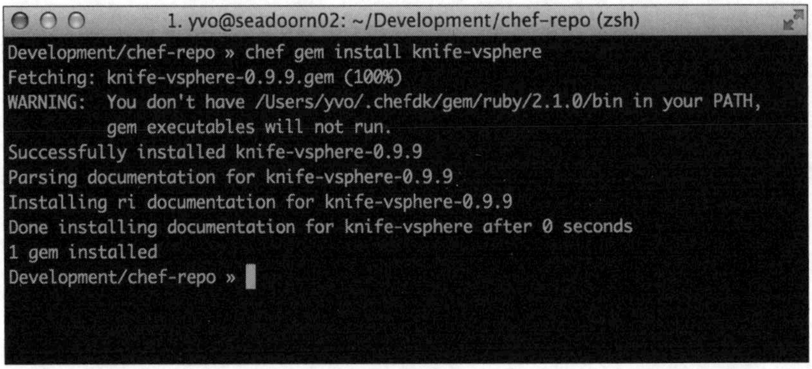
1. yvo@seadoorn02: ~/Development/chef-repo (zsh)
Development/chef-repo » chef gem install knife-vsphere
Fetching: knife-vsphere-0.9.9.gem (100%)
WARNING: You don't have /Users/yvo/.chefdk/gem/ruby/2.1.0/bin in your PATH,
gem executables will not run.
Successfully installed knife-vsphere-0.9.9
Parsing documentation for knife-vsphere-0.9.9
Installing ri documentation for knife-vsphere-0.9.9
Done installing documentation for knife-vsphere after 0 seconds
1 gem installed
Development/chef-repo »

Figure 9-1 Installing the knife-vsphere plugin

> **NOTE**
>
> Your output may vary from the screenshot because of updates made to ChefDK since publication or if you've experimented outside of this book with Chef and ChefDK (for example, installed other gems).

Configuring the knife.rb File

After you have successfully installed knife-vsphere, we need to do a bit more configuration to get Chef to talk to your vSphere server.

Inside your chef-repo directory, there is a .chef directory. The .chef directory contains files like your private key that is used to properly sign requests to a Chef Server's API, but it also contains a configuration file for Knife, appropriately, called knife.rb, as shown in Figure 9-2.

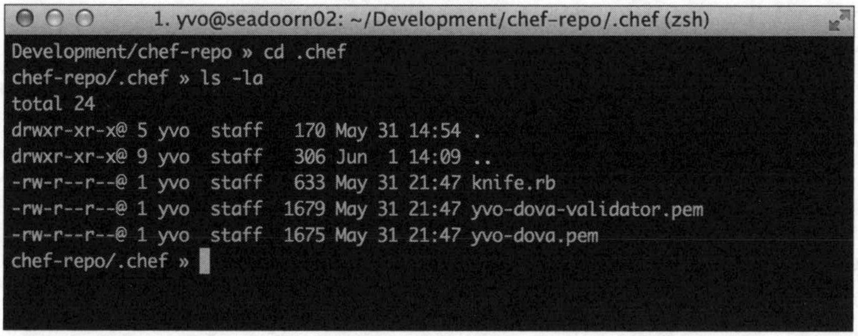

Figure 9-2 .chef directory

Using a reliable text editor (meaning not WordPad/Notepad on Windows or TextEdit on OS X) such as Notepad++, Sublime Editor, or Bluefish, open the knife.rb file that is stored inside the .chef directory (see Figure 9-3).

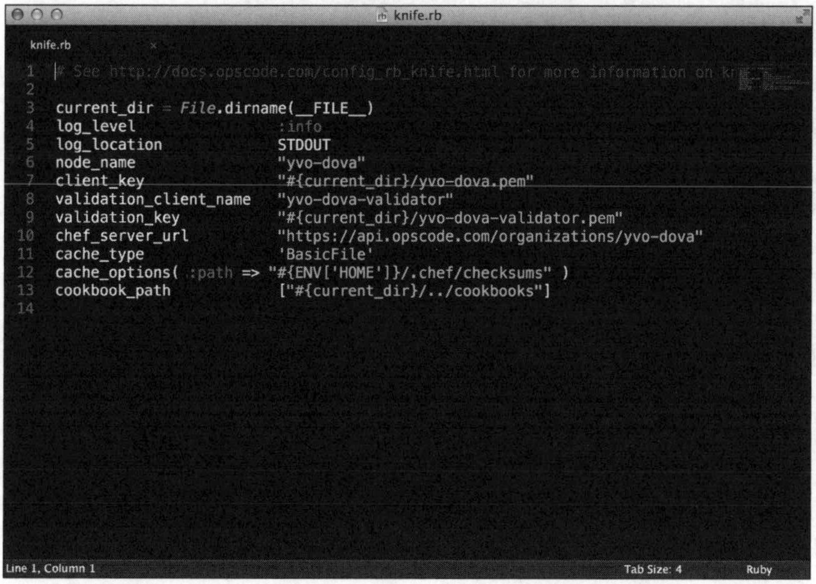

Figure 9-3 Opening knife.rb in a text editor

Add the following lines with the appropriate information for the vSphere environment you want the knife-vsphere plugin to use:

```
knife[:vsphere_host] = "Your.Host.Or.IP.Address.Here"
knife[:vsphere_user] = "YourUserNameHere"
```

```
knife[:vsphere_pass] = "YourPasswordHere"
knife[:vsphere_dc] = "YourvSphereDCHere"
```

Optionally, add the following line if your vSphere server is using a self-signed or nonstandard certificate authority Secure Sockets Layer (SSL) certificate.

```
knife[:vsphere_insecure] = true
```

Once finished, add the necessary lines, save the file in your text editor, and return to the terminal or Windows PowerShell window.

Validating the Configuration

Inside of the terminal or Windows PowerShell, execute the `knife vsphere datastore list` command to validate that you are able to successfully connect to your vSphere vCenter server, as demonstrated in Figure 9-4.

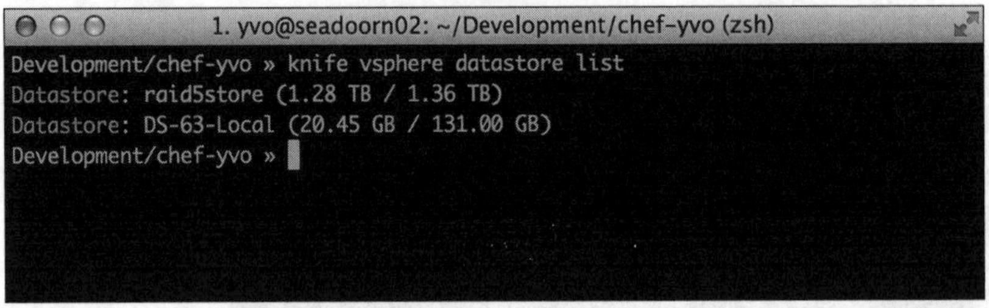

Figure 9-4 Confirming connection to the vSphere vCenter server

Depending on your environment, the preceding command will return the available datastores that are associated with the vSphere DC you specified in your knife.rb file. Because we used a `list` command, no actual changes were made to your vSphere configuration.

Putting It All Together

As mentioned earlier, the real power of Knife is combining both the Chef Server and vSphere server. In the following example, there are a few assumptions. In Chapter 8, the provisioning of a virtual machine (VM), bootstrapping, and adding items to a run list were done in various steps.

What if there were a way to string it all together into a single command:

1. Provision a host with specific memory/CPU/IP settings

2. Bootstrap the host with a current version of Chef
3. Define a run list in the same command so that the node executes immediately after installing Chef client

Unfortunately this is where some of this exercise is left up to you to complete because of the vastly different ways your vCenter server may have been set up.

So, here are some assumptions:

- You have a customization specification designed for an RHE-based (including CentOS or OEL) operating system.
- You have a VM template saved as the RHEL6 OS type.
- You have the ability to clone a template.

> **NOTE**
>
> While CentOS or Scientific Linux may be selectable as guest operating systems in VMware, to properly use the customization specification, the template needs to be saved to a Red Hat-based OS. In my testing, no harm other than that your CentOS template shows up as a Red Hat image was seen.

Here is a sample command that will do it all, in one swoop:

```
knife vsphere vm clone YourVMName --template YourLinuxTemplate
--cips YourVMIPaddress --cdnsips YourVMDNSServer --chostname
UnQualifiedDNSNameforCustomisation --cdomain DomainNameforCustomisation
--start --bootstrap true --distro chef-full --ssh-user SSHUser
--ssh-password SSHPassword --run-list "ARunList"
```

For example:

```
knife vsphere vm clone awebapp01 --template centbase --cips 172.31.8.101/22
--cdnsips 8.8.8.8 --chostname awebapp01 --cdomain opscode.us --start
--bootstrap true --distro chef-full --ssh-user username --ssh-password
Password --run-list "role[base],role[webserver]"
```

Let's break down what this command does exactly:

- `knife vsphere vm clone`: This command tells Knife and vSphere that we are about to clone an image.
- *`YourVMName`*: This is the name of the VM how it shows up in vSphere.
- `--template` *`YourLinuxTemplate`*: This is the specific template name we would use to clone out of.

- `--cips` *`YourVMIPaddress`*: (Optional, with customization template) Specify the IP address in classless interdomain routing (CIDR) notation (for example, 172.31.8.101/22).
- `--cdnsips` *`YourVMDNSServer`*: (Optional, with customization template) Specify the DNS server for the VM.
- `--chostname` *`UnQualifiedDNSNameforCustomisation`*: (Optional, with customization template and hostname not registered in the Domain Name System [DNS]) Specify the hostname; this proves very useful if you haven't registered it yet with DNS.
- `--cdomain` *`DomainNameforCustomisation`*: (Optional, with customization template) Specify the host's domain name.
- `--start`: Instructs the VM to start after being cloned.
- `--bootstrap true`: Instructs the VM to be bootstrapped after being cloned and started.
- `--distro chef-full`: Instructs the VM to use the default bootstrap template.
- `--ssh-user` *`SSHUser`*: The user used to connect to the VM after it is up to bootstrap it.
- `--ssh-password` *`SSHPassword`*: The password used to connect to the VM after it is up to bootstrap it.
- `--run-list "`*`role[base],role[webserver]`*`"`: The run list that should be used to bootstrap the new VM and saved to the Chef Server as the defined run list.

After you execute this command, your workstation will be interacting with three separate targets for the new machine to come online, and there are five separate phases to complete the process, as illustrated in Figure 9-5.

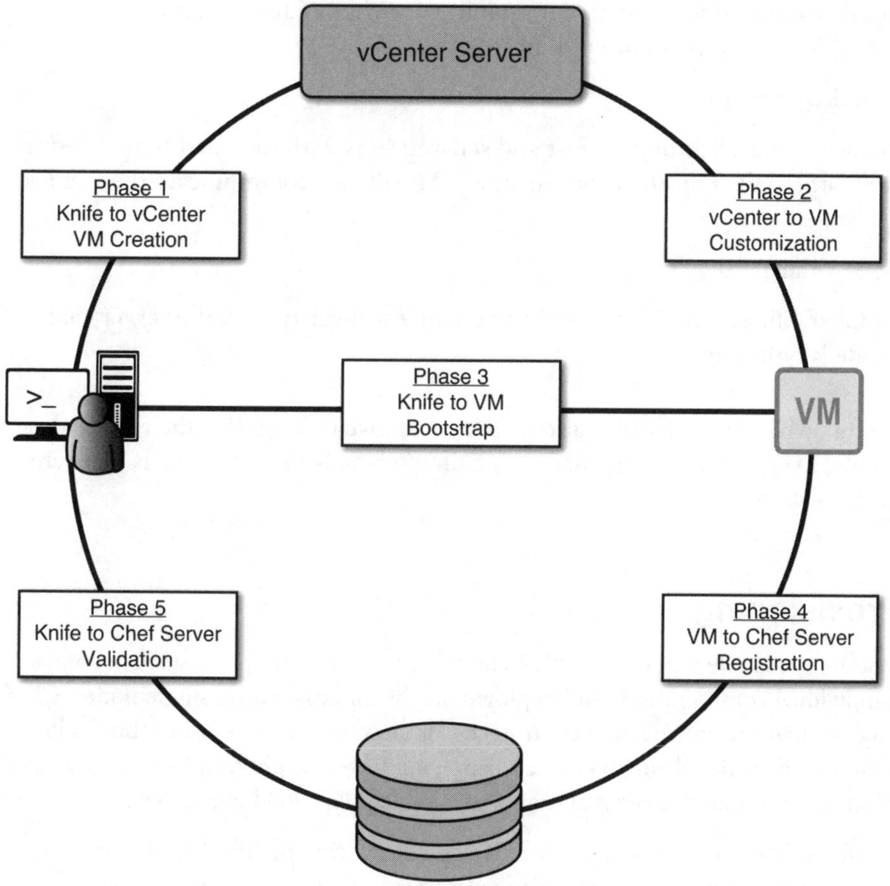

Figure 9-5 Five phases of `knife vsphere clone`

- Phase 1: VM creation

  Knife will communicate with vSphere to clone the VM.

- Phase 2: Customization

  The vCenter server will apply the customization template to the new VM.

- Phase 3: Bootstrap

  After vCenter completes, it will notify knife it has completed. Knife will wait for Secure Shell (SSH) to become available on the new host. After it is up, Knife will copy over the validator key, a sample client.rb, and execute a script to download

Chef. (By default, it is set up to communicate to chef.io; however, you can change this to point to an internal host.)

- Phase 4: Registration

  Chef client is installed on the host and self-registers with the Chef Server (using the validator key). The client on the new VM will also communicate the run list to the server.

- Phase 5: Validation

  Once Chef Client runs for the first time, Knife will verify with the server that the node is online and exit.

Beyond setting up new VMs, you can also do administrative tasks like list the various data stores available. Every command exposed with knife-vsphere is to manage VMs registered with vSphere.

Chef Provisioning

Chef provisioning was released in mid-2014 and takes Chef a level up the stack beyond managing individual configurations and deployments of applications on single nodes. Chef provisioning can manage entire application stacks, or clusters, where orchestration is key. Chef provisioning does this through code and applying the same philosophy to entire stack configuration (for example, ordering matters, executable policy held in recipes).

Whereas knife-vsphere focuses on a single VM and configuring the run list of that single VM, Chef provisioning can spin up an entire pool of servers on your VMware environment.

Chef Provisioning Architecture

There are two components to Chef provisioning:

- The first component is the introduction of a new resource in Chef called the *machine* resource. The machine resource is used to declare, in a Chef recipe, the machines you want to set up. The machines will be set up in the order they are written in the recipe. However, just defining a bunch of machines without actually defining a place where to put them isn't very useful.
- The second component to Chef provisioning is called the *provisioner*, which uses a driver or plugin approach. Each driver is a separate Ruby gem that can be installed inside of the ChefDK environment.

The two components are used together, but because of the flexibility and extensibility of Chef provisioning, the best practice is that the machine resource configuration should live in a separate file from your driver configuration. An intentional design decision related to Chef provisioning is that a majority of the *drivers* will be written by the community as opposed to Chef. Chef will provide the facility (Chef provisioning), whereas companies or open source users will provide the driver to integrate with a specific product. The chef-provisioning-vsphere driver is, as of this writing, maintained by Rally Software.

Getting Started with Chef Provisioning

Open a terminal or Windows PowerShell window and change directories to your chef-repo directory. A quick example is to enter `'cd ~/Development/chef-repo'` on OS X or `'cd $env:userprofile\Development\chef-repo'` on Windows.

Type in the `chef gem install chef-provisioning chef-provisioning-vsphere` command to install chef-provisioning and chef-provisioning-vsphere, as demonstrated in Figure 9-6.

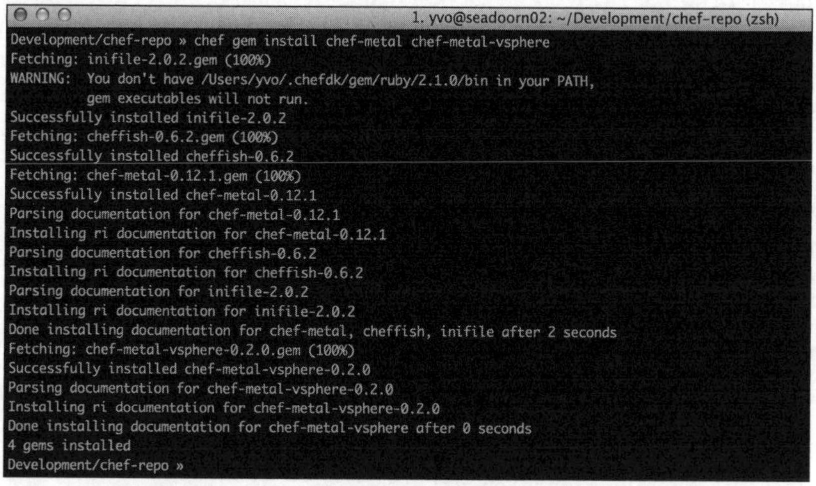

Figure 9-6 Installing chef-provisioning and chef-provisioning-vsphere

> **NOTE**
>
> Your output might vary from the screenshot because of updates made to ChefDK since publication or if you've experimented outside of this book with Chef and ChefDK (for example, installed other gems).

Spinning Up Some Nodes

> **CAUTION**
>
> Chef provisioning is still under heavy development, and it is very possible that at publishing time the instructions might be slightly altered. The gists referenced in this section will be updated to ensure that the examples will continue to work.

Open a text editor and create a file with the following contents or download the content directly from a GitHub gist located at http://bit.ly/1nv8GHn (or https://gist.github.com/yvovandoorn/519f91d84e786fe4b5d7).

```
require 'chef_metal_vsphere'
with_chef_server https://api.opscode.com,
  :client_name => Chef::Config[:node_name],
  :signing_key_filename => Chef::Config[:client_key]
with_vsphere_provisioner vsphere_host: 'vcenter-host-name',
  vsphere_insecure: true,
  vsphere_user:     'you_user_name',
  vsphere_password: 'your_password'
with_provisioner_options('bootstrap_options' => {
  datacenter:          'datacenter_name',
  cluster:             'cluster_name',
  resource_pool:       'resource_pool_name',
  datastore:           'datastore_name',
  template_name:       'name_of_template_vm',
  template_folder:     'folder_containing_template_vm',
  vm_folder:           'folder_to_clone_vms_into',
  customization_spec: 'standard-config',

  ssh: {
    user:                   'username_on_vm',
    password:               'name_of_your_first_pet',
    port:                   22,
    auth_methods:           ['password'],
    user_known_hosts_file: '/dev/null',
    paranoid:               false,
    keys:                   [ ],
    keys_only:              false
    }
  })
```

Save the file as **vsphere-metal.rb** at the root of your chef-repo directory.

Note that you will need to configure the appropriate sections in the vsphere-metal.rb file. Items that will need configuration include the following:

- vcenter-host-name
- vsphere_user
- vsphere_password
- datacenter
- cluster
- resource_pool
- datastore
- template_name
- template_folder
- vm_folder
- customization_spec
- user
- password

> **NOTE**
>
> For Chef provisioning to work, the user who is doing the bootstrapping inside the new VM must have NOPASSWD sudo access enabled.

Open another text editor window and create a file with the following contents or download the content directly from a GitHub gist located at http://bit.ly/1nv8GHn (or https://gist.github.com/yvovandoorn/519f91d84e786fe4b5d7):

```
require 'chef_metal'

with_chef_server "https://api.opscode.com",
  :client_name => Chef::Config[:node_name],
  :signing_key_filename => Chef::Config[:client_key]

1.upto 2 do |n|
  machine "metal_#{n}" do
```

```
    action [:create]
    recipe 'ntp'
    converge true
  end
end
```

Save both files in the root of your chef-repo directory.

Open a terminal or Windows PowerShell window and change directories to your chef-repo directory. A quick example is to enter `'cd ~/Development/chef-repo'` on OS X or `'cd $env:userprofile\Development\chef-repo'` on Windows.

To execute Chef provisioning, we will be executing Chef client directly on your workstation as opposed to a VM.

Execute the following command:

```
'chef-client -z vsphere-metal.rb machine.rb'
```

This will spin up an in-memory Chef Server and provision the two hosts with Network Time Protocol (NTP) run lists. By your specifying the `use_chef_server` in the configuration, the nodes added will also be registered to your hosted Chef account.

Imagine not just community cookbooks of how to set up specific applications on one server, but instead, entire cookbooks that define entire virtual infrastructures in an order that you've defined and can be tested to ensure they will work. Goodbye to maintaining a playbook or a wiki for your infrastructure; instead, it is all handled in a recipe.

Summary

This chapter covered the different ways a vSphere environment can be managed using Chef. Knife can be used to do actual administration of your vSphere environment in addition to bootstrapping new hosts, and Chef provisioning can be used to fully take advantage of your vSphere environment by creating recipes that contain entire stack configurations for specific applications or entire infrastructures.

Chapter 10

Introduction to Ansible

Ansible is a configuration management solution developed by Michael DeHaan (also known for the Cobbler deployment system). Ansible is commercially supported by Ansible, Inc.

Topics covered in this chapter include the following:

- Ansible architecture
- Ansible groups
- Ansible ad hoc command execution
- Ansible playbooks
- Ansible roles
- Ansible Galaxy

Ansible Architecture

Ansible is written in Python, and it is an agentless solution. The server where Ansible is installed is referred to as the *controller*, and the servers to which instructions are to be deployed are referred to as *managed nodes*. Deployment instructions are written in YAML. The controller's instructions are executed on the managed nodes using Python. The controller requires Python version 2.6 to be installed. The managed nodes need to run Python version 2.4 or later. Python version 2.5 or later is recommended on the managed nodes because of a JSON interpreter dependency.

> **NOTE**
>
> Python 3 is not currently supported. If your Linux distribution does not come with Python 2.x versions installed, you must install a Python 2 version, preferably 2.5 or later, and set the `ansible_python_interpreter` variable in your Ansible Inventory file discussed later in the chapter.

All communication between the controller and managed nodes occurs via Secure Shell (SSH). Because SSH is pretty much the standard for accessing Linux servers, this simplifies preparing the infrastructure for Ansible: Just verify that the user executing Ansible commands has an entry in the authorized_keys file residing on each managed node. If the system administrator does not have his or her SSH key in the authorized_keys file for any reason, there are alternative authentication options, such as using the `--user` and `--ask-pass` flags during Ansible executions. For any Ansible jobs that require elevated privileges, you can use the following pairs of runtime flags for this purpose:

- `--su` and `--ask-su-pass`
- `--sudo` and `--ask-sudo-pass` (must have entries in the managed nodes' sudoers files)

For simplicity, the sample code for Chapters 10 and 11 assume that you are executing the Ansible plays as the root user of your controller and that this user's SSH key has been added to the authorized_keys file on each of your managed nodes.

Figure 10-1 illustrates the communication between the controller and managed nodes.

One significant difference between Ansible and other configuration management technologies like Puppet and Chef is that the controller can be any machine, including the system administrator's laptop. If there is a group of administrators executing the Ansible playbooks, it might be a good idea to designate a single machine to be the controller. Ansible, Inc. has a solution to address this called Ansible Tower, which provides a central management point with a user interface (UI), application programming interface (API), and command-line interface (CLI) for teams of administrators to keep track of playbooks and which jobs will be run. This book does not cover Ansible Tower, but you do want to be aware of it for management purposes.

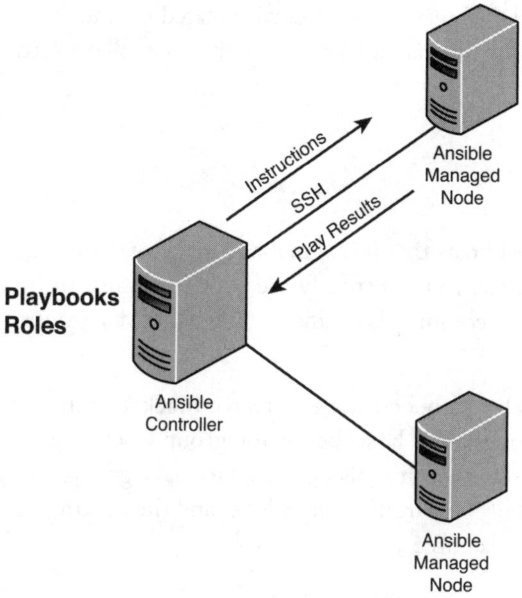

Figure 10-1 Ansible component topology

Preparing your Ansible Test Lab

The examples in Chapters 10 and 11 use a three machine setup:

- Ansible Controller—Ubuntu 12.04
- Managed Node #1—Ubuntu 12.04
- Managed Node #2—CentOS 6.5

The quickest way to setup the environment would be to use Vagrant (discussed in Chapter 3). The resource allocations can be 1 vCPU and 512 MB RAM for the controller and managed node #1. We will eventually install a database server on managed node #2, so give that node 2–4 GB RAM. The book's GitHub page will have a sample Vagrantfile that you can use as a base to start building your test lab.

The version of Ansible available in the controller's default operating system package repositories might be outdated. Follow the instructions hosted on the Ansible documentation site to get the latest stable version for the controller (http://docs.ansible.com/intro_installation.html).

For ease of use, make sure the public SSH key for the controller node is listed in the authorized_keys file on both managed nodes. Otherwise, you will need to specify your username and password every time you execute Ansible plays on the managed nodes.

The controller will need to have access to a DNS server with records created for the managed node IPs, or you can make entries for the managed nodes in the controller's /etc/hosts file.

Ansible Groups

Ansible keeps track of the hosts and groups of hosts that it will manage in an inventory file. The default path is /etc/ansible/hosts. However, you can specify the path at runtime or by editing the ansible.cfg file. It is possible to run commands against individual hosts, groups of hosts, and even groups of groups.

Each group in the inventory file is indicated by a label enclosed between brackets (for example, [group_name]), with a listing of that group's hosts below the group label. Hosts can belong to multiple groups. As mentioned earlier, it is also possible to make groups of groups by appending `:children` to the end of the parent group's label and then listing the member groups below it. Listing 10-1 shows examples.

Listing 10-1 Ansible Inventory File

```
[web]
mnode01.devops.local
mnode03.devops.local
[db]
mnode02.devops.local
mnode04.devops.local
[missioncritical:children]
web
db
```

It is possible to create complex inventory files using wildcards, ranges, and so on (for example, `mnode[01:10].devops.local`). If you want to verify that your inventory file is valid, you can use the `ansible all --list-hosts` command to verify this.

Ansible Ad Hoc Command Execution

The commands that Ansible can execute are known as *modules*. Examples include `ping`, `command`, `user`, and `setup`. You can see the full list of modules on your Ansible Controller by typing the command `ansible-doc -l`. The `ansible-doc` command can also provide detailed information for each of the modules in a format similar to a Linux man page (for example, `ansible-doc yum`). Users are free to create their own modules to add functionality not currently available with Ansible, and you can write these modules in any language supported by the controller's operating system.

For most configuration management workflows, you will utilize playbooks to execute modules, but, in a few cases, ad hoc command execution can come in handy: verifying the accessibility of managed node, executing one-off tasks like system reboots, and so on. Listing 10-2 shows some sample ad hoc Ansible module executions.

Listing 10-2 Ansible Ad Hoc Command Execution

```
ansible all -m ping
ansible mnode02.devops.local -m command -a '/sbin/reboot'
ansible web -m user -a 'name=vmtrooper state=present comment="Test" uid=1000'
ansible web -m user -a 'name=vmtrooper state=absent remove=yes'
```

Ad hoc commands begin with the executable `ansible` and are followed by the pattern of servers that the module will be executed on. That pattern can consist of an explicit hostname or one of the group labels from the inventory file. Next, the `-m` switch (short for `--module-name`) is used to indicate which module will be executed.

The ad hoc commands will run as your current user. So, if you are not logged in as root, you need to use the `--su` or `--sudo` options discussed earlier. If your SSH key is not present in the authorized_keys file on the managed node, it will also be necessary to use the `--ask-pass` option. The earlier example for adding a user can be rewritten as follows for a nonroot user executing the code:

```
ansible web -m user -a 'name=vmtrooper state=present comment="Test"
uid=1000' --ask-pass --sudo --ask-sudo-pass
```

Of course, change the command options as needed based on your company's security conventions (for example, authorized_keys entries, sudo versus su, and so on).

> **NOTE**
>
> Ansible supports command completion for its options in addition to the option abbreviations. For example, you could type `--module-n ping` instead of `--module-name ping`, and Ansible will understand what you mean.

The Ping Module

The ping module verifies that the target servers are accessible by the user that the command is executed as. In Listing 10-2, I'm using the `ping` command with the `all` pattern to verify that all the servers in my Ansible inventory are accessible by the Ansible controller.

The Command Module

The command module allows you to run a local executable on the target servers. You will need to specify the full path on the target server to the executable that you want to run using the `-a` switch, which stands for *argument*.

The User Module

The user module is useful for adding or removing a user according to the needs of an application that you may be deploying across multiple servers. The data that you can specify with the argument switch includes the username, whether the user should be present or absent, the UID, and any other pertinent information about the user. As you might have noticed, each module's argument structure may vary. Be sure to consult the `ansible-doc` command to verify correct syntax for the module that you want to use.

The Setup Module

Before we move on, let's take a look at one more critical module: the setup module. This module helps us gather facts (for example, operating system, hypervisor, and so on) about the systems in our inventory file. As with other configuration management systems, these system facts can be used for making important decisions about how commands are executed on our target servers. At this point, I recommend running the setup module (`ansible all -m setup`) to get an idea of what system facts are returned about your managed nodes. When we discuss Ansible playbook execution for multiple platforms, we will take a closer look at how system facts help us to optimize our code.

Ansible Playbooks

Playbooks are collections of deployment instructions, also referred to as *plays*. The benefit of using playbooks is that you can combine the execution of multiple Ansible modules to perform application rollouts. Also, the imperative execution of playbooks dictates the order that your Ansible plays are executed in, making it easier for other system administrators to understand the logical flow. Playbooks should be stored in Git or another source code management (SCM) system for easy maintenance of your configuration management workflows.

Ansible playbooks are written in YAML, which you learned about in Chapter 5. So, the syntax should look a little familiar. Let's take a look at a simple playbook to set up a web server on one of our managed nodes (see Listing 10-3).

Listing 10-3 Web Server Playbook: apache.yml

```
---
- hosts: web
  tasks:
  - name: deploy apache
    yum: pkg=httpd state=latest
  - name: apache config file
    copy: src='files/httpd.conf' dest='/etc/httpd/conf/httpd.conf'
    notify:
    - restart httpd
  - name: apache service runs
    service: name=httpd state=started
  handlers:
    - name: restart httpd
      service: name=httpd state=restarted
```

The apache.yml playbook is stored in a directory called apache with two subdirectories: files and templates. The first line of the playbook uses the keyword `hosts:` to specify which hosts we will run this play on (the web group of servers in our /etc/ansible/hosts file). The web host group and all the tasks that belong to it comprise a single play.

NOTE

It is possible to have multiple plays in a single playbook. If we want to execute tasks on another group of hosts (for example, a db group), that `hosts: db` declaration and its tasks are considered another play within the playbook.

Next, the `tasks:` keyword marks the beginning of the modules that will be executed on the hosts in the web group. Each task consists of at least two components. The `name:` is an identifier that lets anyone reading the code know what this particular task is meant to do. We will see a little bit further down the code that the name value may be useful for reference purposes. The next component of the task is the Ansible module that will be executed. For our first task, this is the yum: module. There are only two arguments that we are concerned about: `pkg` to tell yum to deploy the httpd package, and `state` to specify that the latest version of httpd should be installed. Alternatively, you could have specified `present` if you are not concerned about the version of the package.

You'll notice in our first task that we are explicitly calling the yum package manager for CentOS. Ansible does not have a generic package installer module. This allows the playbook author to be specific about which package manager she wants to use. In a later example, you take a look at using a conditional statement to act differently based on the operating system that is running (that is, use apt with Debian-based systems and yum with Red Hat-based systems).

The next task is a bit more interesting because we are using the `notify:` parameter. This task is aptly named `apache config file` because we are using it to define which configuration file that httpd will use. In this task, we use the copy: module with two arguments: `src`, the location relative to the playbook file that contains the file that we want to copy; and `dest`, the location on the target servers where the file will be copied to. The `notify:` task parameter indicates the name of an Ansible handler that will execute a certain function in response to changes in our configuration file.

The last task tells Ansible to ensure that the httpd service is running once the package is deployed. This task uses the `service:` Ansible module with two arguments: `name`, which specifies the service to manage; and `states`, to specify whether the service should be running or stopped.

The `handlers:` section of the play looks similar to the `tasks:` section. However, the items listed here serve the special purpose of responding to a notify action. It is here that we define our `restart httpd` handler using the `name:` line, and the Ansible module that we are using (`service:`) to restart the httpd service. An important handler behavior to be aware of is that the handler is executed only once for the Ansible run. So, if you make multiple changes to the configuration file, the service will be restarted only after all the changes are made.

After saving and closing the file, you can execute it at the command line by using the `ansible-playbook` binary:

```
root@mnode01:~/apache# ansible-playbook apache.yml
```

In its current state, the playbook must be executed from within the Apache folder. Later on, we will take a look at how Ansible roles can be used to execute plays against hosts without worrying about our paths.

Conditional Expressions and Variables

Our apache playbook is ready to deploy web servers for Red Hat-based systems. However, what if we also have Debian-based systems (for example, Ubuntu) in production? We would need to handle multiple operating system types gracefully.

The `when:` conditional statement allows us to adjust which Ansible tasks are executed on a host according to our preferences. In our example, we will decide which package to deploy, the configuration file to use, and the service to manage based on the operating system family that our managed nodes belong to. Listing 10-4 shows a modified playbook that contains instructions for managed nodes whose operating systems belong to the Red Hat and Debian operating system families.

Listing 10-4 Ansible `when:` Conditional Statement for Module Execution Based on Facts

```
---
- hosts: web
  tasks:
# Deploy the Web Server
  - name: Deploy Apache for Red Hat Systems
    yum: pkg=httpd state=latest
    when: ansible_os_family == 'RedHat'
  - name: Deploy Apache for Debian Systems
    apt: pkg=apache2 state=latest
    when: ansible_os_family == 'Debian'

# Copy the correct Config File
  - name: Apache Config File for Red Hat Systems
    copy: src='files/httpd.conf' dest='/etc/httpd/conf/httpd.conf'
    notify:
    - restart httpd redhat
    when: ansible_os_family == 'RedHat'
  - name: Apache Config File for Debian Systems
    copy: src='files/apache2.conf' dest='/etc/apache2/apache2.conf'
    notify:
    - restart httpd debian
    when: ansible_os_family == 'Debian'

# Generate the correct Web Content
  - name: Apache Content File for Red Hat Systems
    template: src='files/index.html' dest='/var/www/html/index.html'
      mode=0644
    when: ansible_os_family == 'RedHat'
  - name: Apache Content File for Debian Systems
    template: src='files/index.html' dest='/var/www/index.html' mode=0644
    when: ansible_os_family == 'Debian'
```

```
# Verify Web Service is running
  - name: Apache Service Runs for Red Hat Systems
    service: name=httpd state=started
    when: ansible_os_family == 'RedHat'
  - name: Apache Service Runs for Debian Systems
    service: name=apache2 state=started
    when: ansible_os_family == 'Debian'

# Restart Web Service in response to config file change
  handlers:
    - name: restart httpd redhat
      service: name=httpd state=restarted
    - name: restart httpd debian
      service: name=apache2 state=restarted
```

Comments (prepended with #) have been added to provide clarity and to help with understanding the playbook. Each major step in the web server deployment play has two sets of instructions: one set for Red Hat systems and another set for Debian systems. Ansible will decide which task to execute on the target node by evaluating the `when:` statement, which uses the `ansible_os_family` system fact to provide module execution guidance.

Alternatively, we can use Ansible's `group_by` function, which can automatically create additional host groups based on some condition (for example, `ansible_os_family`). Listing 10-5 shows another way of structuring our playbook using `group_by`. You start off with the web host group from your /etc/ansible/hosts file, and you tell Ansible to create additional groups from the web host group using the `ansible_os_family` system fact as selection criteria. With our systems, that means two groups (one for `RedHat` and one for `Debian`) will be created at runtime, and these host groups can be used in the remainder of the playbook. Listing 10-5 shows separate instructions for RedHat and Debian host groups that do not rely on the `when:` conditional. It is safe to not include conditional statements in the structure because instructions will only be run according to the host's operating system. For example, our Debian instructions will not be executed on our Red Hat servers.

Listing 10-5 Ansible `group_by` Function for Module Execution Based on Facts

```
---
- hosts: web
  tasks:
  - name: Group Servers By Operating System Family
    action: group_by key={{ ansible_os_family }}
- hosts: RedHat
```

```
  tasks:
  - name: Deploy Apache
    yum: pkg=httpd state=latest
  - name: Apache Config File
    copy: src=files/httpd.conf dest=/etc/httpd/conf/httpd.conf
    notify:
    - restart httpd
  - name: Apache Service Runs
    service: name=httpd state=started
  handlers:
    - name: restart httpd
      service: name=httpd state=restarted

- hosts: Debian
  tasks:
  - name: Deploy Apache
    apt: pkg=apache2 state=latest
  - name: Apache Config File
    copy: src=files/apache2.conf dest=/etc/apache2/apache2.conf
    notify:
    - restart httpd
  - name: Apache Service Runs
    service: name=apache2 state=started
  handlers:
    - name: restart httpd
      service: name=apache2 state=restarted
```

Both examples from Listings 10-4 and 10-5 solve the problem of modifying playbook execution according to operating system type. However, there is a lot of repeated code, and Ansible has additional capabilities to help us optimize our plays. Listing 10-6 shows the use of variables to reduce the number of tasks needed in our playbook.

Listing 10-6 Ansible `when:` Conditional Statement for Module Execution Based on Facts

```
---
- hosts: web
  vars_files:
"vars/{{ ansible_os_family }}.yml"
  tasks:
  - name: Deploy Apache for Red Hat Systems
```

```
    yum: pkg=httpd state=latest
    when: ansible_os_family == 'RedHat'
  - name: Deploy Apache for Debian Systems
    apt: pkg=apache2 state=latest
    when: ansible_os_family == 'Debian'
  - name: Apache Config File
    copy: src=files/{{ conffile }} dest={{ confpath }}
    notify:
    - restart httpd
  - name: Apache Service Runs
    service: name={{ webserver }} state=started
  handlers:
    - name: restart httpd
      service: name={{ webserver }} state=restarted
```

There is a new element in our playbook: `vars_files`. This keyword tells Ansible where we are storing variables for use in the playbook. Listing 10-7 shows the contents of the YAML files that contain our variable values.

Listing 10-7 RedHat.yml and Debian.yml Variable Files

```
#RedHat.yml
---
webserver: 'httpd'
conffile: 'httpd.conf'
confpath: '/etc/httpd/conf/httpd.conf'
contentpath: '/var/www/html/index.html'

#Debian.yml
---
webserver: 'apache2'
conffile: 'apache2.conf'
confpath: '/etc/apache2/apache2.conf'
contentpath: '/var/www/index.html'
```

In our playbook, our variables are stored in a directory called vars that is located in the same directory as the playbook. There are two files (RedHat.yml and Debian.yml) whose names correspond to the values returned by the `ansible_os_family` system fact. When we want to use any variable, whether system fact or user defined, we need to enclose it with double curly brackets so that Ansible knows to substitute the text for the stored value (for example, `{{ ansible_os_family }}`).

Because Ansible requires you to explicitly indicate the package manager for your managed nodes' operating system, we still need to have separate tasks for deploying Apache on a Red Hat–based system versus on a Debian-based system. However, the rest of our tasks use generic modules (copy, service, and so on), and this allows us to use our imported variables to eliminate repetitive tasks.

The Apache Config File task is the first to use variables. The `src` argument for the copy module uses the `conffile` variable, and the `dest` argument uses the `confpath` variable. Even the handler definition is able to make use of variables, and we see that it uses the `webserver` variable to indicate which services will be restarted when the configuration file is changed.

If you compare the playbook in Listing 10-4 with the playbook in Listing 10-6, you see that the optimized code requires three fewer tasks and one less handler. This savings might not seem significant. However, in a much larger playbook, variable use can lead to more significant code optimization.

Ansible Roles

Organizing our files is a simple task currently because we are dealing with just deploying Apache. However, what if we want to deploy other types of servers? Do we just keep adding additional plays for databases, application servers, and so on to our current YAML file? Even if we apply modular design and separate our plays out into individual YAML files, what is the best way to organize the supporting files like configuration files, variable files, and so forth? Do we keep them in common directories, or do we create different subdirectories according to function?

Ansible's authors considered these questions and implemented the roles functionality to address them. System administrators can group related files with a particular directory structure according to the function that they will fulfill. Figure 10-2 shows a tree structure based on a role for our Apache web servers.

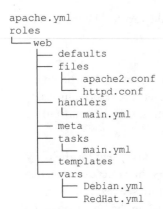

```
apache.yml
roles
└── web
    ├── defaults
    ├── files
    │   ├── apache2.conf
    │   └── httpd.conf
    ├── handlers
    │   └── main.yml
    ├── meta
    ├── tasks
    │   └── main.yml
    ├── templates
    └── vars
        ├── Debian.yml
        └── RedHat.yml
```

Figure 10-2 Ansible role directory structure

The roles directory and the apache.yml file sit at the same level on the file system (for example, /src/apache.yml and /src/roles/), and the remainder of the directories and files reside in the roles directory (/src/roles/web/files/, /src/roles/web/handlers, and so on). Alternatively, you could store your web role in /etc/ansible/roles, and that is a practice we use in the next chapter. However, to keep things simple, we will keep our web role located in the same directory as our apache.yml file.

Before we discuss the required code changes to accommodate the role structure, let's review the purpose of each of the folders in the role:

- **defaults:** If your role accepts parameters when you call it (you'll see an example in the next chapter), you can place a YAML file that contains default values that aren't specified with the role in the main playbook (for example, default passwords).
- **files:** Any files that you would like to copy to the target hosts. For the Apache server, this would be the configuration files.
- **handlers:** The instructions for executing actions in response to notifications from a playbook task (for example, restarting Apache services after the configuration file changes).
- **meta:** References to other Ansible roles that your current role depends on.
- **tasks:** The location for your playbook tasks.
- **templates:** Jinja2 files that can be used to generate content dynamically according to system facts or other variables.
- **vars:** Variables that will be used by your playbooks.

NOTE

It is not necessary to manually create the role directory structure. Ansible includes a utility that will generate it for you: `ansible-galaxy init web`.

Ansible Galaxy is introduced later in this chapter, but for now, it is sufficient to know that this utility helps you generate the correct role structure so that you can share it with the Ansible community if you want to.

By utilizing the role directory structure, you do not have to provide explicit paths when accessing content in the various directories. Ansible can interpret which folder to look into based on the module that you are using. For example, in Listing 10-3, the copy module's `src` argument required the explicit path to the configuration file if we were not storing it in the same directory as our playbook file (`copy: src=files/httpd.conf`). When we adopt the role structure, we follow the correct Ansible conventions and place the configuration file in the role's files subdirectory. In our playbook, it would only be necessary to specify the name of the file, and Ansible will automatically interpret the correct path to the file.

You need to make a few changes to your playbook file for the role structure to function correctly. First, the apache.yml file now contains references to the web role instead of the actual play tasks and handlers (see Listing 10-8).

Listing 10-8 Updated apache.yml

```
---
- hosts: web
  roles:
    - web
```

The name of the role listed (`web`) must match the name of the subdirectory residing in the roles folder. Then, your playbook's tasks and handlers are divided into separate files that are each called main.yml in the tasks and handlers subdirectories, respectively (see Listing 10-9).

Listing 10-9 Apache Deployment Tasks Stored in the Web Role's Tasks and Handlers Subdirectories

```
#web/tasks/main.yml
---
include_vars: "{{ ansible_os_family }}.yml"
  - name: Deploy Apache for Red Hat Systems
```

```
    yum: pkg=httpd state=latest
    when: ansible_os_family == 'RedHat'
  - name: Deploy Apache for Debian Systems
    apt: pkg=apache2 state=latest
    when: ansible_os_family == 'Debian'
  - name: Apache Config File
    copy: src={{ conffile }} dest={{ confpath }}
    notify:
    - restart httpd
  - name: Apache Service Runs
    service: name={{ webserver }} state=started

#web/handlers/main.yml
---
include_vars: "{{ ansible_os_family }}.yml"
  - name: restart httpd
    service: name={{ webserver }} state=restarted
```

The filename main.yml indicates to Ansible that these tasks and handlers should be automatically loaded when the role is referenced from another file. The role structure requires referencing variables in a different way. Instead of using the `vars_files:` keyword, we use the `include_vars:` keyword. Also, we no longer need to specify the vars subdirectory because Ansible will automatically know where to look for our variables files.

These changes might seem confusing at first, but they help tremendously with keeping the code organized according to the function it is supposed to fulfill. This comes in handy if you are working with a LAMP stack, for example, and you have separate web, database, and PHP roles. You can make changes to the database role without potentially affecting the web and application server roles.

Templates

Ansible supports Jinja2 templates for generating role content. Jinja2 is a technology used by Python application frameworks such as Django and Flask for dynamic web content that is generated at runtime. Jinja2 is similar to the Embedded RuBy (ERB) technology introduced in Chapter 4 for Puppet except that it uses Python-like conventions for its code structure.

Jinja2 templates are useful for configuration files and for application content. We will use a Jinja2 template to dynamically generate our web server's index.html file instead of discussing the various options and settings necessary to generate an Apache configuration file. Our index.html file's content will change based on the operating system of the target host. Listing 10-10 shows a sample Jinja2 template for our web content.

Jinja2 utilizes many conventions from Python. So, a basic knowledge of Python can be useful if you would like to develop your own templates. For our example, we use Python's string management to evaluate text and an `if-then-else` statement to determine what text is printed out

Listing 10-10 index.html.j2 Web Content Template

```
#jinja2:  variable_start_string: '[%' , variable_end_string: '%]'
<html><body><h1>Ansible Rocks!</h1>
<p>This is the default web page for
{# Print the correct Operating System name with the right article i.e. "a"
vs "an"#}
{% if ansible_distribution[0].lower() in "aeiou" %}
  an
{% else %}
  a
{% endif %}
<b> [% ansible_distribution %] </b> server.</p>
<p>The web server software is running and content has been added by your
<b>Ansible</b> code.</p>
</body></html>
```

The first line is a special directive for the Jinja2 template interpreter indicating that we are using a nonstandard method of interpolating system facts. We do this because the standard double bracket convention can sometimes cause issues with templates in Ansible.

Note that there are different prefixes for the blocks of Jinja2 statements:

- `{# #}` encloses comments.
- `{% %}` encloses conditional logic and other Python code. Our `if-then-else` statement is deciding which article (either *a* or *an*) is grammatically correct to place in front of the operating system's name.
- `[% %]` encloses system facts according to directive from the first line of the template file. Again, this convention is customizable according to the first line of the template. In our example, we are using the `ansible_distribution` system fact to detect which operating system our target server is running.

NOTE

Experienced Python developers may notice that we are using an `endif` statement. This is not a common practice with standard Python. However, it is helpful to Jinja2 to understand where your conditional statement ends.

When we have finished our Jinja2 file, we place it in the templates subdirectory of the web role and create a task in the role to utilize the template (see Listing 10-11).

Listing 10-11 Adding a Task to Create HTML Content

```
tasks/main.yml
---
include_vars: "{{ ansible_os_family }}.yml"
   - name: Deploy Apache for Red Hat Systems
     yum: pkg=httpd state=latest
     when: ansible_os_family == 'RedHat'
   - name: Deploy Apache for Debian Systems
     apt: pkg=apache2 state=latest
     when: ansible_os_family == 'Debian'
   - name: Apache Config File
     copy: src={{ conffile }} dest={{ confpath }}
     notify:
     - restart httpd
   - name: Apache Content File
     template: src=index.html.j2 dest={{ contentpath }} mode=0644
   - name: Apache Service Runs
     service: name={{ webserver }} state=started
```

We add the task with the name Apache Content File, and we use the template module, which will copy the template and place it in the destination path that we specify.

Ansible Galaxy

Ansible Galaxy is an online repository of Ansible roles located at https://galaxy.ansible.com/. Before setting out to write the next great Ansible role for some functionality in your environment, it would be worthwhile to see whether the Ansible community has already resolved the problem and posted code that you can use.

When you find an Ansible role that you would like to use, you specify its name with the `ansible-galaxy install` command (for example, `ansible-galaxy install bennojoy.mysql`). The role is then placed in /etc/ansible/roles and immediately available for use by any of your playbooks.

Contributing code to Ansible Galaxy is fairly easy. In the Add a Role section of the website, specify your GitHub account, the repository that contains your role, and optionally an alternate name that you want your role's title to be on the Galaxy site. By default, the name of your GitHub repository will be the name that Galaxy displays for your role.

Summary

In this chapter, you learned the basics of how to create an Ansible playbook to deploy a web server. Ansible roles can help you organize your playbook code for code reuse, portability, and ease of maintenance. The next chapter covers how to deploy an entire LAMP stack using the Ansible skills that you have developed up to this point.

References

[1] Ansible documentation. http://docs.ansible.com/

Chapter 11

Systems Management Tasks with Ansible

This chapter focuses on using Ansible for multitier deployments. Specifically, the chapter presents an example of how to deploy a LAMP (Linux-Apache-MySQL-PHP) stack with Ansible.

Topics covered in this chapter include the following:

- Web server deployment
- The application tier
- The database tier
- Role structure optimization
- VMware resource management

Web Server Deployment

There is not much work to be done for our web role because we did a good job of completing it in Chapter 10. To keep our code better organized, though, we will move the folder containing our web role to /etc/ansible/roles.

NOTE

Going forward, we will be placing all of our Ansible roles in the /etc/ansible/roles directory on the controller. This allows us to execute our Ansible playbooks from any location on the controller. Your role path can be updated by editing /etc/ansible/ansible.cfg on the controller.

Another change we will make is to add a task to deploy and enable Network Time Protocol (NTP) so that our servers' clocks can be consistent. See Listing 11-1 for the additional code that we add to our role.

Listing 11-1 Adding NTP Deployment Tasks to /etc/ansible/roles/web/tasks/main.yml

```
---
  - include_vars: "{{ ansible_os_family }}.yml"
  - name: Deploy Apache for Red Hat Systems
    yum: pkg=httpd state=latest
    when: ansible_os_family == 'RedHat'
  - name: Deploy Apache for Debian Systems
    apt: pkg=apache2 state=latest
    when: ansible_os_family == 'Debian'
  - name: Apache Config File
    copy: src={{ conffile }} dest={{ confpath }}
    notify:
    - config file update
  - name: Apache Service Runs
    service: name={{ webserver }} state=started
  - name: Deploy NTP on Ubuntu Servers
    apt: pkg=ntp state=latest
    when: ansible_os_family == 'Debian'
  - name: Deploy NTP for Red Hat Systems
    yum: pkg=ntp state=latest
    when: ansible_os_family == 'RedHat'
  - name: NTP Service Runs
    service: name={{ ntpserver }} state=started
```

Remember, when you are adding new packages with Ansible, you do need to provide a task to verify that the service is running if that's the desired state.

The Application Tier

The application tier in our deployment will be a simple PHP server. PHP gets installed on the same server that is running the Apache web server. However, we will still make a separate PHP role instead of adding the new code to the existing web role. This allows for more flexibility if we want to swap out a different type of web server or application server later on.

Listing 11-2 shows the playbook that we will use to deploy PHP.

Listing 11-2 PHP Deployment Tasks in /etc/ansible/roles/php/tasks/main.yml

```
---
  - include_vars: "{{ ansible_os_family }}.yml"
  - name: Deploy PHP packages for Red Hat Systems
    yum: pkg={{ item }} state=latest
    with_items: phppkg
    when: ansible_os_family == 'RedHat'

  - name: Deploy PHP packages for Debian Systems
    apt: pkg={{ item }} state=latest
    with_items: phppkg
    when: ansible_os_family == 'Debian'

  - name: Restart Apache after deploying PHP
    service: name={{ webserver }} state=restarted

  - name: PHP Content File
    copy: src=index.php dest={{ phppath }}
```

The tasks look similar to our web server deployment tasks with one notable difference. We are using the `with_items` looping mechanism to install multiple packages using a single package deployment task. The `with_items` loop accepts a YAML sequence (similar to a Python list or array) or the name of a variable that contains a YAML sequence as its input. In our code, `phppkg` is one of our variables from the file that we include in the first line. (See Listing 11-3 for the values.) Another notable task in the playbook is the restart of the Apache service. Some distributions may require this step for Apache to recognize that PHP is installed.

Listing 11-3 PHP Role Variable Files

```
#/etc/ansible/roles/php/vars/RedHat.yml
---
webserver: 'httpd'
phppkg:
  - php
  - php-mysql
phppath: '/var/www/html/index.php'
```

```
#/etc/ansible/roles/php/vars/Debian.yml
---
webserver: 'apache2'
phppkg:
  - php5
  - php5-mysql
phppath: '/var/www/index.php'
```

The Database Tier

Let's take a look at how we can deploy MySQL with Ansible. It is interesting to note that Ansible comes with modules for managing MySQL and PostgreSQL databases. We'll take advantage of those modules in our role to create a sample database and a user with permissions on that database.

Our role structure will be very similar to what was used in our web and PHP roles (see Listing 11-4).

Listing 11-4 MySQL Deployment Tasks in /etc/ansible/roles/db/tasks/main.yml

```
---
  - include_vars: "{{ ansible_os_family }}.yml"

  - name: Deploy MySQL for Red Hat Systems
    yum: pkg={{ item }} state=latest
    with_items: dbpkg
    when: ansible_os_family == 'RedHat'

  - name: Deploy MySQL for Debian Systems
    apt: pkg={{ item }} state=latest
    with_items: dbpkg
    when: ansible_os_family == 'Debian'

  - name: MySQL Service Runs
    service: name={{ dbservice }} state=started

  - name: Configure MySQL root password
    mysql_user: name=root password={{ dbpasswd }}
    ignore_errors: yes
```

```
  - name: MySQL DB Create
    mysql_db: name=test state=present login_user=root login_password=
      {{ dbpasswd }}

  - name: Set User Permission
    mysql_user: name=ansible password=ansiblerocks priv=test.*:ALL,GRANT
state=present login_user=root login_password={{ dbpasswd }}
```

NOTE

The `ignore_errors` parameter in the "Configure MySQL root password" task suppresses errors in case you run this playbook multiple times. It is optional, but Ansible will generate errors otherwise.

We use the `with_items` loop again to indicate a list of packages to be installed for MySQL. For Ansible's MySQL modules to work properly, we need to have the Python MySQL libraries installed. So, we add it to the list of packages in the two variable files (see Listing 11-5).

The `dbpasswd` variable for the password parameter (see Listing 11-4) will be set either by a value from the defaults directory or by a parameterized call of the db role in our playbook file. Listing 11-6 shows an example of using parameters when specifying a role, and Listing 11-7 shows our example's default database password value stored in the role's defaults directory.

Listing 11-5 db Role Variable Files

```
#/etc/ansible/roles/db/vars/RedHat.yml
---
dbpkg:
  - mysql-server
  - MySQL-python
dbservice: 'mysqld'

#/etc/ansible/roles/db/vars/Debian.yml
---
dbpkg:
  - mysql-server
  - python-mysqldb
dbservice: 'mysql'
```

Listing 11-6 Parameterized Role Call from the Database Playbook File

```
#Playbook YAML file in your working directory that references the db role
# ~/db.yml
---
- hosts: db
  roles:
    - { role: db, dbpasswd: 'ansibleabc'}
```

Listing 11-7 db Role Default Value File

```
#/etc/ansible/roles/db/defaults/main.yml
---
dbpasswd: 'ansiblerocksabc'
```

Security-conscious system administrators will be concerned that a default password is stored in plain text. As of Ansible version 1.5, you can use `ansible-vault` to encrypt any file in your role with the AES algorithm. The syntax is fairly simple. Once you have created your YAML file, use the `ansible-vault encrypt` command to secure it. For example, if your data file is named main.yml, the syntax is `ansible-vault encrypt main.yml`. The `ansible-vault` command asks for the password and then asks you to confirm it.

The `ansible-vault` feature is very useful in that it does not encrypt all of the files that make up your role. Instead, because you specify which file will be encrypted, you can dedicate a specific YAML file to contain sensitive data and encrypt it. The remainder of your role files will remain in plain text and can be version controlled using Git or some other tool.

When you run your Ansible playbook, you specify a new option (`--ask-vault-pass`) with `ansible-playbook`. For example, if your playbook file is called db.yml, your command execution would be `ansible-playbook db.yml --ask-vault-pass`. Before the playbook can execute, you are asked for the vault password.

Role Structure Optimization

You may have multiple essential system packages that you want to deploy on all of your servers. Instead of including them within each role, it would be a good idea to create a *base image* role that deploys and manages all your essential packages (NTP, SELinux, and so on). I will create a role called base to represent a base image that I want all of my servers to have. My base role will contain the NTP package deployment instructions (see Listing 11-8).

Listing 11-8 Base Role for Essential System Packages

```
#/etc/ansible/roles/base/tasks/main.yml
---
  - include_vars: "{{ ansible_os_family }}.yml"
  - name: Deploy NTP on Ubuntu Servers
    apt: pkg=ntp state=latest
    when: ansible_os_family == 'Debian'
  - name: Deploy NTP for Red Hat Systems
    yum: pkg=ntp state=latest
    when: ansible_os_family == 'RedHat'
  - name: NTP Service Runs
    service: name={{ ntpserver }} state=started
```

Even though the NTP package name (ntp) is the same for both the CentOS and Ubuntu operating systems, the name of the service differs. So, we still need to create different variable files according to the operating system family, as shown in Listing 11-9.

Listing 11-9 Base Role Variable Files

```
#/etc/ansible/roles/ntp/vars/RedHat.yml
---
ntpserver: 'ntpd'

#/etc/ansible/roles/ntp/vars/Debian.yml
---
ntpserver: 'ntp'
```

Now that we have the base role defined, we can remove the NTP deployment tasks from the web role, and we can create a new playbook file to deploy the entire LAMP stack (lamp.yml). The lamp.yml file will be used to execute the various roles according to the groups that the servers belong to (see Listing 11-10).

Listing 11-10 lamp.yml

```
---
- hosts: web
  roles:
      - base
      - web
      - php
```

```
- hosts: db
  roles:
      - base
      - db
```

Because we are placing all of our roles in /etc/ansible/roles, it does not matter where our lamp.yml file resides on the controller. Once we execute this playbook, Ansible knows to automatically check the appropriate paths for the specified roles.

VMware Resource Management

Ansible recently introduced support for managing VMware vSphere virtual machines (VMs). As the Ansible community continues to develop new features for VMware vSphere management, we may dedicate an entire chapter of a future edition of this book to Ansible's VMware integrations. For now, we will introduce Ansible's vsphere_guest module and discuss its capabilities within this chapter.

The vsphere_guest module is one of Ansible's core modules for provisioning cloud workloads. Standalone ESXi is supported. However, we will focus on managing VMware vSphere workloads via VMware vCenter.

The module has a dependency on the open source project pysphere. So, the server that you select to run your VMware management tasks from needs to have pysphere installed via pip, a Python package installer, either manually (`sudo pip install pyshphere`) or by adding prerequisite tasks to your VMware management playbook to install pysphere for you (see Listing 11-11).

Listing 11-11 VMware Virtual Machine Creation

```
- hosts: vmware
  tasks:
    - name: Deploy pip for Ubuntu Servers
      apt: pkg=python-pip state=latest
      when: ansible_os_family == 'Debian'
    - name: Deploy pip for Red Hat Systems
      yum: pkg=python-pip state=latest
      when: ansible_os_family == 'RedHat'
    - name: Deploy the pysphere Python package
      pip: name=pysphere
    - name: Deploy an Ubuntu VM on VMware vSphere
      vsphere_guest:
```

```
vcenter_hostname: vcenter.devwidgets.io
username: vmtrooper@devwidgets.io
password: devopsrocks123
guest: web server 01
state: powered_off
vm_extra_config:
  notes: This is a web server to run Apache in production
vm_disk:
  disk1:
    size_gb: 10
    type: thin
    datastore: datastore1
vm_nic:
  nic1:
    type: vmxnet3
    network: VM Network
    network_type: standard
vm_hardware:
  memory_mb: 512
  num_cpus: 1
  osid: ubuntu64Guest
  scsi: paravirtual
esxi:
  datacenter: Production
  hostname: vsphere01.devwidgets.io
```

In my Ansible inventory file (see Chapter 10 for a refresher), I create a group of hosts called vmware that I specify in Listing 11-11 as the managed nodes to run the VMware management tasks (`- hosts: vmware`). You will need to limit the number of hosts that run the VMware commands so that vsphere_guest does not generate an error for creating duplicate VMs. This can either be done by placing a single managed node in the vmware group or by using the `limit` option with the `ansible-playbook` command:

```
ansible-playbook create-vm.yml --limit vmware[0]
```

The vmware group is treated like a list, and you specify a list index value in brackets after the group name. Python's conventions for the list index will apply here. (For example, 0 would indicate the first host in the group, 1 would indicate the second managed node, –1 would indicate the last managed node in the group.)

The playbook in Listing 11-11 first satisfies the vsphere_guest prerequisites: Verify that pip and pysphere are installed. As we have done with previous Ansible code, we provide tasks for the different operating systems in our test environment (Debian and Red Hat-based systems).

Finally, we specify our vsphere_guest instructions so that we can create a VM using Ansible. There are multiple parameters that can be used during VM creation, but we narrowed down our sample code to the bare minimum that would be most useful:

- `vcenter_hostname`: The VMware vCenter server that we will use to create the VM.
- `username`: The user with sufficient privileges to create a VM.
- `password`: The user's vCenter password.
- `guest`: The name of the VM being created. It must be unique.
- `state`: Whether the VM should be powered on after creation.
- `vm_extra_config`: Specify notes about the VM and set options such as vCPU and memory hot-add.
- `vm_disk`: The VM's storage location.
- `vm_nic`: The VM network that the VM will be connected to.
- `vm_hardware`: Specify characteristics such as the number of vCPUs, the amount of RAM, and the OS that the VM will run.
- `esxi`: Specify the VMware vSphere data center and host that the VM will be created on.

In the `vm_hardware` parameter, the `osid` value for your desired operating system can be obtained from the VirtualMachineGuestOsIdentifier documentation in the VMware vSphere API Reference (see the "References" section at the end of this chapter). Table 11-1 shows a listing of a few popular operating systems and their corresponding VirtualMachineGuestOsIdentifier values.

Table 11-1 VMware vSphere Operating System Identifiers

Operating System	VirtualMachineGuestOsIdentifier
Ubuntu Linux (multiple versions)	ubuntu64Guest
CentOS Linux (multiple versions)	centosGuest
Red Hat Linux 7	rhel7_64Guest
Windows Server 2012 R2	Windows8Server64Guest

> CAUTION
>
> If you select another operating system to use with the code in Listing 11-1, verify that the remainder of the VM's parameters (for example, `vm_hardware`) are compatible with it.

After running the playbook in Listing 11-1, the VM will be created and available in vCenter, as shown in Figure 11-1.

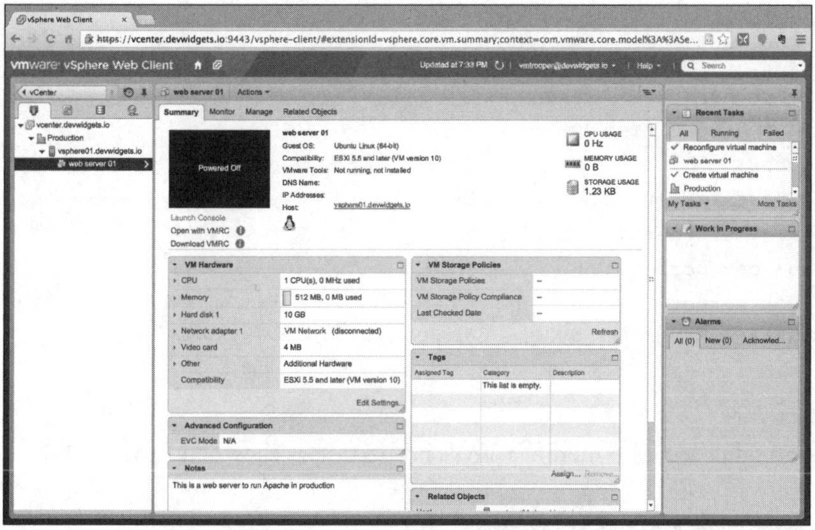

Figure 11-1 Ansible VMware guest deployment results

The vsphere_guest module will not install the VM's operating system on your behalf. However, you can gather facts about the VM, such as its MAC address. You can use this information with whichever OS deployment tool that your team uses. The system administrator can obtain the VM's facts by running the vsphere_guest module ad hoc and using the `vmware_guest_facts` parameter:

```
ansible vmware -m vsphere_guest -a "vcenter_hostname=vcenter.devwidgets.io
username=vmtrooper@devwidgets.io password=devopsrocks123 guest='new vm001'
vmware_guest_facts=yes"
```

VMs can be deleted by setting the `state` parameter to `absent` and setting the `force` parameter to `yes` just in case the VM is powered on (see Listing 11-12).

Listing 11-12 VMware Virtual Machine Deletion

```
- hosts: vmware
  tasks:
    - name: Deploy pip for Ubuntu Servers
      apt: pkg=python-pip state=latest
      when: ansible_os_family == 'Debian'
    - name: Deploy pip for Red Hat Systems
      yum: pkg=python-pip state=latest
      when: ansible_os_family == 'RedHat'
    - name: Deploy the pysphere Python package
      pip: name=pysphere
    - name: Remove a specified VM
      vsphere_guest:
        vcenter_hostname: vcenter.devwidgets.io
        username: vmtrooper@devwidgets.io
        password: devopsrocks123
        guest: web server 01
        state: absent
        force: yes
```

The vsphere_guest module can also modify a VM's properties, as shown in Listing 11-13.

Listing 11-13 VMware Virtual Machine Modification

```
- hosts: vmware
  tasks:
    - name: Deploy pip for Ubuntu Servers
      apt: pkg=python-pip state=latest
      when: ansible_os_family == 'Debian'
    - name: Deploy pip for Red Hat Systems
      yum: pkg=python-pip state=latest
      when: ansible_os_family == 'RedHat'
    - name: Deploy the pysphere Python package
      pip: name=pysphere
    - name: Deploy an Ubuntu VM on VMware vSphere
      vsphere_guest:
        vcenter_hostname: vcenter.devwidgets.io
        username: vmtrooper@devwidgets.io
        password: devopsrocks123
        guest: web server 01
```

```
state: reconfigured
vm_extra_config:
  notes: This is an updated web server to run Apache in production
vm_hardware:
  memory_mb: 1024
  num_cpus: 2
esxi:
  datacenter: Production
  hostname: vsphere01.devwidgets.io
force: yes
```

The first change is to edit the VM state to the `reconfigured` value. If the change that I am making requires a VM shutdown and restart, I can include the `force` parameter to do this automatically. Finally, I update the memory (`memory_mb`), number of vCPUs (`num_cpus`), and the VM's description (`notes`) to the new values that I want the VM to have.

Summary

Ansible roles can help make application deployments easier. Your system deployment tasks are then a matter of calling the right roles with any necessary parameters. This chapter also discussed how the vsphere_guest Ansible module can be used to create, modify, delete, and obtain facts about VMware vSphere VMs. The next chapter takes a look at the desired state configuration (DSC) configuration management system that Microsoft introduced in PowerShell 4.0 for Windows servers.

References

[1] Ansible documentation: http://docs.ansible.com/

[2] VMware vSphere SDK: https://www.vmware.com/support/developer/vsphere_mgmt_sdk/index.html

Chapter 12

Introduction to PowerShell Desired State Configuration (DSC)

PowerShell has quickly grown to be the standard automation tool for both the Microsoft Windows and VMware ecosystems. Many VMware administrators have utilized PowerCLI, VMware's PowerShell snap-in, to perform tasks and collect information about their virtual environments. Microsoft professionals have seen tremendous investment by the company to make Microsoft Windows Server and Microsoft applications manageable with PowerShell.

The tools you have learned about so far in this book served as the precursor to Microsoft's latest feature of PowerShell: Desired State Configuration. Commonly referred to with the acronym DSC, this feature enables Windows administrators to natively manage their environments with similar functionality to what is found with Puppet. This chapter covers the fundamentals of DSC and how it works.

Topics covered in this chapter include the following:

- What is PowerShell DSC?
- PowerShell DSC requirements
- PowerShell DSC components
- PowerShell DSC configurations
- PowerShell DSC modes
- PowerShell DSC resources

What Is PowerShell DSC?

DSC is Microsoft's first effort to enable PowerShell to be declarative, much like Puppet. This means that rather than scripting all the logic and instruction required to accomplish the task, it instead uses the existing underlying framework. The DSC framework already contains the necessary instructions and logic to carry out the requested task. This does not mean that automation no longer requires the use of the familiar imperative programming style. This is simply another, highly scalable, method for maintaining a Windows environment. Users no longer are required to script or program the entire series of steps to get their desired result. They must merely instruct DSC which tasks need to be performed against which system and with what parameters. The rest is handled within the DSC framework.

The need for PowerShell's imperative capabilities will not wane anytime soon. In truth, most administrators will continue to use PowerShell more or less the same for most tasks, such as gathering information. Adopting DSC extends PowerShell's ability to both apply and maintain consistency in how a Windows server or application is configured with considerably less scripting required because it is built in to the framework to accomplish those tasks.

DSC can be used in many ways for managing a Windows server environment. In distributed organizations, these tasks are managed by the operating system (OS) teams and less so by the VMware administrator. Naturally, smaller organizations may have key contributors who are responsible for both the operating system and the virtual environment. This book focuses primarily on these technologies from the vantage point of a VMware administrator. Therefore, it is important to understand the most common use cases of DSC that your development teams may utilize.

Common functionality for PowerShell DSC includes the following resources:

- Managing and monitoring configuration state
- Enabling or disabling Windows roles and features
- Stopping and starting Windows services and application processes
- Deploying software
- Managing
    - Environmental variables
    - Files and directories
    - Groups and users
    - Registry settings

- Writing messages to log
- Running PowerShell scripts (including PowerCLI if installed)

PowerShell DSC Requirements

PowerShell 4.0 is installed on Windows Server 2012 R2 and Windows 8.1 by default and can also be installed on Windows Server 2008 R2 with Service Pack 1 or on Windows 7 Service Pack 1. DSC also requires a full installation of the Microsoft .NET Framework 4.5, also installed by default on Windows Server 2012 R2 and Windows 8.1. PowerShell 4.0 is backward compatible to run scripts written in previous versions, but DSC functionality is available only with PowerShell 4.0. In addition, PowerShell 4.0 requires WS-Management 3.0 and WMI 3.0, which are included as part of the Windows Management Framework (WMF) 4.0. At the time of this writing, Microsoft has released the Windows Management Framework 5 preview. Although this version is not explored in this book, it is important to note that it does include a wide range of fixes, optimizations, and performance improvements.

NOTE

Be sure to review the additional system requirements for Windows Management Framework 4.0 before installing, because there are some application incompatibilities. Also be sure to install Windows Integrated Scripting Environment (ISE) prior to WMF 4.0 on Windows Server 2008 R2 with SP1 if you plan to use ISE to write PowerShell 4.0 scripts. Finally, Microsoft KB2883200 is required on Windows Server 2012 R2 and Windows 8.1

PowerShell DSC Components

PowerShell DSC is made of several components that enable it to configure Windows systems. This section reviews these key components to give you an idea about the overall architecture at work.

Native Cmdlets

First and foremost PowerShell DSC is built on Microsoft Windows PowerShell. Therefore, there is a set of PowerShell cmdlets and functions built in to DSC that you'll see throughout this chapter. To access them, start a PowerShell session and enter the following command:

```
Get-Command -Module PSDesiredStateConfiguration
```

Figure 12-1 shows the output of nine options.

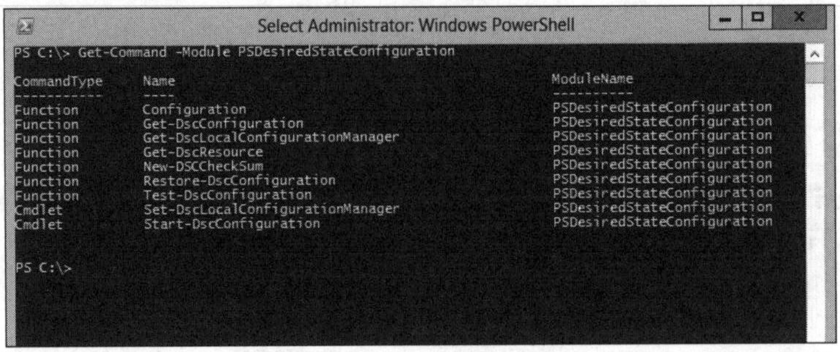

Figure 12-1 Desired state configuration command list

Managed Object Format File

At the heart of DSC is the Managed Object Format (MOF) file. A PowerShell script typically produces this file, as discussed later in this chapter. However, an MOF file can be written directly in a text editor and accepted by DSC if properly formatted. This is an interesting development for Microsoft because this means that even other products have the potential to produce MOF files for use both in Windows and Linux environments. In fact, at the time of this writing, Microsoft has released the first customer technology preview (CTP) of PowerShell DSC for Linux systems. This goes beyond the scope of this book because it is only in preview, but it is interesting to note when considering how DevOps organizations will likely utilize multiple tools for delivering resources. Microsoft is clearly working to make PowerShell DSC consumable for a broad range of environments and use cases.

> **NOTE**
>
> The path for the MOF file used by DSC can be either local or a UNC path. This can be extremely valuable for teams that want to centrally manage their MOF files, especially using pull mode. If you are using a UNC path, the node will have to be able to access that path.

Local Configuration Manager

The Local Configuration Manager (LCM) is the local engine on each DSC-enabled system that calls the resources in the configuration script. Not only is this a critical component of the DSC architecture, it is also customizable to the unique requirements of each node. These properties can dictate LCM's behavior with respect to the frequency it checks for updates, how it behaves when new configurations are found, and whether the node needs to function in push or pull mode. The `Set-DscLocalConfigurationManager` cmdlet is used to apply the customized settings.

Because DSC gives you the option to set LCM settings, it is important to know that the `Get-LocalConfigurationManager` cmdlet will provide you the current settings applied to LCM for your system, as shown in Figure 12-2. This figure shows the default settings found on a Microsoft Windows 2012 system.

```
PS C:\Users\Administrator> Get-DscLocalConfigurationManager

AllowModuleOverwrite           : False
CertificateID                  :
ConfigurationID                :
ConfigurationMode              : ApplyAndMonitor
ConfigurationModeFrequencyMins : 30
Credential                     :
DownloadManagerCustomData      :
DownloadManagerName            :
RebootNodeIfNeeded             : False
RefreshFrequencyMins           : 15
RefreshMode                    : PUSH
PSComputerName                 :
```

Figure 12-2 DSC Local Configuration Manager default settings

We can make an initial change to the LCM configuration with the short example in Listing 12-1. Here we are simply changing a few options for LCM and showing the changes to the system in Figure 12-3. A note is provided to demonstrate where configuration information would be applied to this script. This allows the development team or system administrators to apply both the LCM configurations and the required node settings needed.

```
PS C:\Users\Administrator> Set-DscLocalConfigurationManager -Path "C:\Users\Administrator\Documents\DevOps"
PS C:\Users\Administrator> Get-DscLocalConfigurationManager


AllowModuleOverwrite           : False
CertificateID                  :
ConfigurationID                :
ConfigurationMode              : ApplyAndAutoCorrect
ConfigurationModeFrequencyMins : 45
Credential                     :
DownloadManagerCustomData      :
DownloadManagerName            :
RebootNodeIfNeeded             : True
RefreshFrequencyMins           : 15
RefreshMode                    : PUSH
PSComputerName                 :



PS C:\Users\Administrator>
```

Figure 12-3 Setting DSC Local Configuration Manager configuration

Listing 12-1 Making an Initial Change to the LCM Configuration

```
Configuration LCMExample
{
    Node "localhost"
    {
     LocalConfigurationManager
      {
       ConfigurationModeFrequencyMins = 45
       ConfigurationMode = "ApplyAndAutocorrect"
       RebootNodeIfNeeded = $true
       AllowModuleOverwrite = $false
      }
     # Resource blocks added below when needed
    }
}

# Apply the configuration by entering the following in PowerShell
$path = "C:\Users\Administrator\Documents\DevOps"
LCMExample -OutputPath $path
Set-DscLocalConfigurationManager -Path $path
```

NOTE

Microsoft Windows PowerShell Integrated Scripting Environment (ISE) is a great tool to use for building your DSC configurations. It is included with the WMF 4.0 installation and is programmed to help you build your configurations. You can then write, run, and save your configurations as needed. Keep in mind that the 32-bit version (x86) of ISE does not support PowerShell DSC configurations.

The result of applying the DSC LCM configuration outlined earlier is an MOF file called <hostname>.mof located in the specified path. It may also complete as a file called localhost.mof. This will depend on what you define at the start of the Node section. In our example, the output file will be localhost.mof because we defined Node as localhost.

PowerShell DSC Configurations

PowerShell DSC configurations are simply scripts, formatted similarly to functions, which are used and run in PowerShell DSC to create the MOF file used by the system/node.

These configurations can get very complex, but you can also understand them by their three primary parts:

- Container
- Node declaration
- Configuration

The simple example in Listing 12-2 shows the basic required components.

Listing 12-2 Basic Required Components

```
Configuration Test01
{
    param ($NODENAME="localhost")
    Node $NODENAME
    {
     WindowsFeature IIS
     {
      Ensure = "Present"
      Name = "Web-Server"
     }
    }
}
```

In this example, we have created a basic configuration for installing the IIS feature in Windows Server 2012. We name the configuration Test01 and set the node to the local host by default. Because we declare a parameter for `$nodename`, this configuration could also be used to create MOF files for any system by passing the system name:

```
Test01 YourNode
```

This will create an MOF file for the provided node name. Because this is PowerShell, it is also possible to use multiple parameters. Use cases for multiple parameters include specifying file paths for copying files or choosing directories and Registry locations.

If we combine the LCM configuration with additional resource blocks, a more complete configuration script will start to form, like the one in Listing 12-3. In this configuration, we are keeping the opportunity open for reuse by having the node name be a parameter, configuring the LCM with our specific configuration requirements, and providing the resources required to get the node into the final desired state.

Listing 12-3 LCM Configuration Example

```
Configuration LCMExample
{
    param ($NODENAME="localhost")
    Node $NODENAME
    {
     LocalConfigurationManager {
        ConfigurationModeFrequencyMins = 45
        ConfigurationMode = "ApplyAndAutocorrect"
        RebootNodeIfNeeded = $true
        AllowModuleOverwrite = $false
        }
     WindowsFeature IIS {
        Ensure = "Present"
        Name = "Web-Server"
        }
     File Scripts {
        Ensure = "Present"
        Type = "Directory"
        SourcePath = "\\scriptserver\Scripts\"
        DestinationPath = "C:\Users\Administrator\Documents\Scripts"
        Recurse = "True"
        }
    }
}
```

If you have already read previous chapters, you may have noticed that the formatting of the DSC configuration file is similar to Puppet in that each configuration resource is added separately. Like Puppet, you can utilize each resource multiple times.

PowerShell DSC Modes

DSC is designed to function in two distinct modes: push and pull. However, it might be easier to think of DSC in three modes: local push, remote push, and pull. Each option provides specific advantages and disadvantages, but all are part of the full capabilities for DSC.

Local Push Mode

Local push mode is the simplest method for using PowerShell DSC. Under this method, the administrator just logs in to the system, runs the configuration script locally, and initiates the configuration locally. The example in the upcoming "PowerShell DSC Configurations" section can be easily implemented on a node locally. Note in Figure 12-4 that all components used for DSC are maintained on the node.

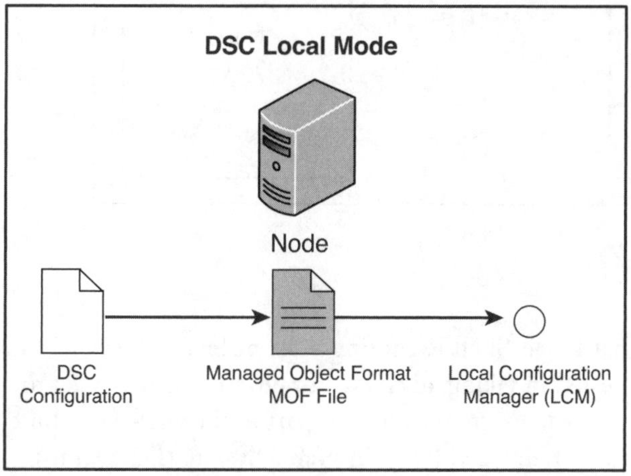

Figure 12-4 DSC local push mode

Remote Push Mode

The second mode, push mode, is also easy to apply but has some additional requirements and caveats. In this mode, an administrator would run the configuration script and execute the configuration to a remote node or nodes as outlined in Figure 12-5. Because PowerShell is in use, multiple nodes can be applied to the same configuration call and have their individual MOF files generated and available. This provides greater scale, especially in an agile environment where multitiered applications are being deployed regularly.

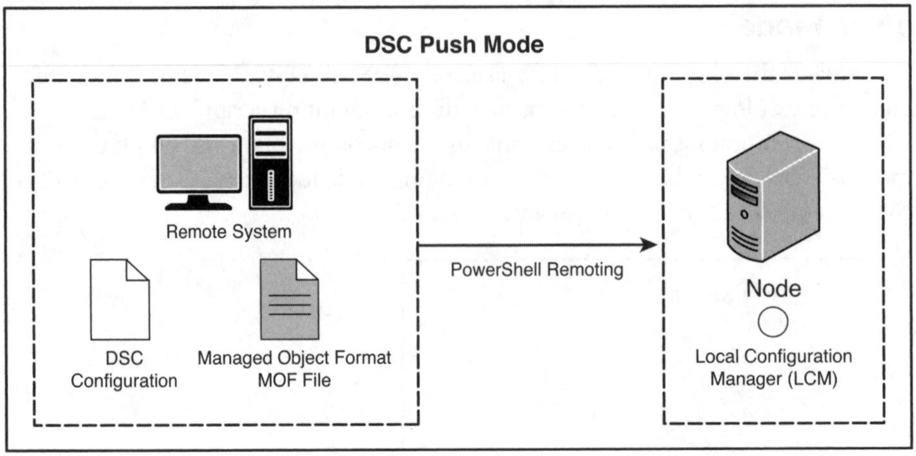

Figure 12-5 DSC remote push mode

The one downside to push mode is that PowerShell Remoting must be enabled on each of the target nodes. Those who are interested in taking advantage of push mode will need to run the `Enable-PSRemoting` cmdlet for each system or have it part of the virtual machine (VM) templates. For push mode to work effectively, Domain Name System (DNS) must also be current. It is advisable to use push mode in environments where all nodes are on the same domain, because PowerShell Remoting is easier to configure and DNS should be current once the node is on the domain.

Remotely executing the DSC configuration also requires that the administrator's PowerShell session is running in administrator mode. You can identify if you are in administrator mode by looking at the title bar of your PowerShell session. If you are not currently in this elevated mode, right-clicking the PowerShell shortcut and selecting Run as Administrator can start a new administrator mode session.

It is also important to note that when using push mode, the target node must have the DSC resources being called locally. If the target node does not have the required resource, the configuration cannot be applied, and you might not see any errors identifying why it has failed. You can check the availability of these resources with the `Get-DscResource` cmdlet, as described in the upcoming "PowerShell DSC Resources" section.

Pull Mode

Pull mode is the most complicated mode to set up, but is also the most flexible. Pull mode utilizes a central server running the DSC service that the node's Local Configuration Manager (LCM) will look to for its MOF file, as diagrammed in Figure 12-6. Pull mode can come in two delivery mechanisms: HTTP/HTTPS or SMB. Unfortunately, the configuration of the pull server can be quite cumbersome. Microsoft and several community contributors have provided resources that you can use to configure an HTTP pull server using DSC itself! These resources install IIS and other dependencies, create required directories, and provide required configuration files.

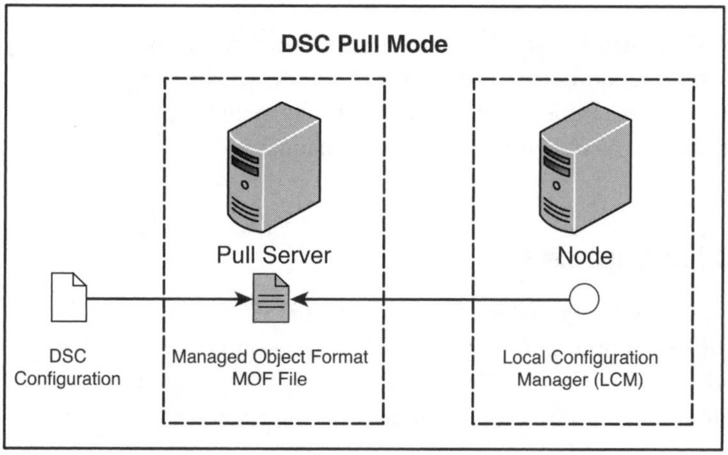

Figure 12-6 DSC pull mode

If your organization chooses to, it can set up the pull server using HTTPS. One common use case for this is if you have systems within a demilitarized zone (DMZ) for which you want to use DSC to maintain their configurations. Using HTTPS for your pull server will require the trusted certificate to be installed on the node before you attempt to request configuration information.

Under an SMB pull server configuration, you simply store the MOF and checksum files onto a network share that is accessible to the nodes. Then the LCM is configured to point to the share path rather than to pull server URL.

NOTE

Checksum files are easily created using the `New-DscChecksum` cmdlet. Make sure that this file is stored in the same directory as the MOF file. Fortunately, the cmdlet's default behavior is to store the .mof.checksum file in the same location as the MOF file: `New-DscChecksum <path to MOF file>`.

Another distinct advantage to pull mode is with respect to missing resources. Unlike push mode, where resources have to preexist on the node before the configuration can be applied, pull mode can copy over required resources to the target node. As a VMware administrator, it might make the most sense for you to encourage your system administrators and developers to adopt pull mode, especially if they plan to implement resources not native to PowerShell 4.

Finally, pull mode is ideal when organizations are interested in monitoring and maintaining compliance. You can configure the behavior of a node for checking in the node's LCM, as discussed later in this chapter. These settings include options for frequency of scanning for changes as well as behavior when changes are identified.

PowerShell DSC Resources

Administrators and developers looking to take full advantage of DSC capabilities will want to investigate the available configuration resources. These resources provide the framework of what is possible natively within DSC. The power of these providers is the ability to combine multiple resources into a single configuration for a node.

PowerShell DSC is enabled on installation of WMF 4.0 with general configuration resources, as mentioned previously in this book. Since the general availability of WMF 4.0, Microsoft has released three "waves" of new resources, thus extending the native capabilities of PowerShell DSC. Be aware that many of these resources are still being improved on, so check back with Microsoft TechNet[1] regularly for updates. You can get a list of available resources on your system with the `Get-DSCResource` cmdlet, as shown in Figure 12-7.

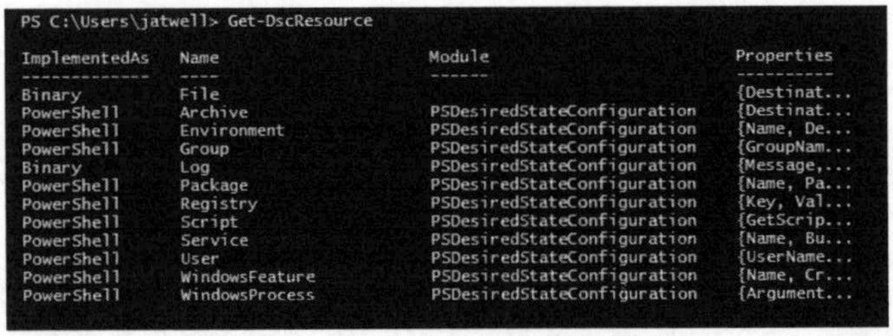

PS C:\Users\jatwell> Get-DscResource
ImplementedAs Name Module Properties
Binary File {Destinat...
PowerShell Archive PSDesiredStateConfiguration {Destinat...
PowerShell Environment PSDesiredStateConfiguration {Name, De...
PowerShell Group PSDesiredStateConfiguration {GroupNam...
Binary Log PSDesiredStateConfiguration {Message,...
PowerShell Package PSDesiredStateConfiguration {Name, Pa...
PowerShell Registry PSDesiredStateConfiguration {Key, Val...
PowerShell Script PSDesiredStateConfiguration {GetScrip...
PowerShell Service PSDesiredStateConfiguration {Name, Bu...
PowerShell User PSDesiredStateConfiguration {UserName...
PowerShell WindowsFeature PSDesiredStateConfiguration {Name, Cr...
PowerShell WindowsProcess PSDesiredStateConfiguration {Argument...

Figure 12-7 `Get-DSCResource` cmdlet

One challenge new users of PowerShell DSC will face is in understanding the properties associated with each DSC resource. Microsoft has continued the tradition of making valuable information available in the PowerShell session. There are two ways to get additional information about the resource properties. The following examples review the properties and syntax for the `Script` resource, as listed previously in Figure 12-7.

Using the `Select-Object` cmdlet, we can expand out the information about the properties:

```
Get-DscResource -Name Script | Select-Object -ExpandProperty Properties
```

NOTE

In this example, we take advantage of the PowerShell pipeline (|), which permits the user to transfer object data returned from one cmdlet (`Get-DscResource`) to be used in the next cmdlet (`Select-Object`). This is a core feature that makes PowerShell so versatile.

This information, whose output is shown in Figure 12-8, tells the user the property's object type and whether it is required.

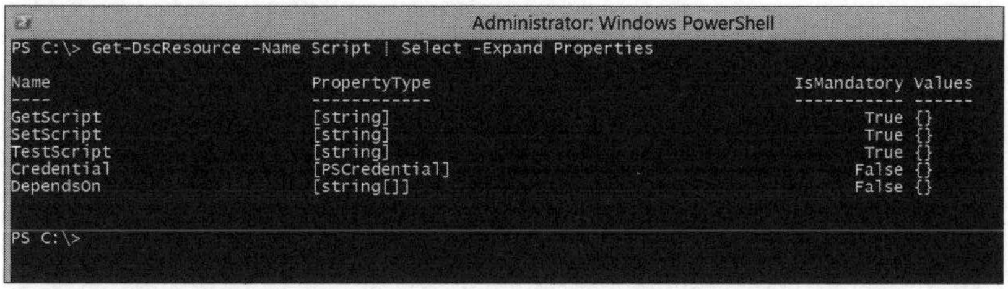

Figure 12-8 `Select-Object` cmdlet

Using the `-Syntax` parameter in the `Get-DscResource` cmdlet, you are presented with the format that you would need to use in the PowerShell configuration script, as shown in Figure 12-9:

```
Get-DscResource -Name Script -Syntax
```

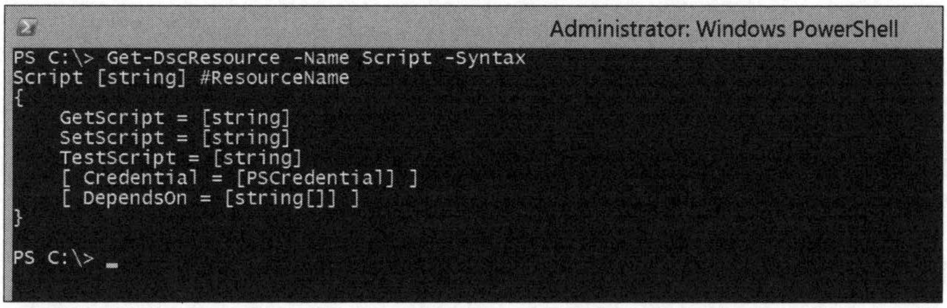

Figure 12-9 `Get-DscResource` cmdlet `-Syntax` parameter

Note that you will be required to replace `#ResourceName` with your specified name for the resource when adding this resource into your configuration script.

Many of the new providers focus on Microsoft Hyper-V, SQL, and Active Directory. While the first one might not be of much use to the average VMware administrator, it is likely that DevOps teams reliant on the Windows platform will be looking to implement the latter two as soon as possible.

The PowerShell community has also been hard at work producing additional resources that you can incorporate into your configurations. Most notably, you should check out the PowerShell.org GitHub[2], where you can find deeper dives into DSC and community-generated resources. Because these resources are community built, they are not supported and should be reviewed before using them, especially in production environments.

Rest assured that Microsoft is moving quickly to release new DSC providers through resource kits. With nine resource kit waves released in under a year, and with many more expected from Microsoft and other vendors, it is safe to say that your development teams will be putting PowerShell DSC to greater use as it matures. The only challenge is that the current released resources are not always guaranteed and should be treated as is. It is easy to identify the currently unsupported resources because their names will be prefixed with an *x*.

NOTE

Microsoft states that the resource kits should be installed on Windows 8.1 and Windows Server 2012 R2. Additional requirements may apply when adding resource kits and community providers to systems running older operating systems. We have tried to provide those prerequisites in this chapter, but we suggest that you read any provided release notes before implementing and using these kits.

Summary

Microsoft has built a very flexible and desired state platform into PowerShell 4 and the Windows Management Framework 4.0. Microsoft Windows PowerShell DSC provides the capability to configure Windows systems dynamically based on configurations deployed as MOF files. This capability enables administrators, developers, and VMware administrators to predefine the characteristics of a Microsoft Windows system and maintain its configuration over time. This is not unique in Linux environments (with the use of Puppet, Chef, and Ansible, as described in previous chapters), but it is a huge step forward for Windows environments. Development for DSC is still in its early stages, and administrators should expect greater capabilities from Microsoft in the months to come that will far exceed the current capabilities outlined in this text.

References

[1] Microsoft TechNet DSC resources: http://technet.microsoft.com/en-us/library/dn282125.aspx

[2] PowerShell.Org GitHub for DSC: http://github.com/PowerShellOrg/dsc

Chapter 13

Implementation Strategies with PowerShell DSC

VMware administrators are in a unique position in a DevOps environment because they tend to be very involved in both the operations and development side of the coin. This position requires them to be agile in how they deliver virtual machines (VMs) and virtual infrastructure to the development teams. Many VMware administrators use PowerCLI, VMware's PowerShell snap-in, for automating tasks and reporting in their VMware vSphere environment. This chapter discusses ways that VMware administrators may look to use PowerCLI, PowerShell 4.0, and PowerShell Desired State Configuration (DSC) to serve the needs of the entire DevOps team.

Topics covered in this chapter include the following:

- Use cases for PowerShell DSC in VMware environments
- Scripted deployments of VMs with PowerCLI
- Incorporating PowerShell DSC in VM templates
- Challenges implementing PowerShell DSC configurations to new VMs
- General lessons learned
- Future use cases for PowerShell DSC in VMware environments

Use Cases for PowerShell DSC in VMware Environments

PowerShell DSC does not have any published resources for managing VMware infrastructure at the time of this writing. Microsoft has released a few initial resources for managing Hyper-V, as discussed further later in this chapter. Today's VMware administrators have a variety of methods they could look to apply DSC configurations to VM operating systems in the environment that they manage. This section outlines the different strategies and the use case for that method. A later section covers some challenges faced when implementing those methods, so that you can understand those challenges before implementing them in your environment:

- Implementing DSC configuration against a VM as part of a PowerCLI deployment script
- Implementing PowerShell DSC in templates
- Using `Invoke-VMScript`

Scripted Deployments of VMs with PowerCLI

PowerCLI, VMware's PowerShell snap-in, enables VMware administrators to deploy new VMs using the `New-VM` cmdlet. This powerful cmdlet can build a VM from a variety of starting points. Most commonly, VMs in a mature VMware environment will be built utilizing templates and operating system customization specifications, as shown in Listing 13-1.

> **NOTE**
>
> VMware OS customizations are not required for VM deployment with `New-VM`, but provide a systematic way for deploying VMs. Information such as the operating system license, domain, and networking configuration can be implemented through using an OS customization specification.

Listing 13-1 Creating a VM

```
###### Creating the VM #####

# The following information is required for connecting to the vCenter
# Server
$vcenter = "vTesseract-vc51"

# $vcenter = Read-Host 'What is your vCenter Server Name?'

# $cred = Get-Credential
<# We recommend you never put credentials in plain text.
Use the above $cred call when running the script interactively.
```

```
Specifying credentials is NOT required when the script is being run by a
user whose logged in credentials match credentials with appropriate vCenter
permissions assigned.
#>


<# Collect or Define VM Info.
 In this section I have defined values.
 You can opt to collect info yourself from environment
 or user VM Info
#>

$VMName = 'devops-02'
# Read-Host 'VM Name?'

# VM Deployment Requirements
$TemplateName = "w2k12r2-01"
# Read-Host 'Template Name?'

$OSSpecName = "W2K12R2"
# Read-Host 'OS Customization Spec Name?'

$DatastoreCluster = "vTesseract-Nas01"
# Read-Host 'Datastore Cluster Name?'

$VMhostCluster = "MGMT"
# Read-Host 'Cluster Name?'

$FolderName = "Devops"
# Read-Host 'Folder Name?'

###### Script Execution Section ######

# Connect to vCenter Server
if($cred -eq $null){
  Connect-VIserver $vcenter
}else{
  Connect-VIserver $vcenter -Credential $cred
}

# Compile New VM Info
```

```
$Template = Get-Template -Name $TemplateName
$OSSpec = Get-OSCustomizationSpec $OSSpecName
$Datastore = Get-DatastoreCluster -Name $DatastoreCluster
# Datastore Cluster assumes Storage DRS is turned on for the Cluster
$Cluster = Get-Cluster -Name $VMhostCluster
$Folder = Get-Folder $FolderName

##### Creates the new VM based on collected info. #####

New-VM -Name $VMName -Template $Template -OSCustomizationSpec $OSSpec '
 -Datastore $Datastore -ResourcePool $Cluster -Location $Folder
```

In Listing 13-1, I have commented out sections where you could use the script to prompt users for input to make it more interactive. Simply set the variable equal to the `Read-Host` statement, as shown in the example in Listing 13-2.

Listing 13-2 Example of User Prompt

```
###### Creating the VM #####

# The following information is required for connecting to the vCenter
# Server
$vcenter = Read-Host 'What is your vCenter Server Name?'
```

You might note that the majority of the script in Listing 13-1 involves gathering the necessary information for the last line where we call `New-VM`. You should use `Get-Help New-VM -Full` to get a fuller representation of what is possible for deploying VMs with the `New-VM` cmdlet.

Incorporating PowerShell DSC in VM Templates

You learned in the preceding chapter that the Local Configuration Manager (LCM) could be configured to point to a central pull server. VMware administrators can work with operating system administrators or development teams to ensure that VM templates have their LCM preconfigured to point to a specific pull server. This allows the manager of the DSC pull server flexibility in dictating the characteristics of the VM that is being deployed.

In addition, this can make it easier for VMware administrators to keep their VM templates current. Proper implementation of Windows Server Update Service (WSUS) and PowerShell DSC pointed to a central pull server means keeping templates current is simpler and more consistent. Maintaining properly patched and updated templates ensures minimal post-deployment configuration and patching required. Reducing time to availability for net new VMs is a cornerstone to effective DevOps.

One of the limitations to using PowerShell DSC with pull server is the requirement that the new VM be able to communicate with that server over the network. Organizations utilizing isolated development environments or deployments in a DMZ may find challenges in successfully using DSC to manage those VMs. The simplest mechanism for support in these environments is to either provide a pull server on the same network or have an open path through a firewall. Because this opens up potential risk, we have put forth effort to find ways of incorporating DSC without the VM's ability to communicate outside of its fenced zone, as discussed later.

Challenges Implementing PowerShell DSC Configurations to New VMs

We discussed earlier the various methods that could be pursued in implementing DSC in a VMware virtual environment. The primary premise around these various mechanisms focuses on minimizing deployment time and providing the greatest flexibility in environments where network segmentation makes centralized DSC management challenging. Improvements in virtual networking make network isolation and management more flexible; however, it was worth exploring alternatives to the traditional pull server architecture to see whether other VMware unique mechanisms for implementing PowerShell DSC might be effective. Note that all challenges pointed out are not showstoppers to implementation. They simply require additional forethought and specific trade-offs based on environment limitations. The most effective method for maintaining VMs with PowerShell DSC remains the use of the pull server.

NOTE

The methods attempted provided varying levels of consistent results and ultimately proved to be marginally beneficial in most cases. Consider your use case before deciding to pursue these methods because the limitations listed might make the solution unsuitable for your needs.

PowerCLI Invoke-VMscript

VMware can take advantage of VMware tools by enabling a cmdlet in PowerCLI called `Invoke-VMscript`. This cmdlet enables an administrator to run a script on a VM by communicating through the ESXi host to the VMware Tools installed on the VM. Naturally, this functionality has a few requirements if using `Invoke-VMscript` with DSC.

1. The VM must be powered on.
2. VMware Tools must be installed and running.
3. PowerShell must be installed on the system.
4. The user running the script must have access to the folder where the VM resides.
5. The user running the script must have Virtual Machine.Interaction.Console Interaction privilege.
6. Port 902 must be open to the ESXi host.
7. The user must be able to authenticate with both the ESXi host and the VM's guest OS.
8. The guest operating system must also have WMF 4.0 with PowerShell 4.0 installed.

The previous requirements are relatively straightforward and are simple enough to include in a script. It is recommended not to include credentials in plain text in a script. This can be avoided by using the `Get-Credential` cmdlet in the script as used in List 13-1. This cmdlet will prompt the person executing the script for credentials and store the response in an encrypted format.

Unfortunately, `Invoke-VMscript` has some limitations that greatly reduce the effectiveness of using it for network-isolated VMs. The primary limitation is that the script parameter for the cmdlet appears to accept only single-line scripts. This is great for many scripting activities but insufficient to properly implement PowerShell DSC. If a VM has network access to a pull server or a configuration script on a network share, there is limited distinct advantage available to the VMware administrator.

This does not mean that `Invoke-VMscript` must be abandoned. It is possible to provide a full path to a PowerShell script file. Using a system with both PowerCLI and PowerShell, it is possible to generate a MOF file, store it in an accessible location, and use `Invoke-VMscript` to initiate the configuration, as shown in Listing 13-3. This code would be included after adding the DSC configuration script webserver and specifying a network location for the generated MOF file.

Listing 13-3 Creating a MOF File

```
# Creating MOF file
$mofpath = "\\<server>\moffiles\$vmname\"
WebServer $VMName -OutputPath $mofpath

$ScriptText = "Set-DscLocalConfigurationManager -Path $mofpath
-ComputerName $VMName"
```

```
# Get the VM object from vCenter
$vm = Get-VM $VMName

# Prompt user for VM guest OS credentials
$guestcred = Get-Credential

# Invoke the script on the Guest OS
Invoke-VMscript -ScriptText $ScriptText -VM $vm -GuestCredential
$guestcred -ScriptType PowerShell -Server $vcenter
```

NOTE

This method certainly resembles using push mode in a remote capacity. However, because we are initiating the DSC configuration script through `Invoke-VMscript`, it does not require PowerShell remoting to be enabled on the target VM. Testing results varied using this technique. Occasionally, the remote system rejected the MOF file. The root cause for this issue was not determined.

PowerCLI Copy-VMGuestFile

If network isolation is an absolute requirement, it is still possible to utilize `Invoke-VMscript` by first copying the MOF file or script to the VM. This can be accomplished using the `Copy-VMGuestFile` cmdlet in PowerCLI. This cmdlet can copy a file from the executing system to the VM's file system through the VM's installation of VMware Tools. This cmdlet has a variety of requirements depending on which version of VMware vSphere you are running:

1. The VM must be powered on.
2. VMware Tools must be installed and running.
3. PowerShell must be installed on the system.
4. The user running the script must have access to the folder where the VM resides.
5. The user running the script must have VirtualMachine.GuestOperations.Modify privilege.
6. Port 902 must be open to the ESXi host.
7. The user must be able to authenticate with both the ESXi host and the VM's guest OS.
8. The guest OS must be supported by the cmdlet.[1]

To implement DSC, you must first copy the configuration script or MOF file to the VM and then use the `Invoke-VMscript` cmdlet as described previously. A simplified example is available in Listing 13-4. Building from previous examples, this script assumes that you've created a script file that includes the configuration, builds the MOF file, and executes the configuration.

Listing 13-4 Implementing DSC via Invoke-VMscript

```
$script = "E:\Scripts\DevOps\WebServer.psd1"
$mofpath = "C:\Users\Administrator\Documents"
$moffile = "C:\Users\Administrator\Documents\WebServer.psd1"
# The following line invokes the configuration and creates a file called
Server001.meta.mof at the specified path
$guestcred = Get-Credential
$BuildMof = WebServer -OutputPath $mofpath

# Get the virtual machine object from vCenter server
$vm = Get-VM devops-02
# Copy the script to the designated directory on the target VM
Copy-VMGuestFile -Source $script -Destination $mofpath -LocalToGuest -VM
$vm -HostCredential $cred -Server $vcenter -GuestCredential $guestcred
# Invoke the copied script on the target VM
Invoke-VMScript -ScriptText $moffile -VM $vm -HostCredential $cred -Server
$global:DefaultVIServer -GuestCredential $guestcred
```

This method enables the VMware administrator to remotely execute DSC configurations on VMs that may be isolated from the network or are incapable of supporting PowerShell Remoting due to security concerns.

NOTE

This method proved to be the most consistent and ultimately the most efficient given the criteria we set out during our testing. Because the requirements are nearly identical to simply using `Invoke-VMscript`, we recommend using `Copy-VMGuestFile` when needing to keep a VM isolated or to avoid enabling remote PowerShell capabilities.

General Lessons Learned

We recognize that some of these use cases do not present themselves as ideal scenarios. However, it is important to understand a wider range of tools at the VMware administrator's disposal. `Invoke-VMscript` and `Copy-VMGuestFile` have limitations that may prevent you from taking advantage of them. It is important to properly assess and qualify your need so that you can choose the most effective method for you.

During our testing, we found that none of the methods performed 100% consistently. This was regularly due to human error, because we were attempting to do things that appear to have been untried before. That said, each method presented in this chapter did prove successful under the right conditions. It is our intent that our efforts provide you with some guidance if you find that you, too, need to pursue these methods to take advantage of PowerShell DSC on systems unable to use native functionality.

Future Use Cases for PowerShell DSC in VMware Environments

Administrators will continue to use PowerShell for a wide range of configuration, management, and reporting tasks. DSC can extend well beyond the configuration of Windows systems and Microsoft applications. As mentioned previously, Microsoft has demonstrated capability to use DSC to manage Linux systems. It is safe to assume that these capabilities could be extended into the VMware ecosystem.

Custom PowerShell DSC resources are certainly a possibility. Providing modules in specific formats enables the resource to create a properly formatted MOF file. Like all PowerShell DSC resources, these MOF files will instruct the resource on the proper end state. The resource will contain PowerShell modules with the required code to implement that change. The formatting requirements are beyond the scope of this book, but can be referenced on Microsoft's TechNet website[2].

The full extensibility of PowerShell DSC has yet to be explored thoroughly because it is still a relatively new feature of PowerShell and Microsoft Windows management. It is safe to say that as this feature matures we will see its capabilities also expand greatly. It would not be surprising to see functionality from PowerShell DSC replicate current VMware features like host profiles and the configuration manager. In addition, VMware administrators may look to maintain VM hardware profiles, folder structures, or network configurations using PowerShell DSC in the not-too-distant future.

Finally, the ecosystem of infrastructure components around VMware data centers continues to evolve and produce more flexible application programming interfaces (APIs) and integration points. We are able to imagine a scenario in the not-too-distant future where PowerShell DSC and its functionality is a strong contributor to the efficiency of the next-generation software-defined data center. Extensibility in storage, network, and computer components are going to yield numerous opportunities for improving how we maintain configuration standards for our entire infrastructure stack.

NOTE

Microsoft regularly releases new waves of PowerShell DSC resources. Before implementing them in your environment, be aware that these resources often have limited support and should be used accordingly.

Summary

You should now have a better understanding of how you might be more empowered to help implement PowerShell DSC in your DevOps environment despite potential challenging limitations. Most likely, the majority of VMware administrators will have limited need for the methods outlined in this chapter.

DSC will continue to grow as a feature of PowerShell 4 and the upcoming PowerShell 5 with a booming library of resources being produced at a rapid pace. Microsoft is pushing hard to include Hyper-V resources, and it is reasonable to expect that VMware and other companies with PowerShell extensibility will eventually follow suit as appropriate use cases become apparent. Regardless of timelines, PowerShell DSC will soon become a mainstay in a Microsoft Windows-centric DevOps environment. As a VMware administrator for that environment, it is important to be knowledgeable about DSC so that you can both speak intelligently to it and also contribute in its successful implementation.

References

[1] VMware developer portal for PowerCLI cmdlet `Copy-VMGuestFile`: https://www.vmware.com/support/developer/PowerCLI/PowerCLI55/html/Copy-VMGuestFile.html

[2] Microsoft TechNet DSC custom resources: http://technet.microsoft.com/en-us/library/dn249927.aspx

Chapter 14

Introduction to Application Containers with Docker

This chapter covers an increasingly popular method of application deployment and management that uses Linux containers powered by Docker. First, we define what applications are and why they can be so complex to manage. Next, we look at how Linux containers actually work. Then we review Docker and its ability to produce portable, self-contained application containers that can deploy in a fast and repeatable manner.

Topics covered in this chapter include the following:

- What is an application?
- Linux containers
- Using Docker

What Is an Application?

An application represents a logical software unit designed to provide a set of features or services. Most software tends to help people perform a specific task such as getting directions to a nearby restaurant or debating trending topics using 140 characters or fewer.

On the surface, users see an application as a simple interface, but as system administrators we know there's complexity hidden within the application or environment in which the application executes.

Hidden Complexity

All applications have dependencies. As system administrators, we typically interact with external dependencies such as third-party packages, language runtimes, system libraries, and databases.

Each dependency usually comes with a variety of configuration options such as defining a database username and password. Many of the tools discussed in previous chapters concentrate on automating applications, application dependencies, and related configurations, but the true complexity of managing applications comes in when our configurations and dependencies conflict with one another. These conflicts are what prevent us from running multiple versions of an application on the same server.

Dependency and Configuration Conflicts

Conflicts occur when two applications require a different set of system libraries or language runtimes that conflict with each other.

In the case of system libraries, we usually see situations where one of the application versions we're installing requires a specific library version. This happens when applications are written against a specific version of a library, a practice that's often encouraged by OS vendors in an attempt to achieve long-term stability. However, there is a cost. What happens when you want to develop a new application that requires a new version of the same library?

The workaround can be very complex to downright impossible. For example, a workaround for installing new and old libraries side by side might be to use different paths and names, such as the following:

- /usr/lib/openssl.so
- usr/lib/openssl-1.0.1.so

The workaround might be successful, but we now have to configure our application to be aware of the difference.

The real solution to the problem of dependency management is isolation.

Linux Containers

Linux containers provide the necessary isolation between applications to eliminate conflicts between runtime dependencies and configurations. Isolation also provides a way for multiple versions of an application to run side by side. This is a powerful concept for zero downtime deployments and the ability to roll back to previous application versions.

Using a container, you can combine an application and its dependencies into a single package, which can become a versioned artifact. One important thing to understand is that a container doesn't provide full virtualization. Instead, each container shares the same hardware and Linux kernel with the underlying host. Although the host and hardware are shared, Linux containers allow you to run a different Linux distribution than the host as long as it's compatible with the underlying kernel.

For example, if a host is running Ubuntu, you're free to run CentOS inside of the container. This is a powerful feature that allows you the freedom to run the best Linux distribution for an application.

There are multiple Linux technologies utilized by containers, although Linux control groups and namespaces provide the majority of the benefits associated with containers such as resource utilization limits and isolation.

Control Groups

Linux control groups, or cgroups, explicitly tell the kernel the amount of resources such as CPU and RAM that it needs to allocate to processes. Because it's possible to add related processes to a single group, a CPU scheduler would have an easier time deciding how to allocate resources to the group members. The use of cgroups is necessary because containers are not like virtual machines, which have a hypervisor controlling all resources and enforcing fair resource allocation. Instead, containers look like regular processes to the operating system, and cgroups attempt to fairly allocate resources.

Namespaces

The isolation provided by Linux containers is made possible by a feature of the Linux kernel called namespaces. Currently there are six namespaces:

- IPC (interprocess communication)
- Mount (file systems and mount points)
- Network (networking)
- PID (processes)
- User (user IDs)
- UTS (hostname)

Each namespace provides a boundary between applications. When running within the bounds of one or more Linux namespaces, an application is said to be running in a container.

The primary purpose of Linux namespaces is to provide process isolation. You can leverage this isolation to build and deploy self-contained application bundles. Each application bundle can have its own file system, hostname, and networking stack.

There are many ways that applications or processes can interact with each other. To fully isolate one process from another, you need to create boundaries at every point of interaction. For application containers, you'll primarily work with the mount, UTS, and network namespaces. The other namespaces focus on security, which is essential for running untrusted applications.

NOTE

So far, we have described isolation for fully trusted applications or processes. While additional Linux namespaces can be utilized to provide better isolation, Linux containers alone do not provide the level of security that can be achieved with full virtualization technologies provided by VMware

Mount Namespace

The mount namespace prevents dependency conflicts by providing full file system isolation between two running processes. In essence, each application sees an independent file system that is not shared with the host operating system. Each application is free to install dependences without conflict.

When you use the mount namespace in combination with chroots, you can create fully isolated Linux installations suitable for running an application.

UTS Namespace

The UTS or hostname namespace provides the ability to assign each application instance a unique hostname.

Network Namespace

The network namespace eliminates port conflicts between two running applications by providing each container its own networking stack. This means that each application can be assigned its own network address, which allows each application to bind to the same TCP port number without conflict.

You can learn more about each namespace by reviewing the kernel documentation.

Container Management

The next question we need to answer is how to create a Linux container. That's a bit difficult because the primary interface to Linux namespaces is via system calls. The good news is that there are userspace tools like LXC that you can use to automate container deployment.

The not-so-good news is that, even when you use LXC, some additional challenges to container management need to be addressed:

- Prerequisites to run a container OS on the host system.
- Configuration files that may need to be edited for resource control.
- Implementations of LXC that may vary between distributions or within the same distribution family.

Using Docker

Docker is a client and server application that makes it easy to utilize Linux containers by providing a standard format for building and sharing those containers. Docker builds on the contributions of LXC, cgroups, namespaces, and other open source Linux projects to simplify container deployments even further than is possible with existing userspace tools.

At a high level, Docker helps automate the creation of Linux containers including isolation at all levels provided by the Linux kernel. Not only is Docker able to streamline the containerization process, it also provides an on-disk format that makes it easy to share containers between hosts and with others.

In a sense, Docker turns applications into self-contained, portable units that can be built once and run anywhere. Where have I heard that before?

Installing Docker

The Docker solution consists of the Docker daemon and Docker client. The Docker daemon is currently only available on x86_64 Linux distributions with Microsoft planning to add support in a future version of Windows Server. The Docker client can run on Linux, Windows, and OS X, which makes it very convenient to execute commands from a remote machine.

> **NOTE**
>
> At the time of this writing, every major Linux distribution has support for Docker.

The most common method for installing Docker is to use your operating system's package manager. Another option is to use a Linux distribution, such as CoreOS, which includes Docker in its base build. Alternatively, you could use boot2docker, a utility that leverages a very small Linux virtual machine (VM) for running containers.

If you run the Docker daemon and client on two different systems, make sure that both are running the same version of Docker.

You can use the `docker version` command to check which version of Docker is installed:

```
$ docker version
Client version: 1.0.1
Client API version: 1.12
Go version (client): go1.2
Git commit (client): 990021a
Server version: 1.0.1
Server API version: 1.12
Go version (server): go1.2
Git commit (server): 990021a
```

Docker Daemon

The Docker daemon is responsible for starting, stopping, and storing application containers on a single host. It also provides a remote application programming interface (API) that you can use to programmatically control containers.

Docker Client

The Docker client is a command-line tool that allows you to interact with the Docker daemon through an API. The Docker client can be installed as a single binary on OS X and Linux operating systems. It is also possible to compile the Docker client for Windows Servers, but coverage of those steps is beyond the scope of this book.

> **NOTE**
>
> You can see a list of all of the actions possible with the client by typing `docker -h` at the command line.

Docker Index

The Docker index is a repository for containers, similar to a code repository like Git. It is possible to have an on-premise Docker Index, or you can use a remote index like the one owned by Docker, Inc. at http://hub.docker.com.

Running a Docker Container

Before we look at how to create a Docker container, let's see how easy it is to get started using a prebuilt Docker image located on a Docker index. We'll use the `docker run` command and the syntax in Listing 14-1. Sample output is also included.

Listing 14-1 Docker Container Deployment

```
$ docker run -d -p 6379:6379 --name redis redis
Unable to find image 'redis' locally
Pulling repository redis
dc10c1051e26: Download complete
511136ea3c5a: Download complete
1e8abad02296: Download complete
f106b5d7508a: Download complete
842b5a724d2d: Download complete
c48940f9fc45: Download complete
013e99580bf7: Download complete
076c6da2d5e4: Download complete
b7db07b1768c: Download complete
5e22b7a89800: Download complete
4b10ba128f08: Download complete
fd9a01509f91: Download complete
6dc9daf74f25906ea4f71ac64ef5fd92019acaf14434b1257d76b207e69855f8
```

The `-d` flag detaches from the container after it's created so that it runs in the background.

The `-p` flag allows you to map exposed ports from the container to ports specified on the command line. In the example, both the external and internal ports are mapped to the same port.

The `-name` flag allows you to launch the container with a unique name. After you name the container, you provide the name of the container image you want to run. In the example, we want to run the redis container image.

You'll see in the output that Docker was unable to find the redis image locally. So, Docker proceeded to download the image one layer at a time. This includes the base image required by the redis image. By default, Docker will attempt to download images from the index maintained by Docker, Inc.

Layers represent an easy way to build up a container image incrementally that speeds up future downloads of updated versions of the same container.

The last line in the output is the container ID. This ID is how we gather additional information about the container. Because we launched this container with the `-name` flag, we can also use the name in place of the container ID.

Listing Running Containers

Docker makes it so easy to launch containers that it can be easy to lose track of which containers are running on a given system. You can view running containers on a system by using the `docker ps` command:

```
$ docker ps
CONTAINER ID  IMAGE         PORTS                   NAMES
66df5215853d  redis:latest  0.0.0.0:6379->6379/tcp  redis
```

From this output, we can tell that the redis container was launched from the redis Docker image with a container ID of 66df5215853d. The `docker ps` output also shows the port mappings of the container. In the case of the redis container, port 6379 on the host is mapped to port 6379 on the container.

Connecting to Running Containers

If you have the redis client installed on the same machine as Docker, you can use the following syntax to connect to your new database instance:

```
$ redis-cli -h localhost -p 6379
```

How did we get these connection parameters? From the previous section, we purposefully mapped the redis application's port (6379) in the container to the same port number on the Docker host. All that is left to do is specify to the redis client the host (localhost) and the port number to connect to.

If you do not have the redis CLI installed locally, no problem! We can just use another container to connect to our redis container.

First, we create a second container on the Docker host, and I will use a simple Ubuntu container:

```
$ docker run -it --link redis:redis --name redis-client ubuntu /bin/bash
```

There are some new flags and options for `docker run` that we did not discuss previously.

The `-i` flag tells Docker that we want to interact directly with the container instead of immediately detaching from it.

The `-t` flag provides a tty for us to run commands in.

The `--link` flag gets us into the realm of Service Discovery a little bit because it informs our new container about important characteristics of our redis container. The `--link` flag will automatically create environment variables in our new container that correspond to information such as the redis container's IP address and application port number. Listing 14-2 shows an example.

Finally, after the name of the container (`ubuntu`), we provide a command for our new container to run (`/bin/bash`). So, when our interactive container comes up, it will place us automatically in the Bash Linux shell.

Listing 14-2 Docker `--link` Environment Variables

```
REDIS_ENV_REDIS_DOWNLOAD_URL=http://download.redis.io/releases/
     redis-2.8.19.tar.gz
REDIS_PORT_6379_TCP_PROTO=tcp
REDIS_ENV_REDIS_DOWNLOAD_SHA1=3e362f4770ac2fdbdce58a5aa951c1967e0facc8
REDIS_NAME=/redis-client/redis
REDIS_PORT_6379_TCP_ADDR=172.17.0.2
REDIS_PORT_6379_TCP_PORT=6379
REDIS_PORT_6379_TCP=tcp://172.17.0.2:6379
REDIS_PORT=tcp://172.17.0.2:6379
REDIS_ENV_REDIS_VERSION=2.8.19
```

After executing the `docker run` command, we will be placed at a command prompt with a randomly generated hostname:

```
root@fe86ff399421:/#
```

Next, we can install the redis-cli using the following commands:

```
# apt-get update
# apt-get install -y redis-tools
```

Last, we connect to the redis container using the environment variables generated by Docker's link functionality:

```
# redis-cli -h $REDIS_PORT_6379_TCP_ADDR -p $REDIS_PORT_6379_TCP_PORT
```

We can now access our redis database and confirm it's working with a couple simple commands:

```
172.17.0.2:6379> set devops rocks
OK
172.17.0.2:6379> get devops
"rocks"
```

Building and Distributing Docker Containers

You may wonder why you would need to build your own containers when there are many great base containers in the Docker community. Well, when you connect to a container and run commands, like in our redis-client example earlier, those changes need to be run every time you create an instance of that container.

Wouldn't it be great if we could distribute our own containers prebaked with the packages and settings that we need? Docker allows us to do just that. Your customizations then become additional layers on top of the base image that you use in a newly generated container.

The Docker container format consists of the file system representation of a container and some metadata known collectively as a Docker image. A Docker image contains the following items:

- A compressed file system
- A metadata file
- A container configuration file also known as the Dockerfile

We will dive a bit deeper into a discussion of the Dockerfile because that is your means of building and customizing your own containers. Before continuing on with the rest of this chapter, open an account on the Docker Hub (http://hub.docker.com). For simplicity, you may want to use the same username as your GitHub account. We discuss the Docker Hub a little later in this chapter.

NOTE

Discussions about which file system is better for your Docker containers (aufs versus btrfs) are beyond the scope of this book. However, Docker containers are by default stored in /var/lib/docker on the Docker host.

Dockerfile

The Dockerfile is a text document that contains the set of commands used to build a container. This is a similar concept to the Vagrantfile that we introduced in Chapter 3 for automating our test environment builds with Vagrant.

Let's take a look at a sample Dockerfile for building an Nginx web server in Listing 14-3.

Listing 14-3 Dockerfile for an Nginx Container

```
# Ubuntu Trusty release selected for the web server
FROM ubuntu:14.04
MAINTAINER Trevor Roberts Jr <vmtrooper@gmail.com>

# Install the add-apt-repository utility
RUN apt-get -qq update && apt-get install -qq -y software-properties-common

# Add the nginx stable repository
RUN add-apt-repository -y ppa:nginx/stable && apt-get -qq -y update

# Install nginx
RUN apt-get install -qq -y nginx
```

We add useful comments using the `#` symbol, like in the first line of Listing 14-3, so that anyone modifying the Dockerfile will understand the thought process in the container composition.

Next, the `FROM` statement tells us which base container to work from. The format of the container identifier that you use with `FROM` is `repository:tag`. In our example, the container is from the Ubuntu repository with the tag 14.04. Some repositories have multiple tagged containers, including one with the tag "latest." If you don't specify a tag, the container image with the tag "latest" is used automatically.

When Docker looks for the container specified with the `FROM` command, it first looks for the image locally. If the image can't be found locally, the Docker daemon looks at remote repositories such as http://hub.docker.com.

Next, the `MAINTAINER` command identifies who maintains the container. Be sure to update this section with your own contact information.

Finally, the `RUN` commands give instructions to the Docker daemon on how to build the container.

Notice that the example uses the `&&` symbol to combine commands in the same line. You can use the `&&` symbol to make related commands part of the same Docker build step. These related commands become part of the same Docker layer and can speed up the download process for your container for others who use it.

For example, the first `RUN` command performs the requisite initial apt repository update and then installs the software-properties-common package. This package contains the add-apt-repository utility that's used in the next `RUN` command.

Because these two command executions are somewhat related, they can be part of the same build step. Remember that the Docker container build process is automated without opportunity for user input. It's important to verify that you include the proper command-line options with your command executions to automate input requests and to optionally suppress output, just as if you were using these commands in a shell script.

Our Dockerfile now needs to be processed to provide a working container image, and the `docker build` command does this for us. The following syntax shows how to build the Dockerfile that we just created:

```
$ docker build -t="your_docker_hub_username/nginx:v1" .
```

The `build` command's `-t` option allows you to specify your repository name and optionally the tag that you want to apply to this container. The repository name consists of your Docker Hub username and the name you want to give to your container (for example, nginx). The tag is "v1" in this example. The tag is optional. If you do not include a tag, this build will be referred to as the "latest" tag in Docker Hub.

Last, you provide the path to the Dockerfile. If you execute the container build from the same directory where you saved the Dockerfile, you use a period (`.`) to tell the daemon to look in the present working directory.

Docker Hub

After you have a working container, you can explore pushing it to an index. You have a few options regarding which index to use:

- An index you've deployed internally
- An index provided by a third-party hosting provider
- The Docker index run by Docker, Inc. at http://hub.docker.com, which is known as the Docker Hub

If you build the container example from Listing 14-3, you can use the following command to push it to the Docker Hub index:

```
docker push your_docker_hub_username/nginx:v1
```

The `push` command tells the Docker daemon to transfer the build steps that are unique to the container. Notice that I said "unique." If you build a container from an existing container, the push process recognizes this when it connects to the Docker Hub and only stores the changes that you introduced. The Docker Hub supports both public and private container repositories.

Docker Versus Virtual Machines

Containers are discrete units of compute resources assigned to a given task similar to VMs. Does that mean that they obviate the use of VMs? Not at all. There are uses for VMs such as security isolation or speed of infrastructure deployment that containers don't currently solve.

Regarding isolation, it's not possible for processes within VMs to affect other processes on the physical host as can be the case with containers. That isn't to say that containers are inherently unsecure. However, if the application in your container needs root access or some other configuration that may be a security concern, it's best to isolate it and any related containers to a VM or group of VMs.

Regarding infrastructure deployment, despite having great technologies like Razor and Cobbler to get our bare-metal servers up and running quickly, VMs are still orders of magnitude quicker to deploy than bare metal servers. If your physical infrastructure has sufficient free capacity, you can deploy VMs to provide the required isolation for your workloads and then deploy your applications in those VMs using containers.

Docker Versus Configuration Management

Docker containers speed up application deployments just like configuration management technologies. Does that mean that we need to get rid of our Puppet manifests or Chef recipes? The answer here is also no.

Configuration management technologies can be used in conjunction with containers for application deployments. One use case is to incorporate execution of configuration management scripts into your Dockerfile. This makes sense because you may have already invested time to ensure the right dependencies are being observed in your configuration management instruction files. Instead of reinventing the wheel in your Dockerfile, execute your configuration management scripts from within the Dockerfile.

Summary

In this chapter, we defined what an application is and looked at how applications are built and deployed. We also examined the limitations of the traditional operating systems and how they add to the complexity of deploying applications. Finally, we discussed how to leverage application containers to reduce many of the complexities that surround building and deploying applications. The next chapter covers details of planning and deploying applications using Linux application containers at scale using a distributed Linux OS running on top of VMware technologies.

References

[1] Docker documentation: http://docs.docker.com

[2] Docker CLI for Windows: http://azure.microsoft.com/blog/2014/11/18/docker-cli-for-windows-clients/

Chapter 15

Running Docker Containers at Scale

Chapter 14 explained how containers are really just fancy Linux processes that, in the case of Docker, ship with all their dependencies using the Docker format. On a single system, processes are usually managed by the init system and the Linux kernel. However, how do we manage containers on multiple hosts? We need an orchestration solution that not only deploys containers, but also we need to handle other logistics such as intercontainer communication, container state management (for example, running, stopped, recover from failure), and so on. This chapter focuses on technologies that enable container management at scale across multiple hosts.

Topics covered in this chapter include the following:

- Container orchestration
- Kubernetes
- Kubernetes deployment
- Platform-as-a-service with Docker

Container Orchestration

Since the Docker project was announced, a few interesting things have happened in the container space. We have seen a significant increase in community interest in using containers for application deployment. Also, there has been an increase in the popularity of what we like to call *container-optimized* operating systems: operating systems that usually ship only with the necessary components and configuration settings to run containers out of the box. This normally means having Docker preinstalled.

The CoreOS Linux distribution has become the most well known of the container operating systems, and for good reason. CoreOS does not ship a package manager such as apt or yum. Instead, all software must be deployed as a Linux container using Docker.

However, to truly run containers at scale, some additional challenges need to be solved such as placement (affinity versus anti-affinity), availability, networking, and so on. There are many tools available to do this, but they often have one thing in common: They all focus on pinning a specific container to a specific host. Although it's true you can deploy a lot of containers this way, it does not scale to the full potential that containers have.

Now that Docker has arrived, we are finding ourselves creating more processes than ever that need to be deployed across an entire cluster. Cluster sizes have grown thanks to virtualization and the ability to deploy anything anywhere.

On a single host, the init system gives us the ability to stop, start, and restart processes. Once up and running, processes are scheduled to get access to hardware and memory. This has been the way system administrators have been managing processes for more than three decades. What we are in need of today is the same ability to schedule these "super" processes (that is, Linux containers) to different machines within the cluster with the ease of running them on a single host. That's where Kubernetes comes in.

Kubernetes

Kubernetes is the container management system from Google that offers a unique workflow for managing containers across multiple machines. Kubernetes introduces the concept of a *pod*, which represents a group of related containers running on the same host that share networking and a file system. A pod is meant to be deployed as a single logical service. The pod concept tends to fit well with the popular pattern of running a single service per container. Kubernetes makes it easy to run multiple pods on a single machine or across an entire cluster for better resource utilization and high availability. Kubernetes also actively monitors the health of pods to ensure they are always running within the cluster.

Kubernetes can achieve this advanced level of clusterwide orchestration by leveraging the etcd distributed key-value store, a project started and maintained by CoreOS. etcd takes care of storing and replicating data used by Kubernetes across the entire cluster. etcd employs the Raft consensus algorithm to recover from hardware failure and network partitions. The combination of Kubernetes and etcd is even more powerful when deployed on CoreOS, an operating system built for this kind of thing.

Kubernetes Workflow

A simple way to think of Kubernetes is to look at it as a project that builds on the idea that the data center is the computer, and Kubernetes provides an application programming interface (API) to manage it all.

The deployment workflow provided by Kubernetes allows us to think about the cluster as a whole and less about each individual machine. In the Kubernetes model, we don't deploy containers to specific hosts. Instead, we describe the containers we want running, and Kubernetes figures out how and where to run them. This declarative style of managing infrastructure opens up the door for large-scale deployments and self-healing infrastructures. Yeah, welcome to the future.

But how does it all work?

Kubernetes pods are great for applications that benefit from co-locating services such as a caching server or log manager. Pods are created within a Kubernetes cluster through specification files that are pushed to the Kubernetes API. The Kubernetes scheduler will select a cluster node to deploy the pods on. If the specification files indicate that the pod should be replicated, the Kubernetes controller manager will verify that the desired number of pods per application specification is deployed.

On each cluster node, two services are running: Kubelet and the Kubernetes Proxy. Kubelet receives the Kubernetes instructions to start the related containers via the Docker API. It is Kubelet's responsibility to keep the scheduled containers up and running until the pod is either deleted or scheduled onto another machine.

The Kubernetes Proxy server is responsible for mapping service TCP ports to application pods. The idea is that consumers of a service could contact any machine in a Kubernetes cluster on the service's assigned port and the request is routed to the correct pod to provide access to the application. This communication is possible due to each pod having its own IP address. Kubernetes uses etcd to keep track of the pod IPs so that it can properly route application access requests to the correct pod and host.

Kubernetes provides a form of service discovery based on labels to make life easier. Each collection of pods can have an arbitrary number of labels that can be used to locate them. For example, to locate a `redis` service running in production, you could use the following labels to perform a label query:

```
service=redis,environment=production
```

Kubernetes Deployment

Our Kubernetes environment consists of a three-node CoreOS cluster. The following software components make up our demonstration environment:

- CoreOS Linux
- etcd

- flannel (a simple network overlay technology that is used to provide IPs to pods)
- fleet (a utility for deploying applications on a CoreOS cluster)
- Kubernetes
- Kubernetes Register (`kube-register`) (an open source project to simplify Kubelet registration with the Kubernetes API server)
- `etcdctl`, `fleetctl`, and `kubectl` (CLI utilities for managing etcd, fleet, and Kubernetes, respectively)

CoreOS and Kubernetes Cluster Management Utilities

Before we deploy the cluster nodes, let's obtain the CLI utilities that will help us manage the environment. You can obtain the binaries at the following locations on GitHub:

- etcdctl—https://github.com/coreos/etcd/releases
- fleetctl—https://github.com/coreos/fleet/releases
- kubectl—https://github.com/GoogleCloudPlatform/kubernetes

The binary for kubectl actually needs to be built before you can use it. The good news is that the Google team made the process very easy to accomplish by providing a container for the build! The only prerequisite is to have Docker installed locally, or boot2docker if your desktop is Windows or Mac OS X.

After you verify that docker is running (ex: docker ps executes successfully), clone the Kubernetes repository locally and change directory to the "kubernetes" directory that you just downloaded. Next, run the following command:

```
$ ./build/run.sh hack/build-cross.sh
```

If Docker is working properly on your system, the build of the kubernetes binaries will proceed successfully, and the kubectl binary for your operating system will be found in the following directory:

```
kubernetes/_output/dockerized/bin
```

At the time of this book's publishing, Windows binaries for fleetctl do not exist. If you have a Windows desktop, you can either attempt to build binaries from the source code or use Vagrant (See Chapter 3) to create a small Linux VM to manage the Kubernetes environment.

The binaries should be copied to a directory in your current PATH (ex: /usr/local/bin). After we select the IP of the etcd server, we will discuss setting the appropriate environment variables that these binaries will need to communicate with the Kubernetes cluster.

CoreOS Cluster Deployment

Deploy three VMs running the CoreOS operating system either by using the CoreOS-built VMware images from their website (recommended) or by manually installing CoreOS. All three VMs must be connected to the same VMware vSphere portgroup or VMware Fusion/Workstation vmnet.

NOTE

The vSphere portgroup or the Fusion/Workstation vmnet that you connect these VMs to will need to have Dynamic Host Configuration Protocol (DHCP) running for the lab setup to work properly. It is recommend that your entire network range not be managed by DHCP so that we can allocate a static IP for the etcd server. For example, if your network name is 192.168.10.0/24, consider having the DHCP service manage addresses on a higher IP range like 192.168.10.100 to 192.168.10.254.

Next, we create cloud-config files to specify how the CoreOS servers should be configured at boot. Fortunately, these files have been created for you in the /configs directory for this environment's GitHub repository (https://github.com/DevOpsForVMwareAdministrators/kubernetes-fleet-tutorial), and you merely need to update the settings in these files that pertain to your environment. The necessary modifications are described later, and we display sample configuration files in Listings 15-1 and 15-2 for etcd and Kubernetes, respectively.

Listing 15-1 etcd Server Configuration File

```
#cloud-config

hostname: etcd
coreos:
  fleet:
    etcd_servers: http://127.0.0.1:4001
    metadata: role=etcd
  etcd:
    name: etcd
    addr: 172.16.171.10:4001
    bind-addr: 0.0.0.0
    peer-addr: 172.16.171.10:7001
    cluster-active-size: 1
    snapshot: true
```

```
  units:
    - name: static.network
      command: start
      content: |
        [Match]
        Name=enp0s17

        [Network]
        Address=172.16.171.10/24
        DNS=172.16.171.2
        Gateway=172.16.171.2
    - name: etcd.service
      command: start
    - name: fleet.service
      command: start
    - name: docker.service
      mask: true
  update:
    group: alpha
    reboot-strategy: off
ssh_authorized_keys:
    - ssh-rsa AAAAB3NzaC1yc2EAAAADAQABAAABAQCXJo3tfAdsvBZp/l6ChpYbKYtTsK-
cAL32VhV7KGjYqUPY9LJhRPlAAfAh6bU1hBf9wLTCWVOAoWwrQg09raJadfCbDsNohMy2t-
P37vGxyCdd/55uejWIkZEVeMJgRiQC7WIL1GMNWXf8dwWDvk4Xx0MbRBUpb5LcwPFnsCyQEV-
cyi0NQT+1odNnjt74rYCBPbVrM1Owski3zizt+JWqSNAPCYaj+Yvy3OulUmkhZIv8OsEeL-
4BACiZNQDAJFhVw7DW4LZicw+GNzavHD7M0Q5UQdIwx43h0Oiw6AEKtHD16TuYgAVs2ult-
K95Xxg3atZO/WCcgBt2ObFRNOaPAjf3p
```

Listing 15-2 Kubernetes Server Configuration File

```
#cloud-config

coreos:
  fleet:
    etcd_servers: http://172.16.171.10:4001
    metadata: role=kubernetes
  units:
    - name: etcd.service
      mask: true
    - name: fleet.service
      command: start
```

```
    - name: flannel.service
      command: start
      content: |
        [Unit]
        After=network-online.target
        Wants=network-online.target
        Description=flannel is an etcd backed overlay network for contain-
ers

        [Service]
        ExecStartPre=-/usr/bin/mkdir -p /opt/bin
        ExecStartPre=/usr/bin/wget -N -P /opt/bin http://storage.googlea-
pis.com/flannel/flanneld
        ExecStartPre=/usr/bin/chmod +x /opt/bin/flanneld
        ExecStart=/opt/bin/flanneld -etcd-endpoint
http://172.16.171.10:4001
    - name: docker.service
      command: start
      content: |
        [Unit]
        After=flannel.service
        Wants=flannel.service
        Description=Docker Application Container Engine
        Documentation=http://docs.docker.io

        [Service]
        EnvironmentFile=/run/flannel/subnet.env
        ExecStartPre=/bin/mount --make-rprivate /
        ExecStart=/usr/bin/docker -d --bip=${FLANNEL_SUBNET} --mtu=${FLAN-
NEL_MTU} -s=btrfs -H fd://

        [Install]
        WantedBy=multi-user.target
    - name: setup-network-environment.service
      command: start
      content: |
        [Unit]
        Description=Setup Network Environment
        Documentation=https://github.com/kelseyhightower/setup-network-
environment
        Requires=network-online.target
        After=network-online.target
```

```
        [Service]
        ExecStartPre=-/usr/bin/mkdir -p /opt/bin
        ExecStartPre=/usr/bin/wget -N -P /opt/bin http://storage.
googleapis.com/snenv/setup-network-environment
        ExecStartPre=/usr/bin/chmod +x /opt/bin/setup-network-environment
        ExecStart=/opt/bin/setup-network-environment
        RemainAfterExit=yes
        Type=oneshot
  update:
    group: alpha
    reboot-strategy: off
ssh_authorized_keys:
    - ssh-rsa AAAAB3NzaC1yc2EAAAADAQABAAABAQDQgbpj/
u2FTiBBSqBElIrcYCSg9YP2V4VRH/ckV7qWxRBlHwCBGgJSoG+h-
63HG59Jlpe7vtCSlXcxNUbV997AsDMPKGRiww6ngWqyr8GJT+3/
LNSRGAKFOjyhfU4VUYRS9fQNdr0FTfWWDKKgTTyQVdrom+jFw5MBERwBS2u2Srmgw6NWC9BEZn/
j7SWfI3HxdmfWvXWbZO6Ujv3mq2/tVw/2WexspfQ7NnkcysrvgjYfvzlUNrwRrqQhaUL-
8N5+2+C09PzyCVCl7WvVJy+PoBOHeOlVxohuLsLQvQEdTozdtiBCW85W5lMzHSjiYNRTAf+Qw-
zuJhD3Lrh3p/MSB9B
```

In Listing 15-1, the following values need to be updated to reflect your lab environment:

- `etcd:` section
  - `addr`: Replace the IP address with a static IP from your own VM network. Do not change the port number (4001).
  - `peer-addr`: Use the same IP used for the value above. Once again, do not change the port number (7001).
- `units:` section
  - `[Match] Name=`: This refers to the name of the VM's network interface. Once the VM boots, you can see this value. Refer to Figure 15-1 for an example whose VM network interface name is enp0s17 located above the login prompt.
  - `- [Network] Address, DNS,` and `Gateway`: These values should match the appropriate settings for your selected IP and portgroup/vmnet.
- `ssh_authorized_keys`: Replace the value with your own Secure Shell (SSH) public key value. Pay attention to the YAML syntax and ensure that a hyphen (-) precedes your entry, just like in the sample file.

In Listing 15-2, the following values need to be updated to reflect your lab environment:

- `fleet:` section
- `- etcd_servers:` Replace the IP address with the static IP used for your etcd server configuration file.
- `units:` section
- `- flannel.service:` Change the `etcd-endpoint` IP to match your etcd server's IP address.
- `ssh_authorized_keys:` Replace the value with your own SSH public key value. Pay attention to the YAML syntax and ensure that a hyphen (-) precedes your entry, just like in the sample file.

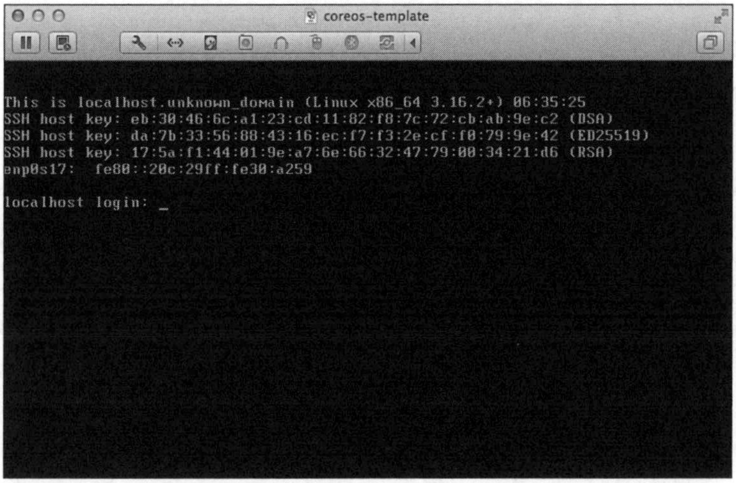

Figure 15-1 CoreOS VM boot prompt

> **NOTE**
>
> The etcd server is the only server that requires a static IP. The two Kubernetes nodes, and any subsequent servers that you add to the Kubernetes cluster, will use DHCP to obtain an IP.

The YAML files need to be written to ISO files (one ISO per YAML) with the following conventions:

- The volume label must be config-2.
- The YAML file must be renamed to user_data and placed in the following folder hierarchy/openstack/latest/ with the openstack directory being in the root of the ISO file.

- Verify that the ISOs are created properly by mounting the ISO on your desktop. The volume label should be displayed as config-2. The root of the ISO should consist of the openstack directory with the user_data file stored in the subdirectory called latest.

etcd Server Configuration

Now, you should have two ISO files: one for the etcd server and the other for Kubernetes cluster nodes. For simplicity, we will refer to the two ISO files as coreos-master.iso for the etcd server and kubernetes-node.iso for the Kubernetes cluster node servers, and we suggest that you follow a similar naming standard.

Attach coreos-master.iso to the CoreOS VM that will be your etcd server, and attach kubernetes-node.iso to the other two VMs. Only reboot the etcd server VM at this point. (We'll take care of the remaining servers a little bit later.)

When we talked about the CLI utilities earlier, we mentioned environment variables that need to be set for the utilities to work properly. Those two environment variables are `ETCDCTL_PEERS` and `FLEETCTL_ENDPOINT`. You will use the IP address of your etcd server and port 4001 as follows:

```
$ export ETCDCTL_PEERS=http://192.168.12.10:4001
$ export FLEETCTL_ENDPOINT=http://192.168.12.10:4001
```

Be sure to substitute your etcd server's IP address for the value in the example, and you may want to place these statements in a file that you can easily source if you ever need to reopen your terminal window.

When your etcd server is done rebooting, you can use the following commands to verify that `etcdctl` and `fleetctl` are working properly:

```
$ etcdctl ls /
$ fleetctl list-machines
```

If neither command generates an error, your etcd server is up and running properly.

You may be wondering why we are only setting up a single etcd server if it's so important to the cluster, and that is a valid concern. In production, you deploy an etcd cluster with an odd number of hosts instead of using a single etcd server setup. This ensures high availability of this vital resource. However, for our demonstration purposes, a single etcd server will suffice.

Network Overlays with Flannel

As mentioned earlier, each pod gets its own IP address. The standard convention is to utilize private IP addressing. This can be accomplished multiple ways (a second network interface card [NIC] on the VM, assigning multiple IPs addresses to a single NIC, and so on). For the purposes of this demo, we utilize the CoreOS flannel project to create a simple overlay network, which will store its mapping information in etcd. The following command assigns a /16 address space for flannel to use:

```
$ etcdctl mk /coreos.com/network/config '{"Network":"10.0.0.0/16"}'
```

We use the default flannel settings, and this assigns a /24 IP address space to each host in the Kubernetes cluster. etcd will contain a mapping that Kubernetes can refer to, to determine which physical host owns a particular private address space. For example, when Kubernetes is up and running, the following etcdctl query will allow you to see the mapping of an overlay network range to a host:

```
$ etcdctl get /coreos.com/network/subnets/10.0.76.0-24
{"PublicIP":"172.16.171.134"}
```

In the sample output, `PublicIP` refers to the IP address of the Kubernetes cluster node, and `10.0.76.0-24` is the IP address space assigned to that server.

Kubernetes Cluster Nodes

Let's verify that we attached the kubernetes-node.iso file to the two remaining CoreOS VMs and reboot them. Monitor the VM console windows to verify when the CoreOS customization is complete. When you see the login prompt in the VM consoles, the servers are ready. You can also use `fleetctl` to verify the nodes' status:

```
$ fleetctl list-machines
MACHINE        IP              METADATA
19de047d...    172.16.171.133  role=kubernetes
775e2223...    172.16.171.134  role=kubernetes
98786c6b...    172.16.171.10   role=etcd
```

You should see three machines listed. One of them has the role `etcd`, and the remaining two servers have the role `kubernetes`. This metadata will be used to identify which nodes should be running the Kubernetes services.

In CoreOS, when you deploy applications, you use systemd unit files that contain application deployment instructions, including which containers to deploy, what types of hosts to deploy the application on, whether there should be any affinity in container placement, and so on. The units directory for this example's repository contains all the deployment instructions that we need to set up our Kubernetes cluster. Listings 15-3 and 15-4 show the details of two of these unit files.

Listing 15-3 kube-scheduler.service

```
[Unit]
Description=Kubernetes Scheduler Server
Documentation=https://github.com/GoogleCloudPlatform/kubernetes

[Service]
ExecStartPre=/usr/bin/wget -N -P /opt/bin http://storage.googleapis.com/
kubernetes/scheduler
ExecStartPre=/usr/bin/chmod +x /opt/bin/scheduler
ExecStart=/opt/bin/scheduler --master=127.0.0.1:8080
Restart=always
RestartSec=10

[X-Fleet]
MachineOf=kube-apiserver.service
MachineMetadata=role=kubernetes
```

Listing 15-4 kube-kubelet.service

```
[Unit]
Description=Kubernetes Kubelet
Documentation=https://github.com/GoogleCloudPlatform/kubernetes
Requires=setup-network-environment.service
After=setup-network-environment.service

[Service]
EnvironmentFile=/etc/network-environment
ExecStartPre=/usr/bin/wget -N -P /opt/bin http://storage.googleapis.com/
kubernetes/kubelet
ExecStartPre=/usr/bin/chmod +x /opt/bin/kubelet
ExecStart=/opt/bin/kubelet \
--address=0.0.0.0 \
--port=10250 \
--hostname_override=${DEFAULT_IPV4} \
--etcd_servers=http://192.168.12.10:4001 \
--logtostderr=true
Restart=always
```

```
RestartSec=10

[X-Fleet]
Global=true
MachineMetadata=role=kubernetes
```

In the unit file, the Unit section provides basic information about the application that is being run as well as the startup order compared to other services in the cluster. The Service section specifies the binary that will be run as well as any startup options. Finally, the X-Fleet section provides details on where in the CoreOS cluster this application should be running. Compare the X-Fleet sections in both Listings 15-3 and 15-4. You will see that they are both set to run only on CoreOS servers that have the role of Kubernetes. However, there are two differences:

- The Kubernetes Scheduler service is part of the Kubernetes control stack. So, we use the `MachineOf` setting to specify affinity with the Kubernetes API service.
- The Kubelet service is meant to run on all Kubernetes cluster nodes. So, we set the `Global` setting to `true` to ensure this happens.

Kubernetes Service Deployment

We will need to modify a few of the files to point to your etcd Server's IP address, specifically the `etcd_servers` value in `kube-apiserver.service`, `kube-kubelet.service`, and `kube-proxy.service`. Once the files are updated, we will use `fleetctl` to deploy the unit files as follows:

```
$ fleetctl start kube-proxy.service
$ fleetctl start kube-kubelet.service
$ fleetctl start kube-apiserver.service
$ fleetctl start kube-scheduler.service
$ fleetctl start kube-controller-manager.service
$ fleetctl start kube-register.service
```

Use the `fleetctl list-units` command to verify that the core Kubernetes services are up and running properly:

```
$ fleetctl list-units
UNIT                            MACHINE                         ACTIVE  SUB
kube-apiserver.service          1f4a2e45.../172.16.171.128      active  running
kube-controller-manager.service 1f4a2e45.../172.16.171.128      active  running
kube-kubelet.service            19de047d.../172.16.171.133      active  running
kube-kubelet.service            1f4a2e45.../172.16.171.128      active  running
```

```
kube-proxy.service          19de047d.../172.16.171.133    active   running
kube-proxy.service          1f4a2e45.../172.16.171.128    active   running
kube-register.service       1f4a2e45.../172.16.171.128    active   running
kube-scheduler.service      1f4a2e45.../172.16.171.128    active   running
```

Earlier, we identified the `kube-register` component as distinct from core Kubernetes. Normally, the Kubernetes API service needs to know the IP addresses of the Kubelet hosts in advance. The `kube-register` service was contributed by Kelsey Hightower, from CoreOS, to automatically register Kubernetes nodes with the API service. This is accomplished by monitoring etcd for servers running the Kubelet service and informing the API service as new servers come online.

It is worth noting that although the Kubernetes deployment process seems complex, the work that we've done up to this point will simplify the addition of more Kubernetes cluster nodes. If you would like to increase the size of the cluster, deploy additional CoreOS VMs with the kubernetes-node.iso file attached to the CD-ROM and use the same virtual network as the rest of the cluster. As these servers boot, they will now be automatically added to the Kubernetes cluster thanks to the `kube-register` service.

Kubernetes Workload Deployment

The `kubectl` utility utilizes the Kubernetes RESTful API to deploy and manage workloads on a Kubernetes cluster. Before you can use it, we need to set an environment variable that will tell `kubectl` which cluster node is running the Kubernetes API service. (You get the IP address from the `fleetctl list-units` command.)

```
$ export KUBERNETES_MASTER="http://172.16.171.128:8080"
```

We can verify that the Kubernetes cluster is up and running properly by using `kubectl` to list the servers that are running the Kubelet and proxy services (known as *minions* in Kubernetes terminology) with the following command.

```
$ kubectl get minions
NAME              LABELS        STATUS
172.16.171.128    <none>        Unknown
172.16.171.133    <none>        Unknown
```

Multitier Application Deployment

Now that we've verified that our Kubernetes cluster is up and running, it's time to deploy applications. Like in previous chapters, we'll take a look at deploying a MySQL database with an Apache web server and the PHP application server. Only this time, we'll be deploying these applications as Docker containers using Kubernetes to manage the placement and availability of the services.

In the earlier chapter about containers, we introduced the Docker hub, and we'll be leveraging it to obtain our workloads. MySQL has a standard container that we will use for the database. We will use a custom container for the web and application server components. When deploying our applications, we will follow the convention of a single application per pod. This can simplify troubleshooting as well as availability design.

Kubernetes accepts instructions in the JavaScript Object Notation (JSON) format. JSON is a plain-text format used to describe data similar to YAML. It is typically used for sending/retrieving data from web APIs as a popular alternative to Extensible Markup Language (XML). Each application deployment will consist of two JSON files: a pod definition file and a service definition file. You can find the JSON files for these examples in the applications directory of this environment's GitHub repository (https://github.com/DevOpsForVMwareAdministrators/kubernetes-fleet-tutorial).

Pod Definition

The first instruction file tells Kubernetes which application to deploy and how it should be deployed. Listing 15-5 shows a JSON file example for a MySQL application deployment.

Listing 15-5 MySQL Pod Definition JSON File (mysql-pod.json)

```
{
  "id": "mysql-server-id",
  "kind": "Pod",
  "apiVersion": "v1beta1",
  "desiredState": {
    "manifest": {
      "version": "v1beta1",
      "id": "mysql-server-id",
      "containers": [{
        "name": "database",
        "image": "dockerfile/mysql",
        "ports": [{
          "containerPort": 3306,
          "hostPort": 3306
        }]
      }]
    }
  },
  "labels": {
    "name": "mysql-server"
  }
}
```

Let's take a look at some of the important elements of our pod definition file. The `id` value is how the pod will be identified to the etcd system. The `kind` value represents which Kubernetes component type we are deploying. The `desiredState` section contains the container specifications, including the container name, the port that the container application uses (`containerPort`), and the host port that the container will communicate through. Finally, the `labels` section is how users and other containers can identify the application you are deploying using the Kubernetes API.

Service Definition

The second instruction file specifies how Kubernetes will direct traffic to our MySQL pod available. Listing 15-6 shows a service file for our database.

Listing 15-6 MySQL Service Definition JSON File (mysql-service.json)

```
{
  "id": "mysqlserver",
  "kind": "Service",
  "apiVersion": "v1beta1",
  "port": 10000,
  "containerPort": 3306,
  "selector": {
    "name": "mysql-server"
  }
}
```

The `port` value will be used by Kubernetes Proxy to advertise the container services to users and other pods. The `selector` is the label of the target pod that traffic sent to this service will be forwarded to. Remember that in Listing 15-5 the label was the last value that was set.

Moving on to the web and application tier, Listings 15-7 and 15-8 show our web and application container's pod and service definition files, respectively.

Listing 15-7 Web and Application Pod Definition JSON File (web-pod.json)

```
{
  "id": "web-server-id",
  "kind": "ReplicationController",
  "apiVersion": "v1beta1",
  "desiredState": {
    "replicas": 2,
```

```
    "replicaSelector": {"name": "web-server"},
    "podTemplate": {
      "desiredState": {
         "manifest": {
           "version": "v1beta1",
           "id": "web-server-id",
           "containers": [{
             "name": "web",
             "image": "vmtrooper/web-app",
             "ports": [{
               "containerPort": 80,
               "hostPort": 80}]
           }]
         }
      },
      "labels": {"name":"web-server"}
    }
  },
  "labels": {
    "name": "web-server"
  }
}
```

Notice that we are using a slightly different structure in the pod definition file. We want to have a replicated web and application tier so that if one of the nodes goes down we have continued availability with little to no downtime.

When we want the Kubernetes Controller Manager to create pod replicas, we specify the `ReplicationController` keyword for the `kind` value. We also specify the number of replicas and the label of the pod that will be replicated. Another new element is the `podTemplate` object, which is used to define all the pod characteristics that the Controller Manager will use when deploying the pod to each server.

Listing 15-8 Web and Application Service Definition File (web-service.json)

```
{
  "id": "webserver",
  "kind": "Service",
  "apiVersion": "v1beta1",
  "port": 10080,
  "containerPort": 80,
```

```
  "labels": {
       "name": "web-server"

  },
  "selector": {
    "name": "web-server"
  }
}
```

There are not many differences for a replicated pod's service definition file, but we include this one here to show that you can also specify labels for services and perform Kubernetes queries for the service based on the label:

```
kubectl get services -l "name=web-server"
```

Now that we have our definition files complete, we can go ahead and launch them using the following syntax. (Pay attention to the keywords that come after `create`.)

```
$ kubectl create -f mysql-pod.json
$ kubectl create -f mysql-service.json
$ kubectl create -f web-pod.json
$ kubectl create -f web-service.json
```

Depending on the speed of your Internet connection, it might take a few minutes for each pod's status to get to the Running state. You can use the following commands to verify the pods' status:

```
$ kubectl get pods
$ kubectl get services
```

Your instances of `web-app` can be accessed on port 10080 on either Kubernetes minion, and you can use the MySQL client to connect to port 10000 on either Kubernetes minion to manage your databases. (Remember that service connections are routed to the correct container host.) Also, if you boot another CoreOS VM with the kubernetes-node.iso file attached, it will automatically become a Kubernetes minion. Your workloads will be accessible by providing the new minion's IP with the correct service port as well. Give it a try!

Platform-as-a-Service with Docker

If you have been following the platform-as-a-service (PAAS) space in the IT industry, the concepts that we discuss in this chapter probably sound very familiar. Pivotal's Cloud Foundry and the other PaaS solutions operate on the same principle as Kubernetes:

Deploy software as containers on arbitrary cluster nodes and manage availability on behalf of the administrator. There are Docker-based PaaS platforms like ActiveState Stackato, Deis, and Flynn for you to experiment with after you've kicked the tires on Kubernetes. If you are just interested in experimenting with other container management solutions, Apache Mesos (used by Twitter and other companies) is another popular solution.

Summary

The deployment of application containers on a cluster is simplified when using a solution like Kubernetes to manage them. Although Kubernetes consists of multiple components, the infrastructure setup can be automated when using CoreOS with Cloud-Config. As VMware works closer with Docker, Inc. and Google for container management, we can expect exciting developments in this space.

References

[1] Kubernetes GitHub repository and documentation: https://github.com/GoogleCloudPlatform/kubernetes

[2] The Raft consensus algorithm: http://raftconsensus.github.io/

Chapter 16

Server Provisioning Using Razor

Razor is an automated provisioning tool that combines server installation and management with configuration tools. It enables you to go from bare metal or a virtual machine (VM) that has no operating system on it and end up with a fully configured node managed by Puppet or Chef.

Topics covered in this chapter include the following:

- How Razor works
- Using Razor
- Using Razor APIs
- Razor components
- Setting up Razor

How Razor Works

Razor combines the power of iPXE, TFTP, DHCP, and DNS to provide a fully automated deployment solution. In addition to being extremely powerful, it also provides APIs to automate all the tasks. Although useful by itself, Razor also provides integration with the configuration tools via Chef and Puppet brokers. The result of all the integrated tools is a mechanism for inventory and server lifecycle management.

Razor runs on its own server as a web application (TorqueBox), with all the supporting tools configured to be available either on the same or separate servers. Razor should have its own network with new machines connected to it. When a new server (configured for network boot) is connected to the Razor network, the following steps happen:

- **Discovery:** Razor detects a new node. It then inspects the node's characteristics by booting it with the Razor microkernel and collecting the information (facts) about the server.
- **Registration:** If the server's facts match an existing tag, the tags are then compared to the policies on the Razor server. The first matching policy is applied to the node.
- **Installation:** Based on the policy applied, the server is installed with an operating system and configured.
- **Handoff:** If the policy contained broker information, server is handed off to Chef or Puppet.

To get an idea of what the actual install through Razor looks like, check out Figure 16-1, where you can see that the node is doing network boot, has connected to Razor, and is loading the microkernel.

> TIP
>
> Set up Razor in a virtual environment by using Vagrant to follow examples in this chapter. This single VM Vagrant environment will provide Razor with dnsmasq configured: https://github.com/eglute/razor-server-vagrant.

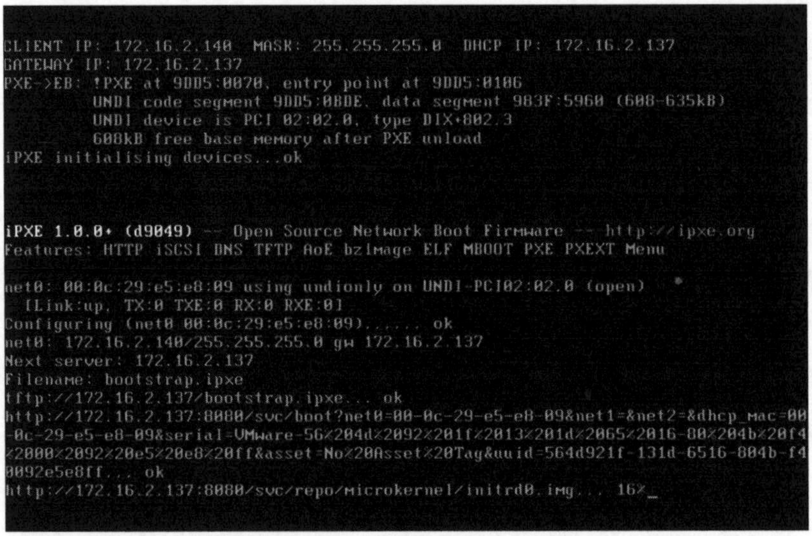

Figure 16-1 Server downloading microkernel

After getting the microkernel, the node will be registered with Razor and will get bootstrapped. Figure 16-2 shows a registered node, its associated task, and loading of the install files.

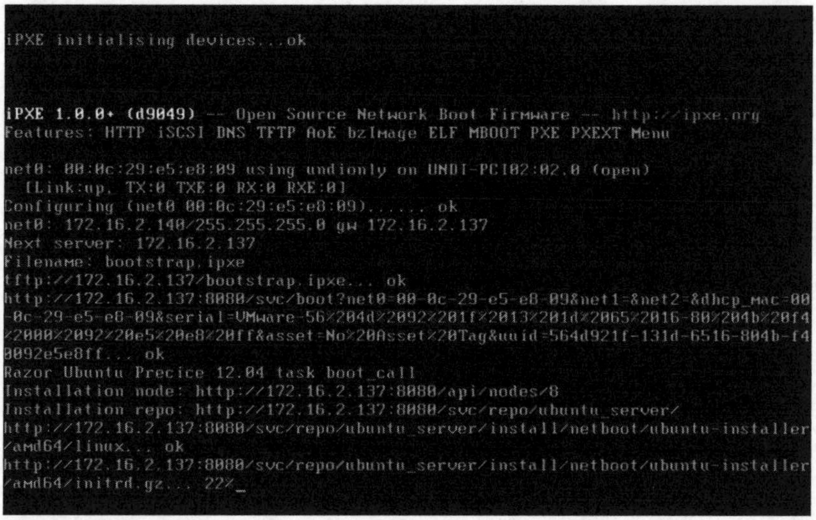

Figure 16-2 Registered node preparing to install Ubuntu server

Finally, once everything is ready, the server will install the OS. In the case of Figure 16-3, the node is installing using the Ubuntu preseed file that was defined in the Ubuntu task.

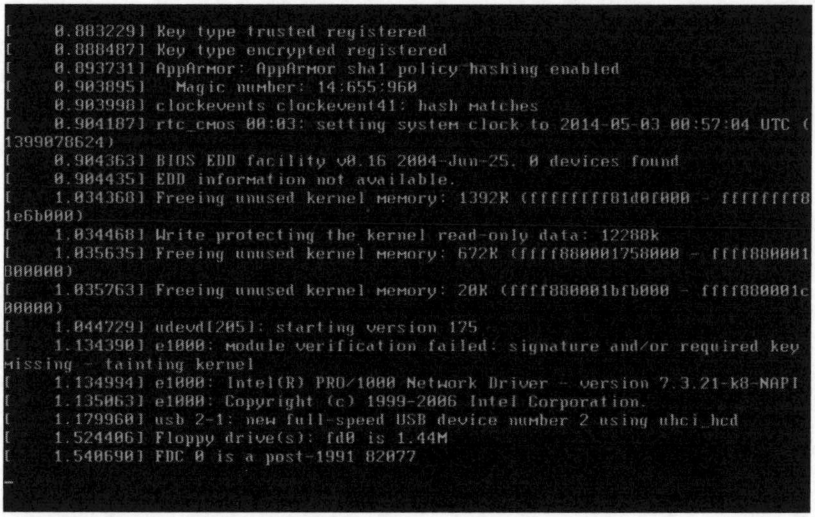

Figure 16-3 Server in the process of being installed

NOTE

The current version of Razor is a second-generation Razor, written in JRuby and running on TorqueBox with a PostgreSQL back end. The first version of Razor was Ruby and Node.js based, backed by the MongoDB database, and provided slightly different functionality than the current one. If you were an early adopter and want to move to the current version of Razor, you will have to do it manually. There is no upgrade/migration path from the original version to the next.

Using Razor

If you have Razor installed and configured, using Razor is pretty straightforward. Razor follows a set of conventions that make it easy to use all the commands.

NOTE

Razor is currently under very active development. Check command reference guide, http://docs.puppetlabs.com/pe/3.2/razor_reference.html, for the latest command syntax, because it may have changed slightly since the publishing of this book.

For now, we will assume that you have Razor installed and working properly, and cover the installation and all the components further in this chapter. Once all the components are installed, you need to do some basic setup. First, you need to point the Razor client to the Razor server:

```
$ razor --url http://$IP_ADDRESS:8080/api nodes
```

Where `$IP_ADDRESS` is the hostname or the IP address of your Razor server:

```
$ razor --url http://razor:8080/api nodes
```

Note that you need to point the Razor client to the Razor server only once. After the address is set, list available commands by typing `razor` or `razor -h` commands. Listing 16-1 shows an example.

Listing 16-1 Razor Client Help and Available Commands

```
$ razor
Usage: razor [FLAGS] NAVIGATION
    -d, --dump                    Dumps API output to the screen
    -u, --url URL                 The full Razor API URL, can also be  set
                                  with the RAZOR_API environment variable
```

```
                                  (default http://localhost:8080/api)
-h, --help                        Show this screen

Collections:
    brokers
    nodes
    policies
    repos
    tags
    tasks

  Navigate to entries of a collection using COLLECTION NAME, for example,
  'nodes node15'  for the  details of a node or 'nodes node15 log' to see
  the log for node15

Commands:
    add-policy-tag
    create-broker
    create-policy
    create-repo
    create-tag
    create-task
    delete-broker
    delete-node
    delete-policy
    delete-repo
    delete-tag
    disable-policy
    enable-policy
    modify-node-metadata
    modify-policy-max-count
    move-policy
    reboot-node
    reinstall-node
    remove-node-metadata
    remove-policy-tag
    set-node-desired-power-state
    set-node-ipmi-credentials
    update-node-metadata
    update-tag-rule
```

```
Pass arguments to commands either directly by name ('--name=NAME')
or save the JSON body for the  command  in a file and pass it with
'--json FILE'.  Using --json is the only way to pass  arguments in
nested structures such as the configuration for a broker.
```

As you can see, Razor commands are split up into two sections: *collections* and *commands*. The collections are tied to the objects (things) that are part of Razor, and commands are all the actions that can be performed on the individual items in the collections. View a list of all collections by a entering a command in this format:

```
$ razor <collection>
```

To view details about each collection, append a specific item:

```
$ razor <collection> <item name>
```

So, to view details for a task, it would be as follows:

```
$ razor tasks microkernel
```

Actions are performed on the various collection items or their combination.

Razor Collections and Actions

Collections in Razor are lists of objects, or virtual assets, that are or will be tied to physical devices. There are six possible collections; each of them will have different actions that can be executed on their individual items:

- Repositories
- Tasks
- Brokers
- Tags
- Policies
- Nodes

The only prebuilt collection is *Tasks*; the other ones you will have to build yourself before any node can be installed.

Tasks

Razor tasks describe the process that should be performed while provisioning the machines. Each task comes with a corresponding YAML metadata file and a set of templates. Razor comes with several built-in tasks, and other custom tasks can be added by the user. As shown in Listing 16-2, view all available tasks by entering `razor tasks` command.

Listing 16-2 Built-In Razor Tasks

```
$ razor tasks
From http://localhost:8080/api/collections/tasks:
    id: "http://localhost:8080/api/collections/tasks/centos"
  name: "centos"
  spec: "/razor/v1/collections/tasks/member"
    id: "http://localhost:8080/api/collections/tasks/debian"
  name: "debian"
  spec: "/razor/v1/collections/tasks/member"
    id: "http://localhost:8080/api/collections/tasks/microkernel"
  name: "microkernel"
  spec: "/razor/v1/collections/tasks/member"
    id: "http://localhost:8080/api/collections/tasks/noop"
  name: "noop"
  spec: "/razor/v1/collections/tasks/member"
    id: "http://localhost:8080/api/collections/tasks/redhat"
  name: "redhat"
  spec: "/razor/v1/collections/tasks/member"
    id: "http://localhost:8080/api/collections/tasks/ubuntu"
  name: "ubuntu"
  spec: "/razor/v1/collections/tasks/member"
    id: "http://localhost:8080/api/collections/tasks/ubuntu_precise_amd64"
  name: "ubuntu_precise_amd64"
  spec: "/razor/v1/collections/tasks/member"
    id: "http://localhost:8080/api/collections/tasks/ubuntu_precise_i386"
  name: "ubuntu_precise_i386"
  spec: "/razor/v1/collections/tasks/member"
    id: "http://localhost:8080/api/collections/tasks/vmware_esxi"
  name: "vmware_esxi"
  spec: "/razor/v1/collections/tasks/member"
    id: "http://localhost:8080/api/collections/tasks/windows"
  name: "windows"
  spec: "/razor/v1/collections/tasks/member"
```

Each task represents an operating system that can be installed, if a corresponding repository is added to Razor. The task and repository will be tied together in a policy. To view the details of each task, you need to go to Razor's install directory tasks folder. Depending on your system, the location might be /opt/razor/tasks. Listing 16-3 shows a YAML metadata file to install an ESXi example.

Listing 16-3 vmware_esxi.yaml file for vmware_esxi task

```
---
os_version: 5.5
label: VMWare ESXi 5.5
description: VMWare ESXi 5.5
boot_sequence:
  1: boot_install
  default: boot_local
```

This `vmware_esxi` task would install ESXi 5.5 by utilizing the boot_install.erb file found under the razor/tasks/vmware_esxi directory. This file contains a script to automate iPXE commands, and it can referenced in Listing 16-4.

Listing 16-4 boot_install.erb file for ESXi 5.5

```
#!ipxe
echo Razor <%= task.label %> task boot_call
echo Installation node: <%= node_url  %>
echo Installation repo: <%= repo_url %>

echo Booting ESXi installer via pxelinux to support COMBOOT modules fully
echo Unfortunately, this double bootloader is necessary to run the ESXi
installer

sleep 3
# These are the magic that direct pxelinux.0 to our HTTP based config...
set 209:string pxelinux_esxi.cfg
set 210:string <%= file_url('') %>
imgexec <%= file_url('pxelinux.0', true) %>

:error
prompt --key s --timeout 60000 ERROR, hit 's' for the iPXE shell, reboot in
60 seconds && shell || reboot
```

If you want to add your own custom tasks, you need to replicate the structure of an existing task. For more details on writing custom tasks, refer to the documentation: http://docs.puppetlabs.com/pe/3.2/razor_tasks.html.

Nodes

The nodes collection is the most important in Razor because it represents the machines that Razor is managing. Nodes contain all the "facts" from the machine. Nodes currently registered with the Razor server can be viewed by entering the `razor nodes` command (see Listing 16-5).

Listing 16-5 List of Current Nodes Registered with Razor

```
$ razor nodes
From http://localhost:8080/api/collections/nodes:

    id: "http://localhost:8080/api/collections/nodes/node1"
  name: "node1"
  spec: "/razor/v1/collections/nodes/member"

    id: "http://localhost:8080/api/collections/nodes/node2"
  name: "node2"
  spec: "/razor/v1/collections/nodes/member"
```

Inspecting the details for an individual node will provide a lot of information. That is because Razor collects and stores a lot of identifying information about each server. These facts are used to identify nodes. Check out Listing 16-6 for the details available for an individual node.

Listing 16-6 Details for an Individual Node

```
$ razor nodes node1
From http://localhost:8080/api/collections/nodes/node1:

            id: "http://localhost:8080/api/collections/nodes/node1"
          name: "node1"
          spec: "/razor/v1/collections/nodes/member"
       hw_info:
                    asset: "no asset tag"
                      mac: ["00-0c-29-cd-fc-ee"]
                   serial: "vmware-56 4d 61 fd b3 73 ee 95-8a d3 dd 4c 07 cd fc
ee"
                     uuid: "564d61fd-b373-ee95-8ad3-dd4c07cdfcee"
      dhcp_mac: "00-0c-29-cd-fc-ee"
        policy:
                     id: "http://localhost:8080/api/collections/policies/
```

```
ubuntu_one"
                   name: "ubuntu_one"
                   spec: "/razor/v1/collections/policies/member"
            log:
                 log => http://localhost:8080/api/collections/nodes/node1/log
           tags: [
                     id: "http://localhost:8080/api/collections/tags/
ubuntu_small"
                   name: "ubuntu_small"
                   spec: "/razor/v1/collections/tags/member"
                 ]
          facts:
                          architecture: "x86_64"
                   blockdevice_sda_size: 21474836480
                 blockdevice_sda_vendor: "VMware,"
   interfaces: "eno16777736,eno33554960,lo"
                  ipaddress_eno16777736: "172.16.2.141"
                 macaddress_eno16777736: "00:0c:29:cd:fc:ee"
                    netmask_eno16777736: "255.255.255.0"
< … >
      processorcount: "1"
                              uniqueid: "007f0100"
                               virtual: "vmware"
                            is_virtual: "true"
       metadata:
                 ip: "172.16.2.141"
          state:
                    installed: "ubuntu_one"
                 installed_at: "2014-04-23T11:50:31-07:00"
                        stage: "boot_local"
       hostname: "host"
  root_password: "secret"
   last_checkin: "2014-04-23T11:31:06-07:00"
```

The node details (see Listing 16-6) will contain the physical characteristics of the server (facts), the information about how the node was created (which policy applied), the last time it checked in, and how to find its log information.

> CAUTION
>
> Because Razor identifies nodes by their physical characteristics, updating hardware on a node that is registered with Razor can really confuse Razor. Removing or replacing a primary NIC can make Razor think that is a new node.

In addition to having default facts, Razor allows users to add custom metadata to each node. This custom metadata permits users to add business or operations-specific identifying data. Check out the command reference guide for how to add custom metadata: http://docs.puppetlabs.com/pe/3.2/razor_reference.html#modify-node-metadata.

The node's log information will contain the different steps executed in the node's creation (see Listing 16-7).

Listing 16-7 Viewing Node's Activity Log

```
$ razor nodes node1 log
From http://localhost:8080/api/collections/nodes/node1/log:

  timestamp: "2014-04-23T11:27:18-07:00"
      event: "boot"
       task: "microkernel"
   template: "boot"
       repo: "microkernel"
   severity: "info"

< … >
timestamp: "2014-04-23T11:50:30-07:00"
      event: "store_metadata"
       vars:
               update:
                          ip: "172.16.2.141"
   severity: "info"

  timestamp: "2014-04-23T11:50:31-07:00"
      event: "stage_done"
      stage: "finished"
   severity: "info"
```

There are multiple steps in installing the node, and the logs will show the status and failures (if any) during the process. Once the node finishes installing, there will also be a log created in the node's /tmp directory. There, the razor_complete.log may contain useful information of what went wrong during the install.

> **NOTE**
>
> Currently, the way to add a node to Razor is by installing a new server and registering it through the microkernel. You could use the `noop` task to register an existing server, but in the future there will be an explicit way to add an existing server to the Razor. Check release notes for the newest features.

Any node can also be deleted from Razor. To delete a node, simply execute the deletion command, `razor delete-node --name` *`<node name>`*, as demonstrated in Listing 16-8.

Listing 16-8 Deleting an Existing Node

```
$ razor delete-node --name node3
From http://localhost:8080/api:

  result: "node destroyed"
```

If the same server is booted again, the node will be re-created in Razor.

To reinstall an existing node, execute the reinstall command, `razor reinstall-name --name` *`<name4>`*, as demonstrated in Listing 16-9.

Listing 16-9 Reinstalling an Existing Node

```
razor reinstall-node --name node4
From http://localhost:8080/api:

  result: "node unbound from ubuntu_two and installed flag cleared"
```

Once the node reboots, it will go through the microkernel again and will be reinstalled. If applicable, a new policy may be applied during reinstall.

IPMI Support

Currently, Razor supports a set of IPMI functionality. If your hardware supports it, you may be able to reboot and set the node's state through Razor. First, you will need to set the IPMI credentials. Create an ipmi.json file with relevant details, and then use it to set the credentials on the node, as demonstrated in Listing 16-10.

Listing 16-10 ipmi.json File for Setting IPMI Credentials

```
{
  "name": "node1",
  "ipmi-hostname": "node1",
  "ipmi-username": "root",
  "ipmi-password": "secret"
}
```

Setting IPMI data on a node is done by executing the command `razor set-node-ipmi-credentials --json <json filename>`, as demonstrated in Listing 16-11.

Listing 16-11 Setting IPMI Credentials on a Node

```
$ razor set-node-ipmi-credentials --json ipmi.json
From http://localhost:8080/api:

  result: "updated IPMI details"
```

Once the IPMI credentials are set, you can reboot and set the power state of the node through Razor.

Building Razor Collections

To get Razor going, you need to add some initial information. Build the objects in this order:

- Add a repository.
- Add a broker.
- Add a tag.
- Add a policy.

Creating objects can be done by passing attributes on a command line, or creating JSON files and passing the JSON file as an argument. It is a lot easier to use JSON files than to list all the information on the command line, especially when creating a policy.

Adding a Repository

A repository is a container that stores the actual bits needed to install a node. It is going to be an ISO file or a link to an ISO file. The basic syntax for creating a repo is as follows:

```
$ razor create-repo --name=<repository name> --iso-url <URL>
```

The repository name can be an arbitrary name of your choice. The repository can be created by either passing a URL link or by using a local file. When the ISO file is remote, it may take awhile to create the repo, because it takes awhile to download. Check the log files to see whether the repository creation has finished.

```
$ razor create-repo --name=ubuntu_server --iso-url http://releases.
ubuntu.com/precise/ubuntu-12.04.4-server-amd64.iso
```

If you want to use a locally available ISO, the same command-line syntax will allow for pointing to it:

```
$ razor create-repo --name=ubuntu_server --iso-url file:///root/ubuntu-
12.04.4-server-amd64.iso
```

Note that the file and the path need to be available to the user under which Razor is running.

> TIP
>
> Adding a repository is something that needs to be done only once for each image.

After the repository is created, the ISO file will be unpacked into a directory under /var/lib/razor/repo-store or similar. In Puppet Enterprise, the default path will be /opt/puppet/var/razor/repo/.

Adding a Broker

Razor brokers are the way to hand off a provisioned server to the configuration management tools. A broker consists of a configuration file and a script. The script runs after all the main installs are done and sets up Puppet or Chef clients on the machine. Currently, four broker types are available:

- **Noop (`noop`):** Use a Noop broker if you do not want to do any more automation on the newly installed server through Razor.
- **Chef (`chef`):** The Chef broker installs Chef client on the newly installed server, registers it with the Chef Server, and executes the initial run list.

- **Puppet (`puppet`):** The Puppet broker installs the Puppet agent and registers it with the Puppet master.
- **Puppet Enterprise (`puppet-pe`):** The Puppet Enterprise broker configures the new node to register with the Puppet master.

To add a simple Noop broker, all you need to do is use the `create-broker` command:

```
$ razor create-broker --name=noop --broker-type=noop
```

The syntax to add a broker is as follows:

```
$ razor create-broker --name <name> --broker-type <type> --configuration
<configuration>
```

where configuration must be in a JSON format.

Unless you are adding a Noop broker, it is much simpler to use a JSON-formatted configuration file for this command:

```
$ razor create-broker --json <file.json>
```

Each broker configuration file will consist of three parts: name, broker type, and configuration. The configuration is specific to the broker type, and will differ across different brokers.

A Puppet broker JSON configuration file would look like Listing 16-12.

Listing 16-12 Sample puppetbroker.json File for Creating a Puppet Broker

```
{
  "name": "puppet",
  "configuration": {
     "server": "puppet.example.org",
     "environment": "production"
  },
  "broker-type": "puppet"
}
```

To create a Puppet broker, all you need to do is pass a JSON configuration file. You may name the JSON files as you want; in this example, we will call it puppetbroker.json, as in Listing 16-13.

Listing 16-13 Creating a Razor Broker

```
$ razor create-broker --json puppetbroker.json
From http://localhost:8080/api:

    id: "http://localhost:8080/api/collections/brokers/puppet"
  name: "puppet"
  spec: "/razor/v1/collections/brokers/member"
```

Creating a Chef broker is much more complex because of the configuration options required. A sample configuration file is provided in the broker directory where Razor is installed, sample_chef_broker.json, and also shown in Listing 16-14.

Listing 16-14 Creating Razor Chef Broker sample_chef_broker.json File

```
{
    "name": "openstack_chef_broker",
    "configuration": {
        "install_sh": "http://opscode.com/chef/install.sh",
        "version_string": "11.4.4",
        "chef_server_url": "https://chef.example.com:443",
        "validation_client_name": "chef-validator",
        "run_list": "role[allinone]",
        "environment": "openstack",
        "chef_client": "chef-client",
        "validation_key": "MIIok0h+mSHr1Pbi+v2950H1/7mzd71hXAcRHbmrdy-
tAR+RjgtyibkkZTdSxjLP6o2qEuji0I7DL8cckHG56AvuAKhYoadu+9J/2ahmYr18CSqOmg4S-
bh6CPm5edpqaAVTbE3Ec+1wN0IMl8KWtmGCrjpXzH1MDdaLZpIIYqC9DUVgLbd/
i61hbiiYlky5wPdIKlKwilRl7alfsGKTUrVq1DuYiIZsDYrnY-LOERbzU6yUxWSIasfVP-
JGpT9LvstChFjyjv/73etmhXwwIDAQABAoIBAHH1p1upll-VJNMSAhSmLZfTe6Q9nT8unRF-
H1egcsni8dPXYyVzDQ1ztV3RFNDLjP01ZThqkjoA4TnkHvRnC90yR049eQNxn+7pctcTNW61aA-
glomMhBcFt7LlcDiiXfD3dVhoIDv4ijpfsNCDvEVain9Dv+krjGVP+dWKLKr2azZbrAnyJKJjKb-
8DkwFET7UADFgUiCwJCW7RyAAxL40WE1hyYGq03cum5+M+2MGTcCiiAumqIRjYyTioNl73zf/
ckBKRBNb6DkVGa1drAwXqMtA0MAaJlQBoJJF9SehSf7rAKVMvQ+esS9kNXZhECgYEA28FK-
bU3K4mU2khZ8lJgomfelWV48sjeIH3OEuLK7WdKg2LAnNajiLAOHYi0egKiMJPnNyZ8u-
vOY0JABLHQXv10QKaNlHGqy+aRiRSb1Ya6SlbCg8hMoT29yWGa8k7AclLJSn20/dg0GAEQtegi/
k3EEZq0CgYEA148QtVh4ng80d9P81rJEDkraAkKUNJPHBSKFqo1rNwSDsyxxTEXIzZSPYS1m-
jsdB4IxraiNm3WDhb+EldcSlXvmBDjYJck1WyLCw1JuyAS2VCEtdc38aPWGYZ157de-
cuzkR8CU2TKw48KGSRTtwL8yYqTknqpAmnqf/KkWfVNi8CgYEA1a0AnX+Cwtf/
U9UhlarN78fosxj6k5+DcHF2n9DKcvBnDctalMZ+BKX5wfB1NEyu2FU9T8rEO1DragYPA01+h-
CXYqVJ73OgSzUXiH31IuIID9u/0LyseTWOWoIxWJzdTh44xJ+wJlwNuYXxgjgVGaVZk-
```

```
2niXWTLxtTNEdCz0RpECgYAlholhGIq+8WSv656bfaMtXciAFjkYwhUmhrEAVOgyRr3qpjT/
EzL23wLq5u1ws617OtbEPm984I2+XVKZIuerFgJqh+uzE1WlUGUoTgZ6AAZu0DfvkFPwFZpjfGY/
y0QxsmhpcjDJkQvV+FP3h4UpCh7ZTDLl5axjgt0v3QSYDwKBgFde/5TO8N8U6lHr1YX+yY8w-
bQ9sVWPU8qruL5Qx11an1tm9Ja1Wbg8Sn0/A7h7Y331V4cDmVraUreULiTQwSO7N26IxQ3Rg/
MQG3szUgP0MWYmjuG0c8zaFB73rnBpZ8xakF/xcRTt2Pb62dkw1VqFhzNc50bN+QvGmtE-
osIB9z"

},
    "broker-type": "chef"
}
```


As you can see from the JSON file (Listing 16-14) needed to create the broker, Chef broker configuration options are much more complex. To explain the different options, we will use the broker configuration requirements file found in the broker's directory, as shown in Listing 16-15. This file describes the requirements for the configuration.

Listing 16-15 Configuration File for Chef Broker configuration.yaml

```
---
install_sh:
  description: "Omnibus installer script URL. (example: http://mirror.
example.com/install.sh) default: http://opscode.com/chef/install.sh"
version_string:
  description: "Chef version (used in gem install). (example: 11.4.4)"
validation_key:
  description: "Contents of the validation.pem file. Since this is json
file, please make it one line no spaces..."
chef_server_url:
  description: "URL for the Chef Server. (example: https://mychefserver.
com:443)"
validation_client_name:
  description: "Validation client name. (example: myorg-validator) default:
chef-validator"
run_list:
  description: "Optional run_list of common base roles. (example:
role[base],role[another])"
environment:
  description: "Chef environment in which the chef-client will run. (exam-
ple: production). Use _default if not using any specific environments."
chef_client:
  description: "An alternate path to the chef-client binary. (example: /
usr/local/bin/chef-client) default: chef-client"
```

The different options guarantee that the Chef broker can be completely customized to fit your environment needs.

> **NOTE**
>
> It is important to note that the `validation_key` value for Razor broker is all on one line. This is due to a requirement for the configuration to be in a JSON format. All the configuration options for a broker get flattened and stored in one line in Razor's database. Normally, the validation key would contain newline characters. Chef broker takes the `validation_key` parameter and reinserts newline characters, thus re-creating the proper validation.pem file structure on the client side.

You need to create only one broker for each configuration environment used with Razor. To view all created brokers, enter the command `razor brokers`, as demonstrated in Listing 16-16.

Listing 16-16 Configuration File for Chef Broker configuration.yaml

```
$ razor brokers
From http://localhost:8080/api/collections/brokers:

    id: "http://localhost:8080/api/collections/brokers/noop"
  name: "noop"
  spec: "/razor/v1/collections/brokers/member"

    id: "http://localhost:8080/api/collections/brokers/puppet"
  name: "puppet"
  spec: "/razor/v1/collections/brokers/member"
```

Each broker will keep count of how many policies are using this particular broker. To view details for a particular broker, enter the command `razor brokers` *`<broker name>`* as shown in Listing 16-17.

Listing 16-17 Viewing Individual Details for the Puppet Broker

```
$ razor brokers puppet
From http://localhost:8080/api/collections/brokers/puppet:

            id: "http://localhost:8080/api/collections/brokers/puppet"
          name: "puppet"
```

```
          spec: "/spec/object/broker"
  configuration:
                        server: "puppet.example.org"
                   environment: "production"
    broker-type: "puppet"
       policies:
                     id: "http://localhost:8080/api/collections/brokers/
puppet/policies"
                   name: "policies"
                  count: 0
```

At the time of this writing , there is no command to list all available brokers. However, if you have access to the Razor server, you can see which ones are available by visiting the brokers' directory under Razor's installation. Similarly, each broker will have its own configuration.yaml file, which is useful in determining the parameters that each broker accepts.

If you need to use a different configuration tool for which a broker does not exist, you can add a custom broker by following the documentation on the Razor GitHub site: https://github.com/puppetlabs/razor-server/wiki/Writing-broker-types.

Adding a Policy

Policies combine repos, tasks, tags, and brokers in a logical arrangement to determine what is going to be installed on a new node and how many times. Policies can be enabled and disabled, and they also keep track of how many times they have been applied to a node. In addition to orchestrating all the other information, policies also set a hostname and password for the node. Currently, the password will be stored in plain text, so it is advisable to change the password of the newly installed node via a configuration tool.

To create a policy, first create the policy.json file (see Listing 16-18), and then use the `razor create-policy` command.

Listing 16-18 policy.json

```
{
  "name": "ubuntu_one",
  "repo": { "name": "ubuntu_server" },
  "task": { "name": "ubuntu" },
  "broker": { "name": "noop" },
  "enabled": true,
  "hostname": "host${id}",
  "root_password": "secret",
```

```
  "max_count": "20",
  "tags": [{ "name": "ubuntu_small", "rule": ["=", ["num", ["fact",
"processorcount"]], 1]}]
}
```

Listing 16-18 shows the attributes of the policy, which are as follows:

- `name`: Name of the newly created policy. Must be unique.
- `repo`: Name of the repository that will be used to install on the node. Must be already created.
- `task`: Name of the task that will be used. Note that the task and the repo must be both of the same type; that is, use centos task for a centos installation and so on.
- `broker`: Name of the broker that was created. Must already exist.
- `enabled`: Whether the policy should be enabled. If enabled is set to false, the Razor will ignore this policy while looking for matching policies to install on a node.
- `hostname`: A pattern used to set the hostname on the newly installed node. Expression `${id}` will evaluate to a number from a database, and the nodes will increase by one. In this example, the first node will have hostname node1, the second node2, and so on.
- `root_password`: This will be the root password set on the new node. Change it after installing the node, because this password is stored in plain text.
- `max_count`: How many servers should be installed using this policy. If you want only one server installed with this particular policy, set it to 1.
- `tags`: Determine to what kinds of nodes this policy should be applied. Additional tags can be added to the policy later as well.

To add a policy, execute the `razor create-policy --json <filename>` command, as shown in Listing 16-19.

Listing 16-19 Creating a Policy

```
$ razor create-policy --json policy.json
From http://localhost:8080/api:

    id: "http://localhost:8080/api/collections/policies/ubuntu_one"
  name: "ubuntu_two"
  spec: "/razor/v1/collections/policies/member"
```

To list available policies, execute the `razor policies` command, as demonstrated in Listing 16-20.

Listing 16-20 Listing Existing Policies

```
$ razor policies
From http://localhost:8080/api/collections/policies:

    id: "http://localhost:8080/api/collections/policies/ubuntu_one"
  name: "ubuntu_one"
  spec: "/razor/v1/collections/policies/member"

    id: "http://localhost:8080/api/collections/policies/ubuntu_two"
  name: "ubuntu_two"
  spec: "/razor/v1/collections/policies/member"
```

Details of the policy can be inspected by viewing it. To view it, use the `razor policies` *`<policy name>`* command, as demonstrated in Listing 16-21.

Listing 16-21 Viewing Policy Details

```
$ razor policies ubuntu_one
From http://localhost:8080/api/collections/policies/ubuntu_one:

             id: "http://localhost:8080/api/collections/policies/ubuntu_
one"
           name: "ubuntu_one"
           spec: "/razor/v1/collections/policies/member"
           repo:
                    id: "http://localhost:8080/api/collections/repos/
ubuntu_server"
                  name: "ubuntu_server"
                  spec: "/razor/v1/collections/repos/member"
           task:
                    id: "http://localhost:8080/api/collections/tasks/
ubuntu"
                  name: "ubuntu"
                  spec: "/razor/v1/collections/tasks/member"
         broker:
                    id: "http://localhost:8080/api/collections/brokers/
noop"
                  name: "noop"
```

```
                spec: "/razor/v1/collections/brokers/member"
        enabled: true
      max_count: 20
  configuration:
                hostname_pattern: "host"
                   root_password: "secret"
           tags: [
                    id: "http://localhost:8080/api/collections/tags/
ubuntu_small"
                  name: "ubuntu_small"
                  spec: "/razor/v1/collections/tags/member"
]
          nodes:
                   id: "http://localhost:8080/api/collections/policies/
ubuntu_one/nodes"
                 name: "nodes"
                count: 2
```

Note that the details contain not only all the information that was added on its creation, but also a node count.

Adding a Tag

Tags are composed of a name and a rule. They are used in policies to determine whether the policy should be applied to the node by evaluating the server's characteristics. A characteristic could be anything from size to the type of Ethernet card or a MAC address.

A tag's rule is composed of an operator and one or more arguments. When applied to the policy, the tag will be evaluated as an if/then expression: If the server's details match this tag, then apply the policy.

Tags can be created separately or as part of the policy. To create a policy for unique MAC addresses, we will first create a JSON file, macs_tag.json, as shown in Listing 16-22.

Listing 16-22 macs_tag.json File

```
{
    "name": "unique_macs",
    "rule": [
        "in",
        [
            "fact",
```

```
            "macaddress"
        ],
        "de:ea:db:ee:f0:00",
        "de:ea:db:ee:f0:01"
    ]
}
```

Then, creating a tag is simple by using the `razor create-tag --json <filename>` command, as demonstrated in Listing 16-23.

Listing 16-23 Creating a Tag

```
$ razor create-tag --json macs_tag.json
From http://localhost:8080/api:

    id: "http://localhost:8080/api/collections/tags/unique_macs"
  name: "unique_macs"
  spec: "/razor/v1/collections/tags/member"
```

> **TIP**
>
> When creating JSON formatted documents, there are some very handy validation and formatting tools, available both as command-line tools as well as web applications. One such web tool is http://jsonlint.com/.

Tags can also be added to a policy and deleted from a policy. To add an existing tag to a policy, we will create another JSON file, another_tag.json, as shown in Listing 16-24.

Listing 16-24 another_tag.json File

```
{
  "name": "ubuntu_one",
  "tag" : "unique_macs"
}
```

Here, `"name"` is the name of an existing policy and `"tag"` is the name of an existing tag.

Similarly, we could create a file where the new tag is created and added at the same time. Compare Listings 16-24 and 16-25.

Listing 16-25 another_tag.json File Alternate Version

```
{
    "name": "ubuntu_one",
    "tag": "processor_count_2",
    "rule": [
        "=",
        [
            "fact",
            "processorcount"
        ],
        "2"
    ]
}
```

Either format will work when adding a new tag to an existing policy:

```
$ razor add-policy-tag --json another_tag.json
```

Now, if we inspect the tag portion of the policy, we will see that the policy has two new tags, as shown in Listing 16-26.

Listing 16-26 Tags Portion of Updated ubuntu_one Policy

```
tags: [
                      id: "http://localhost:8080/api/collections/tags/
ubuntu_small"
                    name: "ubuntu_small"
                    spec: "/razor/v1/collections/tags/member"

                      id: "http://localhost:8080/api/collections/tags/
unique_macs"
                    name: "unique_macs"
                    spec: "/razor/v1/collections/tags/member"

                      id: "http://localhost:8080/api/collections/tags/
processor_count_2"
                    name: "processor_count_2"
                    spec: "/razor/v1/collections/tags/member"
                ]
```

Tags can also be updated and deleted in a similar fashion. However, extra care must be taken when doing so because the existing policies will be affected.

Using Razor APIs

So far, all the examples were done using the Razor client. However, the client is just a thin wrapper that makes RESTful calls to the server. You may have already observed that the output of the commands and the details for each collection item contain IDs with a URL. That is not a coincidence. In fact, when executing Razor commands, you may pass a `-d` flag to any Razor command, and you will get output in a raw JSON format of what was returned from the server of what was returned from the server. Also, you do not have to use the client: The structure of the APIs makes it very easy to write your own automation tools to interact with the Razor server. For example, if you make a call to list all the tags through the client, you will get the output shown in Listing 16-27.

Listing 16-27 Tag Details for ubuntu_small Using Razor Client

```
$ razor tags ubuntu_small
From http://localhost:8080/api/collections/tags/ubuntu_small:
        id: "http://localhost:8080/api/collections/tags/ubuntu_small"
      name: "ubuntu_small"
      spec: "/razor/v1/collections/tags/member"
      rule: [
              "="
              ["num", ["fact", "processorcount"]]
              1
            ]
     nodes:
                  id: "http://localhost:8080/api/collections/tags/ubuntu_
small/nodes"
                name: "nodes"
               count: 3
  policies:
                  id: "http://localhost:8080/api/collections/tags/ubuntu_
small/policies"
                name: "policies"
               count: 1
```

The highlighted URLs can be used directly in making calls to the Razor server. The output in Listing 16-28 is from an identical call via API to view the details of the tag named ubuntu_small.

Listing 16-28 API Call to View Tag Details for ubuntu_small

```
$ curl http://localhost:8080/api/collections/tags/ubuntu_small
{"spec":"http://api.puppetlabs.com/razor/v1/collections/tags/
member","id":"http://localhost:8080/api/collections/tags/ubuntu_
small","name":"ubuntu_small","rule":["=",["num",["fact","processorcount"]],
1],"nodes":{"id":"http://localhost:8080/api/collections/tags/ubuntu_small/
nodes","count":3,"name":"nodes"},"policies":{"id":"http://localhost:8080/
api/collections/tags/ubuntu_small/policies","count":1,"name":"policies"}}
```

Similarly, you could make calls to the Razor server directly from your own custom tools just using the API. Because most of the Razor client commands required JSON input, the API calls will likewise take the same JSON input for creating and modifying collection items.

Razor Components

Razor consists of several components and supporting tools that are required for the application to work.

Razor Server

The Razor server is the brains of the operation and the main Razor component. It is written in JRuby and runs on the TorqueBox application platform. TorqueBox is based on the JBoss application server and provides built-in clustering, high availability, and load balancing. The Razor server requires PostgreSQL for its back end, and supports having dev/test/prod modes on one server. Users interact with the server via the Razor client or directly through the RESTful API.

Razor Microkernel

The Razor microkernel is a small Linux image that boots on nodes and inventories them. The current version of the microkernel is based on Fedora and uses MAC addresses as unique identifiers. After discovery, if there are no matching policies configured for the server, the server will present the login screen for the microkernel. However, you will not usually need to log in to the microkernel itself. The microkernel is 64-bit image, and therefore it supports only 64-bit machines.

> **NOTE**
>
> Razor can provision only 64-bit machines.

Razor Client

The Razor client is a command-line client that can be installed on any machine that has network access to the Razor server. The client needs to be installed separately. For security reasons, it is best to keep the client on the same server as Razor server because currently there is no authentication provided by the client itself.

> TIP
>
> The Razor client should use a Ruby interpreter compatible with Ruby 1.9.3. Although the Razor client will run just fine under JRuby, it will do so very slowly. Use Ruby environment managers such as rbenv or RVM to switch between different versions.

The Razor client can be installed as a Ruby gem. If you are installing the Razor server and client on the same machine, take care not to use JRuby for the client. If you notice that the client returns extremely slowly, check the Ruby version; JRuby makes it very slow.

Setting Up Razor

You can set up Razor in several ways. If you are using Puppet Enterprise, Razor comes with it. However, you need to test Razor in a completely separate environment before deploying it to production. You should test Razor in a virtual environment first, to see how it actually works and get a sense for its power.

PE Razor

Razor can be installed in a few different ways. If you are using Puppet Enterprise, Razor is already available there; however, you still need to install additional components. The missing pieces are a DHCP server, DNS server, and an image repository.

Puppet Install

If you already have Puppet running, it takes only two lines to install Razor:

```
puppet module install puppetlabs/razor
puppet apply -e 'include razor'
```

However, you still need to install and configure the database yourself.

Install from Source

If you are not using Puppet, you need to install Razor from its source. Installation instructions are provided on the Razor GitHub site: https://github.com/puppetlabs/razor-server/wiki/Installation. Unless you are very adventurous, do not install from trunk, and follow the latest releases. Installing from a release is the same as installing from source code. The latest release can be found here: https://github.com/puppetlabs/razor-server/releases.

> TIP
>
> If you are setting up a test environment, start out with Vagrant. Several prebuilt Vagrant environments are available.
>
> This Vagrant environment sets up a three-server environment with Puppet Enterprise, DHCP, and Razor VMs running: https://github.com/npwalker/pe-razor-vagrant-stack.
>
> This single-VM environment will provide the latest release of Razor with dnsmasq configured: https://github.com/eglute/razor-server-vagrant. Also, this installation contains a script, provision.sh, that can very easily be adapted to run on a standalone server outside of Vagrant.

Manual Release Install

This is the easiest way to install Razor if you are not using Puppet or Puppet Enterprise. Follow release install directions on the Razor wiki: https://github.com/puppetlabs/razor-server/wiki/Installation.

Other Services

To make Razor work, additional services are required. The back end for Razor is PostgreSQL, and it may need to be installed and configured if it was not installed as part of the Razor install.

Razor will need access to OS images that will be used in your installation. Razor understands how to access local files as well as remote files. If you use remote images, the Razor server will require HTTP access to retrieve them. After retrieving an image, Razor expands it and stores it locally under its repo directory.

Razor also requires DHCP and DNS services. IP addresses are assigned to newly installed nodes through DHCP. You may use the DHCP server of your choosing. If your environment is small, dnsmasq will work just fine for both DHCP and DNS.

A dnsmasq configuration file (dnsmasq.conf) might look like Listing 16-29.

Listing 16-29 Sample dnsmasq.conf File

```
server=$IP_ADDRESS@eth1
interface=eth1
no-dhcp-interface=eth0
domain=razor.local
# conf-dir=/etc/dnsmasq.d
# This works for dnsmasq 2.45
# iPXE sets option 175, mark it for network IPXEBOOT
dhcp-match=IPXEBOOT,175
dhcp-boot=net:IPXEBOOT,bootstrap.ipxe
dhcp-boot=undionly.kpxe
# TFTP setup
enable-tftp
tftp-root=/var/lib/tftpboot
dhcp-range=$IP_ADDRESS,$IP_RANGE,12h
dhcp-option=option:ntp-server,$IP_ADDRESS
```

Note that this will differ based on your environment and installation. In this example, `$IP_ADDRESS` is the starting IP address, and the `$IP_RANGE` is the last IP address that can be allocated to the new nodes by Razor.

> CAUTION
>
> Before deploying Razor to production, test it first.
>
> Razor could affect your existing infrastructure if not configured properly. Rebooting a server on a Razor network could result in a reinstall of an existing machine.

Troubleshooting

If, after you install and configure all the components, the new servers still cannot be booted, check the following:

- Is Razor running? Because Razor is running on TorqueBox, check whether a Java process is running (see Listing 16-30).

Listing 16-30 Check Whether a Java Process Is Running

```
ps -ef | grep java
root      2451  2420  0 Apr23 pts/0    00:04:15 java -D[Standalone] -server
-XX:+UseCompressedOops -Xms64m -Xmx512m -XX:MaxPermSize=256m -Djava.
net.preferIPv4Stack=true -Djboss.modules.system.pkgs=org.jboss.byteman
-Djava.awt.headless=true -Dorg.jboss.boot.log.file=/root/.rbenv/versions/
jruby-1.7.8/lib/ruby/gems/shared/gems/torquebox-server-3.0.1-java/jboss/
standalone/log/server.log -Dlogging.configuration=file:/root/.rbenv/
versions/jruby-1.7.8/lib/ruby/gems/shared/gems/torquebox-server-3.0.1-
java/jboss/standalone/configuration/logging.properties -jar /root/.rbenv/
versions/jruby-1.7.8/lib/ruby/gems/shared/gems/torquebox-server-3.0.1-java/
jboss/jboss-modules.jar -mp /root/.rbenv/versions/jruby-1.7.8/lib/ruby/
gems/shared/gems/torquebox-server-3.0.1-java/jboss/modules -jaxpmodule
javax.xml.jaxp-provider org.jboss.as.standalone -Djboss.home.dir=/root/.
rbenv/versions/jruby-1.7.8/lib/ruby/gems/shared/gems/torquebox-server-
3.0.1-java/jboss -Djboss.server.base.dir=/root/.rbenv/versions/jruby-1.7.8/
lib/ruby/gems/shared/gems/torquebox-server-3.0.1-java/jboss/standalone
-Djruby.home=/root/.rbenv/versions/jruby-1.7.8 --server-config=standalone.
xml -b 0.0.0.0
```

If you don't see a Java/TorqueBox process running, start it up:

```
torquebox deploy --env production
torquebox run --bind-address=0.0.0.0
```

- If there is more than one Razor process running, kill them all and start up TorqueBox again.
- Check the logs: Are there any obvious errors?
- Can the OS image file can be accessed? Check permissions and ownership.
- Can the image be extracted to a folder? Once again, check that the Razor process has access to the location where the ISO will be extracted. It is usually under razor/repo-store. On Puppet Enterprise, the default location is under /opt/puppet/var/razor/repo-store.
- Does DHCP work? DHCP needs to be running on the Razor network. There should be only one DHCP service on the Razor network.
- Does DNS work? If DNS is not configured properly, the Chef broker will not be able to hand off the node to the Chef Server.
- Does the database work properly and have appropriate users and permissions? Check connectivity to the database. If the database is not configured correctly, you cannot perform any Razor client commands; so, at least it will be easy to detect.
- Make sure that the client is pointing to the proper Razor server.

If the Razor is working properly, but the node does not get installed properly, check the files created in the node's /tmp folder. The logs in that directory will contain installation information as well as broker handoff logs.

Summary

Combining Razor with configuration tools makes for a very powerful, fully automated server provisioning solution. Using this deployment system, the installation of customized environments can be performed as fast as the servers come online.

References

[1] Puppet Enterprise Razor documentation: http://docs.puppetlabs.com/pe/3.2/razor_intro.html

[2] Puppet Labs Razor-Server wiki: https://github.com/puppetlabs/razor-server/wiki

[3] Puppet Labs Razor client project: https://github.com/puppetlabs/razor-client

[4] Puppet Labs Razor microkernel project: https://github.com/puppetlabs/razor-el-mk

Chapter 17

Intro to the ELK: Elasticsearch, Logstash, Kibana

Elasticsearch, Logstash, and Kibana, also called the *ELK stack*, are three powerful tools. Elasticsearch is a search server where the data is stored and optimized for indexing. Logstash is a data (log) shipping and cleaning tool. Kibana is the front end for viewing and analyzing data. Each of them can be used as a standalone tool, but the combination of all of them makes a perfect combination for managing logs.

This chapter provides a quick introduction into each tool and explains how to combine them for effective log management. Topics covered in this chapter include the following:

- Understanding the Elasticsearch index
- Working with Elasticsearch data
- Installing Elasticsearch plugins
- Using Elasticsearch clients
- Configuring input to Logstash
- Applying filters in Logstash
- Understanding Logstash output
- Sharing and saving in Kibana

Elasticsearch Overview

Elasticsearch is one of the most brilliant tools that you could have in your DevOps tool chain. The more you get to know it, the more uses you will find for it. Elasticsearch is a powerful indexing and search engine that also provides built-in horizontal scalability and resiliency. It has a RESTful interface, providing easy access for data input and retrieval. Elasticsearch is based on Lucene, a powerful, open source search engine. While using pure Lucene can be a bit more of a challenge, getting started with Elasticsearch is straightforward.

Getting Started

Elasticsearch is a huge topic, and exploring it in depth would fill up several books. However, just getting started with Elasticsearch is easy; the documentation for installation and setup is available on the Elasticsearch site:

Install and configure using Puppet: https://github.com/elasticsearch/puppet-elasticsearch. Chef cookbook: https://github.com/elasticsearch/cookbook-elasticsearch. All others: http://www.elasticsearch.org/guide/en/elasticsearch/reference/current/_installation.html.

Once Elasticsearch is running, test it out by using the `curl` command, as shown in Listing 17-1.

Listing 17-1 Testing Elasticsearch Status

```
curl 'http://localhost:9200/?pretty'
{
  "status" : 200,
  "name" : "Blacklash",
  "version" : {
    "number" : "1.1.1",
    "build_hash" : "f1585f096d3f3985e73456debdc1a0745f512bbc",
    "build_timestamp" : "2014-04-16T14:27:12Z",
    "build_snapshot" : false,
    "lucene_version" : "4.7"
  },
  "tagline" : "You Know, for Search"
}
```

The command in Listing 17-1 will show the status of the cluster and some other information. Although you can get details on the health and status of the Elasticsearch cluster via REST calls, there are some excellent plugins that can provide the same information via a graphical user interface. We cover plugins a little later in this chapter.

Understanding the Index

Elasticsearch is a complex system that hides the complexity from the user. One of the most complex parts is the heart of Elasticsearch, its index. If you look in the data folder, you will notice the Elasticsearch index is a set of special files. Do not try to do anything directly to them; treat them as a database. They grow in size when new data is added and shrinks as the data gets indexed and the index gets optimized (compressed). When you are doing a lot of indexing, you may notice that the index files will grow dramatically, only to shrink down to one-third or one-half in size. This is normal, and there are settings that can be set if you want to optimize indexing.

To create a new index named devops using the `curl` command, refer to Listing 17-2.

Listing 17-2 Creating a New Index

```
$ curl -XPUT 'localhost:9200/devops?pretty'
{
  "acknowledged" : true
}
```

The command in Listing 17-3 will verify the index was created by listing all indices in your cluster.

Listing 17-3 List Elasticsearch Indices

```
$ curl 'localhost:9200/_cat/indices?v'
health index              pri rep docs.count docs.deleted store.size
yellow devops               5   1          0            0       495b
yellow _river               1   1          3            0       10kb
yellow mybooks              5   1        460            0    244.7mb
yellow .marvel-2014.05.02   1   1        765            0      2.4mb
```

Indices can have different statuses and multiple shards. Each Elasticsearch cluster can have multiple indices. How many indices you have depends on how your data is structured.

Working with Data

It is important to understand the data that can be indexed by Elasticsearch. What you want to index will determine the document format. A document is a JSON object that gets stored in Elasticsearch. You may think of an Elasticsearch document as an entry in a nosql database. To make data searching and retrieval easier, documents stored in the index should have a consistent format. The consistency and the format depend on the end user and the data being stored, just like it would in a nosql database. The document format, or JSON schema, can be anything you like, as long as it is a valid JSON format. Each document consists of zero or more fields, or key-value pairs. The value of each pair can be either simple or complex. After data is stored in the index, it is processed internally, or indexed, and made searchable.

To get data into Elasticsearch, you will need to use its APIs. The Elasticsearch APIs are straightforward and easy to use. Listing 17-4 shows an example of adding a simple entry and its response.

Listing 17-4 Adding Data to an Index

```
curl -XPUT 'localhost:9200/devops/chef/1?pretty' -d '
> {
>   "recipes": "vsphere"
> }'
{
  "_index" : "devops",
  "_type" : "chef",
  "_id" : "1",
  "_version" : 1,
  "created" : true
}
```

In this example, we added data to index devops with type chef and ID of 1. The actual data is key-value pair `"recipes: vsphere"`.

Data deposited into Elasticsearch can follow a user-defined schema, or it can be free form. When retrieving data, the results will come back as a whole document. Let's get the same document back, as shown in Listing 17-5.

Listing 17-5 Listing Elasticsearch Indices

```
$ curl -XGET 'localhost:9200/devops/chef/1?pretty'
{
  "_index" : "devops",
  "_type" : "chef",
  "_id" : "1",
  "_version" : 1,
  "found" : true, "_source" :
{
```

```
    "recipes": "vsphere"
}
}
```

Right now, this is pretty easy, but how about searching for data? The simplest search you could perform is without any search parameters:

```
$ curl -XGET 'localhost:9200/devops/_search'
```

A long result will be displayed on one line. Use command-line text formatting or browser tools such as http://jsbeautifier.org/ to get formatted JSON. Listing 17-6 shows the formatted result from the search.

Listing 17-6 Formatted Search Results

```
{
    "took": 1,
    "timed_out": false,
    "_shards": {
        "total": 5,
        "successful": 5,
        "failed": 0
    },
    "hits": {
        "total": 2,
        "max_score": 1.0,
        "hits": [{
            "_index": "devops",
            "_type": "chef",
            "_id": "1",
            "_score": 1.0,
            "_source": {
                "recipes": "vsphere"
            }
        }, {
            "_index": "devops",
            "_type": "puppet",
            "_id": "1",
            "_score": 1.0,
            "_source": {
                "manifest": "jenkins"
            }
        }]
    }
}
```

Do not execute a search that could return all the data from the index unless you are debugging and have no other choice. If you want to inspect all the data, there are plugins that will enable you to inspect all fields and data in a web browser.

```
$ curl -XGET 'http://localhost:9200/devops/_search?q=jenkins'
```

The previous command shows a simple query to search `devops` only for all instances of `jenkins`, which will return all documents that contain `jenkins` in any of the fields, as shown in Listing 17-7.

Listing 17-7 Formatted Search Results, Searched for `jenkins`

```
{
    "took": 1,
    "timed_out": false,
    "_shards": {
        "total": 5,
        "successful": 5,
        "failed": 0
    },
    "hits": {
        "total": 1,
        "max_score": 1.0,
        "hits": [{
            "_index": "devops",
            "_type": "puppet",
            "_id": "1",
            "_score": 1.0,
            "_source": {
                "manifest": "jenkins"
            }
        }]
    }
}
```

The Elasticsearch query language is complex, and it also needs to be in JSON format if using `curl` or other direct application programming interface (API) calls. An example of a simple query that should match any document containing `jenkins` is shown in Listing 17-8.

Listing 17-8 Sample JSON Query to Search for `jenkins`

```
{
    "query": {
        "bool": {
            "must": [],
            "must_not": [],
            "should": [{
                "query_string": {
                    "default_field": "_all",
                    "query": "jenkins"
                }
            }]
        }
    },
    "from": 0,
    "size": 10,
    "sort": [],
    "facets": {}
}
```

You will most likely not be interested in using `curl` to submit complex queries. A better way to query is using scripting language clients or direct code integration with your app. Plugins are also useful when troubleshooting queries or doing one-time searches.

Learn more about the Elasticsearch query language at http://www.elasticsearch.org/guide/en/elasticsearch/reference/current/query-dsl-query-string-query.html.

Installing Plugins

Elasticsearch comes with multiple plugins to help with data input and analysis so that you do not have to do everything by hand. Installing plugins is simple. You can install most of them as follows:

```
$ bin/plugin --install mobz/elasticsearch-head
```

Elasticsearch-head is one of my favorite plugins, and the first one installed after setting up Elasticsearch. This plugin is a simple web front end to provide an overview of the cluster, inspect the data, and perform searches.

Figure 17-1 shows what a cluster overview looks like in the elasticsearch-head plugin.

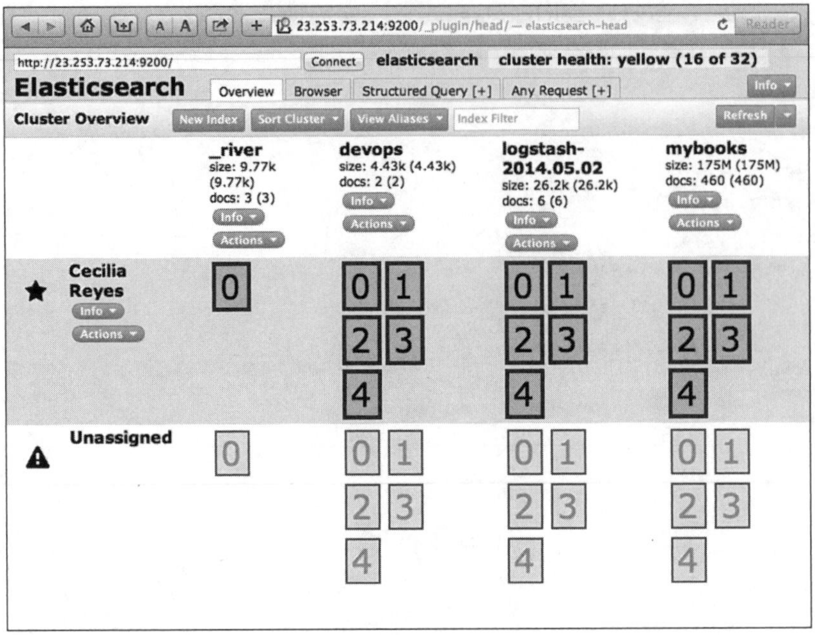

Figure 17-1 Elasticsearch cluster

A lot of data is available under the simple interface. The Cluster Overview tab will show the general status of the cluster, with more details available under each drop-down menu.

The Browser tab (see Figure 17-2) allows for inspection of all data items indexed by Elasticsearch that can be narrowed down by indices, types, and fields. Both Structured Query and Any Request tabs provide wrappers over the querying language along with a way to make any request to the Elasticsearch cluster.

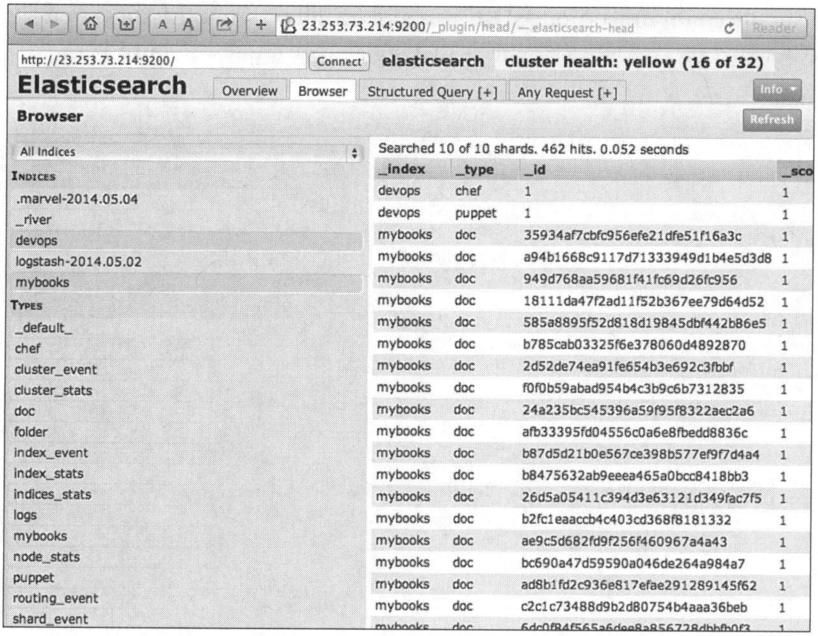

Figure 17-2 Elasticsearch index details and individual documents

> TIP
>
> In the elasticsearch-head interface under the Structured Query tab is a Show Raw JSON button. It is extremely useful to debug a troublesome query.

> TIP
>
> For large Elasticsearch clusters, there is a commercial plugin, Marvel, that provides management, monitoring, and analytics functionality. Free for development use. You can find it at http://www.elasticsearch.org/overview/marvel/.

River Plugins

Besides helpful dashboards, there are a few other types of plugins. If you are looking to index a particular data source, you may need to be looking at river types of plugins. Rivers are pluggable services running within the Elasticsearch cluster. They solve the problem of the data stream ("river"). If, for example, you want to index a MongoDB database, you can simply configure a MongoDB river and get all data into Elasticsearch from the database. Creating a river is as simple as making a `curl` request. Figure 17-3 shows an example.

```
curl -XPUT "localhost:9200/_river/mongogridfs/_meta" -d'
 {
   "type": "mongodb",
     "mongodb": {
       "db": "my_database",         Database name
       "collection": "fs",          Collection to be indexed
       "gridfs": true               Are there GridFS objects?
     },
     "index": {
       "name": "gutenberg",         Index name
       "type": "files"              What kind of objects to index?
     }
 }'
```

Figure 17-3 Create MongoDB river

> TIP
>
> When installing a plugin, make sure that the version of the plugin is compatible with the version of Elasticsearch you are running. For a full list, check out the website: http://www.elasticsearch.org/guide/en/elasticsearch/reference/1.x/modules-plugins.html.

Using Clients

Using `curl` or similar tools is convenient when we need to test something quickly with Elasticsearch. However, many libraries make scripting against Elasticsearch easy. Suppose, for example, that we want to search the data we had indexed with the river, but need to automate it. Multiple language bindings let you interact with the index. We are using the official Ruby client in Listing 17-9 to connect to our search index and search for a specific phrase.

Listing 17-9 Search.rb File

```
require 'rubygems'
require 'elasticsearch'
phrase = "custom phrase"
client = Elasticsearch::Client.new host: 'localhost'
client.cluster.health
search_result = client.search q: phrase
```

The `search_result` will contain the whole result, and the query did not take up half the page, as the earlier example did.

You can find a list of current clients at http://www.elasticsearch.org/guide/en/elasticsearch/client/community/current/clients.html.

When using Elasticsearch, you will usually be updating the index or reading data. When using clients, separate the writing to index tasks from the reading part, and make sure to reopen the same index. Better yet, delegate some of the processing to other tools, like rivers and Logstash.

Logstash Overview

Logstash collects, analyzes, and stores data. It is great for consolidating logs, and once the logs are consolidated, it can provide for easy access without having access to all the different systems.

The way Logstash works can be described in three succinct steps:

1. Input data, something that would be in your auth.log file:

```
May  5 01:46:06 egle-elk1 sshd[16057]: reverse mapping
checking getaddrinfo for 202.57.189.199.client.siamtech.ac.th
[202.57.189.199] failed - POSSIBLE BREAK-IN ATTEMPT!
```

2. Process with filter, configured in the auth.conf file and passed to Logstash:

```
filter {
  if [type] == "syslog" {
    grok {
            match => { "message" => "%{SYSLOGTIMESTAMP:syslog_time-
stamp} %{SYSLOGHOST:syslog_hostname} %{DATA:syslog_program}(?:\
[%{POSINT:syslog_pid}\])?: %{GREEDYDATA:syslog_message}" }
    }
    syslog_pri { }
    date {
         match => [ "syslog_timestamp", "MMM  d HH:mm:ss", "MMM dd
HH:mm:ss" ]
    }
  }
}
```

3. Output, this would be Elasticsearch or a destination of your choice:

```
{
        "message" => "May  5 01:57:13 egle-elk1 sshd[16642]: reverse
mapping checking getaddrinfo for 202.57.189.199.client.siamtech.ac.th
[202.57.189.199] failed - POSSIBLE BREAK-IN ATTEMPT!",
       "@version" => "1",
     "@timestamp" => "2014-05-05T01:57:14.102Z",
           "host" => "egle-elk1",
           "path" => "/var/log/auth.log"
}
```

The content of Step 1 is something you already have. Step 2 can be found in a Logstash recipe, and Step 3 is something Logstash produces. We cover all the steps in this section.

Getting Started

To get started with Logstash, download it from http://logstash.net/. Logstash is a Java application, so it will require a JVM. Follow the setup: http://logstash.net/docs/1.4.0/tutorials/getting-started-with-logstash.

In addition, you need to decide what to use for storage. If you want to use Logstash with Elasticsearch, verify that it is running, and you will be ready for log processing. After you have both Elasticsearch and Logstash running, you need to create a configuration file with your input, filter, and output configuration.

Configuring Input to Logstash

Logstash works with logs. From Logstash's perspective, a log can be defined as anything that has a time stamp. There are several ways to get data to Logstash; the default way is using Logstash agent itself. In addition to using Logstash, you can also configure alternative ways that may suit your environment better. To see a list of other available log shippers, refer to Logstash recipes: http://cookbook.logstash.net/recipes/log-shippers/.

To configure input to Logstash, use the input section in the configuration file. There is a growing list of available inputs available; if you do not see your preferred input available in the documentation at http://logstash.net/docs/1.4.0/, you can add your own. We are going to use one of the recipes found in Logstash's cookbook for our example (these recipes should not be confused with the Chef recipes), http://cookbook.logstash.net/. We used the example on syslog log processing. First, we created a syslog.conf file, as shown in Listing 17-10.

Listing 17-10 syslog.conf File

```
input {
  tcp {
    port => 5000
    type => syslog
  }
  udp {
    port => 5000
    type => syslog
  }
}

filter {
  if [type] == "syslog" {
    grok {
      match => { "message" => "%{SYSLOGTIMESTAMP:syslog_timestamp}
%{SYSLOGHOST:syslog_hostname} %{DATA:syslog_program}(?:\[%{POSINT:syslog_
pid}\])?: %{GREEDYDATA:syslog_message}" }
      add_field => [ "received_at", "%{@timestamp}" ]
      add_field => [ "received_from", "%{host}" ]
    }
    syslog_pri { }
    date {
      match => [ "syslog_timestamp", "MMM  d HH:mm:ss", "MMM dd HH:mm:ss" ]
    }
  }
}

output {
  elasticsearch { host => localhost }
  stdout { codec => rubydebug }
}
```

In this example, input is syslog and output is to Elasticsearch and standard out.

After creating the configuration file, we started Logstash:

```
$ bin/logstash -f syslog.conf
```

Because we had logging to the console enabled, we were able to see the processed logs in the console.

Listing 17-11 shows the document format that will get stored in Elasticsearch and will be available for retrieval.

Listing 17-11 Console Log Output

```
{
                 "message" => "\r",
                "@version" => "1",
              "@timestamp" => "2014-05-02T11:26:19.709Z",
                    "host" => "127.0.0.1:45058",
                    "type" => "syslog",
                    "tags" => [
        [0] "_grokparsefailure"
    ],
    "syslog_severity_code" => 5,
    "syslog_facility_code" => 1,
         "syslog_facility" => "user-level",
         "syslog_severity" => "notice"
}
```

Applying Filters

As you might have noticed, the configuration file in the Listing 17-10 contains a filter section. This is where we tell Logstash how to parse the incoming data. Filters are applied in the order listed, and can contain conditionals and plugins. To save time writing regular expressions, Logstash provides a filter called Grok.

Grok

Grok is a special filter for parsing log data. It was created so that users do not have to write regular expressions, and it is the best way to parse unstructured data. With more than 100 patterns built in, Grok should be able to parse even the most complex data. View available patterns on the project's GitHub page: https://github.com/elasticsearch/logstash/tree/master/patterns. You can also add your own.

If you do want to add your own pattern, or have a Grok expression that is buggy, there is a convenient tool just for that purpose, Grok Debugger: http://grokdebug.herokuapp.com/. Grok Debugger not only helps you debug your pattern, but it also produces a pattern given your input. It also has a convenient way of browsing all available patterns.

Data Transformation

With the help of the filters, data can be transformed and additional fields added while the logs are being processed. So, if you have raw data lines coming in with a simple format, as in Listing 17-12, you can transform, remove, and add additional information.

Listing 17-12 Unformatted Log File Entry

```
May  5 01:46:06 egle-elk1 sshd[16057]: reverse mapping checking getaddrinfo
for 202.57.189.199.client.siamtech.ac.th [202.57.189.199] failed - POSSIBLE
BREAK-IN ATTEMPT!
```

After processing through the filter, we can add additional information, such as in Listing 17-13.

Listing 17-13 Filter for Adding Fields

```
add_field => [ "received_at", "%{@timestamp}" ]
add_field => [ "received_from", "%{host}" ]
```

To remove fields:

```
remove_field => [ "syslog_hostname", "syslog_message", "syslog_timestamp" ]
```

To modify:

```
replace => [ "@source_host", "%{syslog_hostname}" ]
```

What kind of processing can be done on the data? Refer to the documentation for each filter. For example, Listing 17-14 contains all the available filters for Grok.

Listing 17-14 Search.rb File

```
grok {
    add_field => ... # hash (optional), default: {}
    add_tag => ... # array (optional), default: []
    break_on_match => ... # boolean (optional), default: true
    drop_if_match => ... # boolean (optional), default: false
    keep_empty_captures => ... # boolean (optional), default: false
    match => ... # hash (optional), default: {}
    named_captures_only => ... # boolean (optional), default: true
    overwrite => ... # array (optional), default: []
    patterns_dir => ... # array (optional), default: []
```

```
    remove_field => ... # array (optional), default: []
    remove_tag => ... # array (optional), default: []
    tag_on_failure => ... # array (optional), default: ["_grokparsefailure"]
}
```

After the data has been manipulated, it can be directed to multiple outputs.

Understanding Output

Output is where Logstash is going to store the processed log data. There can be more than one output specified at the same time. The preferred destination for Logstash is Elasticsearch, especially if you want to use Kibana for data analysis. More on how to configure Elasticsearch as an output is available in the documentation at http://logstash.net/docs/1.4.0/outputs/elasticsearch. However, for the simplest setup, all that is needed is the host information.

Besides sending output to Elasticsearch, there are multiple other destinations available. In fact, Logstash allows you to send data to more than one destination at a time. Refer to Listing 17-15 for how to direct output to multiple destinations.

Listing 17-15 Multiple Outputs

```
output {
  elasticsearch { host => localhost }
  stdout { codec => rubydebug }
}
```

Some of the other destinations besides Elasticsearch and standard out are email, file, pagerduty, and jira. So, potentially, you could filter the logs, find specific errors, and notify users by paging them, emailing, and creating a jira issue. For testing purposes, you can also use null output.

After data is processed by Logstash and stored in Elasticsearch, it can be visualized and analyzed in Kibana Logstash dashboard.

Kibana Overview

Kibana is a dashboard written to visualize any data that has a time stamp. It is written in HTML and JavaScript. The only requirement Kibana has is a web server and a one-line configuration. To get it running, download Kibana, extract the files, and drop them in the web server. If Elasticsearch is not running on the same server as a Kibana, modify the config.js file to point to your Elasticsearch cluster.

After opening Kibana in a web browser for the first time, you will see a welcome screen with links to a few default dashboards (see Figure 17-4).

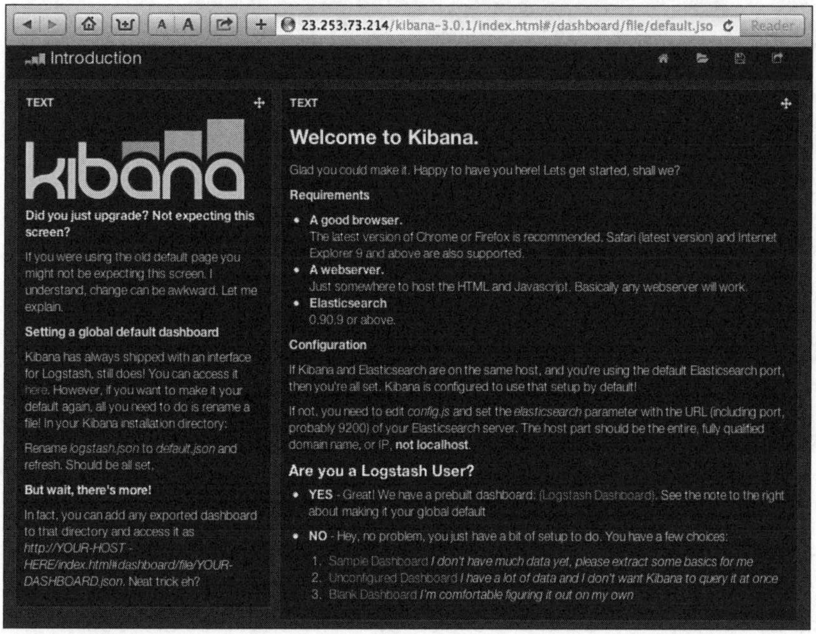

Figure 17-4 Kibana welcome screen

You can build your own dashboard, but we are going to use the Logstash dashboard.

After opening the Logstash dashboard, you will see data loaded automatically and multiple cogs and buttons for customizing the dashboard. To change from the dark dashboard to the light, find the Configure Dashboard cog in the upper-right corner and click on it. After you click it, you will be presented with a Dashboard Settings window and have several options to edit dashboard settings, as shown in Figure 17-5.

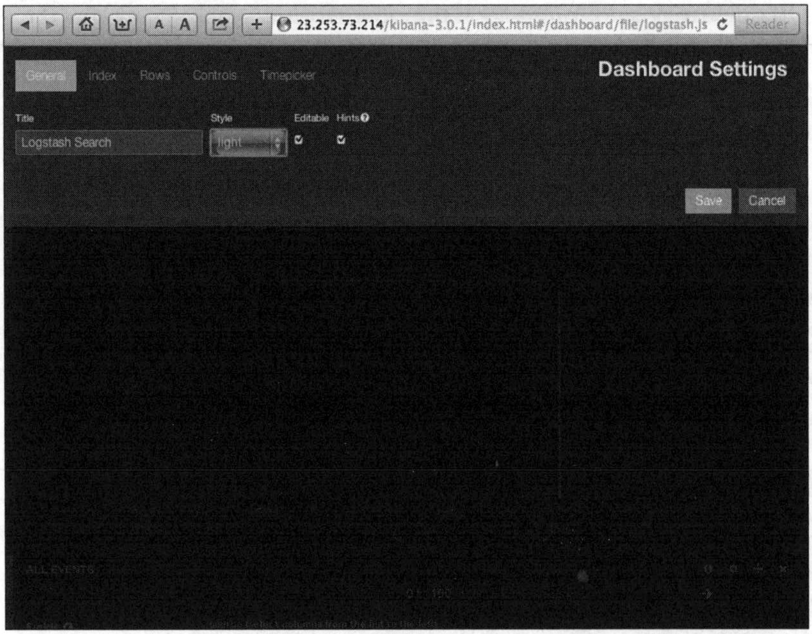

Figure 17-5 Change Kibana style to light theme

In Figure 17-5, you are presented with an option to change the style. We are going to switch to the light. Besides styles, you can also adjust which Elasticsearch index Kibana is pointing to, as well as some other display options under Rows, Controls, and Timepicker options.

Any graph can be clicked on to zoom in for more detail. For bar charts, explore spikes by selecting the time span on suspicious activity. Figure 17-6 shows an example.

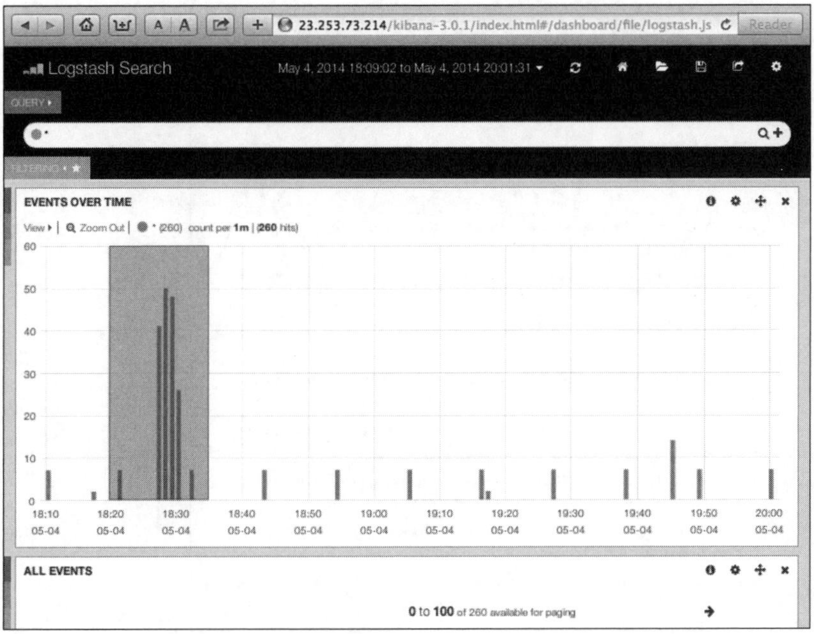

Figure 17-6 Zoom in on date range

Below the Events over Time dashboard, there is a corresponding All Events table. This table contains all the fields displayed by default. You can adjust the view by selecting only desired fields and modifying their order. Figure 17-7 shows an example of only host and message fields displayed in the event table.

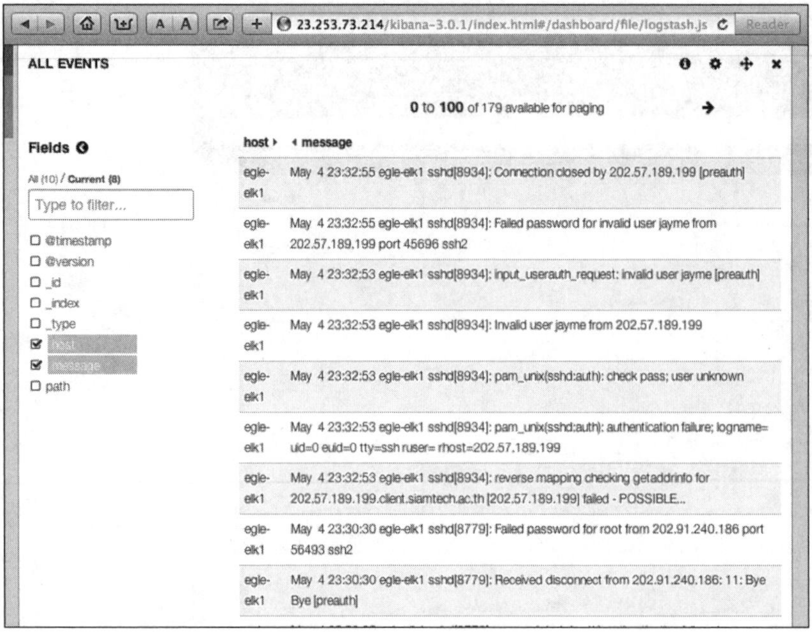

Figure 17-7 Customized events table

Each event is also clickable and available in multiple formats. To view the event's JSON format stored in Elasticsearch, just expand the event and select JSON view (see Figure 17-8).

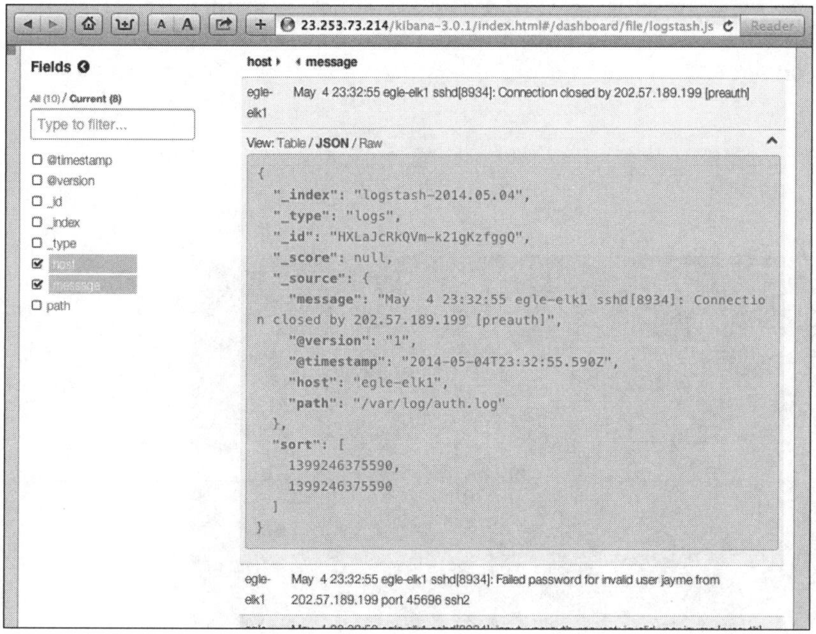

Figure 17-8 Event details JSON view

All the different views can be shared, saved, and viewed again. Do not refresh your browser if have not saved your current view.

Sharing and Saving

Different panels can be shared and must be saved if you want to be able to load them again. Both share and save options are available in the upper-right corner. Saved options can be loaded by clicking the folder icon next to the save icon. As shown in Figure 17-9, when sharing a dashboard, you are provided with the URL that will direct the same exact dashboard that was just created.

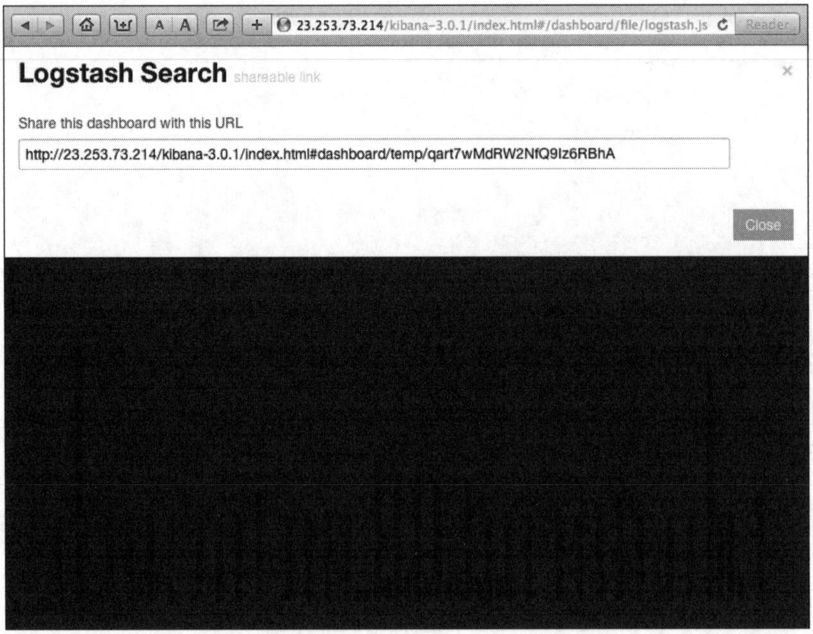

Figure 17-9 Sharing Kibana temporary view

Custom Data Views

Besides the default Logstash dashboard, Kibana allows users to customize what is shown and how data is displayed. If you have geographic data, try adding a map panel. Other panels include ways to display histograms, pie charts, or just simply plain text.

Kibana allows users to explore logs through a GUI instead of learning query languages. Save dashboards, instead of searches.

Summary

Elasticsearch, Logstash, and Kibana are powerful tools that can each be used individually. However, they really shine when combined together, and make for a stellar log management combination. They enable you to process a lot of data and visualize it with a simple setup. The whole ELK stack is available to be installed either via Puppet manifests or by using Chef recipes.

References

[1] Elasticsearch documentation: http://www.elasticsearch.org/guide/

[2] Logstash: http://logstash.net/

[3] Getting Started with Logstash: http://logstash.net/docs/1.4.0/tutorials/getting-started-with-logstash

[4] Grok: http://logstash.net/docs/1.4.0/filters/grok

[5] Kibana: http://www.elasticsearch.org/overview/kibana/

Chapter 18

Continuous Integration with Jenkins

This chapter focuses on continuous integration (CI) systems that DevOps teams use to automatically build and test source code. The build process is triggered automatically as new changes are committed to the source code management (SCM) system. Jenkins is one of the more popular CI tools, and we'll take a look at how to deploy and use it.

Topics covered in this chapter include the following:

- Continuous integration concepts
- Jenkins architecture
- Jenkins deployment
- Jenkins workflow
- Quality assurance teams

Continuous Integration Concepts

Rapid infrastructure deployment, with essential services automatically configured, is great. However, the rapid deployment of bug-free, customer-facing applications is even more critical to your business's success.

Traditional software development teams may have multiple steps between writing code to getting the product out of the door including source code commits, binary builds from source, quality assurance (QA) testing, staging, and finally, production deployment. These steps often include manual processes and handoffs that can introduce bugs above and beyond problems that may already exist in the source code. Wouldn't it be great if there were a way to add a bit more automation to the source code deployment process? This is where CI systems come in.

CI systems allow you to define a pipeline that begins with the source code development and ends with tested and verified code being automatically staged for production deployment. The interim steps listed earlier are performed automatically, including testing, via the CI system.

Continuous Integration or Continuous Deployment?

Because CI is sometimes referred to as *continuous delivery*, this may lead some new DevOps practitioners to confuse it with *continuous deployment*. Organizations that are just getting started with CI systems are more likely to implement *continuous integration*, which can be thought of as *continuous staging*.

With CI, builds are output and undergo final acceptance testing before being manually deployed into production. Organizations that are CI experts may have developed a confidence in their build practices so that new builds are automatically placed into production. This is *continuous deployment* (CD).

Regardless of which practice is employed, CI or CD, the toolsets are the same for each type of workflow. So, we will collectively refer to Jenkins and tools like it as CI/CD in this chapter.

Test Automation

The root causes for application problems can be numerous, but they normally can be boiled down to a few categories: compilation problems, feature bugs, or logical bugs. The "blame" could lie in an operating system (OS) configuration change, a developer introducing a bug, or changes in third-party dependencies, with the second of the three being common.

Why are developers more at risk to introduce these issues? It is common practice for developers to be distributed across agile teams, physical locations, working different schedules, and in different time zones. That fact that these developers have different priorities and levels of expertise compounds this problem. Although these might sound like incredible obstacles to overcome, the solution is simply this: Test often. Several tools, depending on the application's programming language, can significantly reduce risk in the software development process.

The first step is to have your developers think about test cases during or even before the software development process. The industry debates the merits of test-driven development

(TDD), but it is difficult to argue the value of critically thinking about the expected behavior of your code during the software development process.

There are industry-standard tools for developers to create unit tests to verify small functional sections of their code. These tools include JUnit for Java, PyUnit for Python, RSpec and TestUnit for Ruby-on-Rails, and NUnit for Microsoft .NET. These tools facilitate writing tests faster by abstracting the repetitive tasks needed when testing (checking for valid return values, logic, and so on). They are useful for returning feedback quickly because test execution will halt immediately if any of the tests fail.

The idea behind unit testing is that these small tests should cover the majority of application functionality. As development continues, these tests can ensure the following:

1. New features work.
2. Existing features continue to work.
3. Formerly resolved bugs are not reintroduced (regression testing).

The developer tests repeatedly during the software development process, ensuring that all tests pass before even committing source code.

When building a web application, there are some features that can be tested only via a browser. These applications can be tested using tools such as Selenium webdriver and Capybara that can be integrated with the aforementioned testing frameworks. These tools include libraries that enable you to create programs that run a browser session, opening different pages throughout the application and verifying the content on the rendered page. As developers make adjustments to a user interface (UI), they can then run these tests to verify that content still displays correctly.

You would be right in thinking, "This all sounds a bit manual with opportunities for human error." A developer may not be aware of other tests that are dependent on her code. For smaller applications, ant scripts could be created to run all unit tests, but that could be time-consuming and dissuade developers from testing often. It is also possible that some tests might be missed if executed manually.

Fortunately, CI/CD tools such as Jenkins, Travis Continuous Integration (Travis CI), and Go Continuous Delivery (GoCD) enable you to create a pipeline composed of build steps for each of the unit tests. Before the source code can be built in to a packaged binary and sent to staging, it must pass every unit test defined in the CI/CD pipeline (see Figure 18-1).

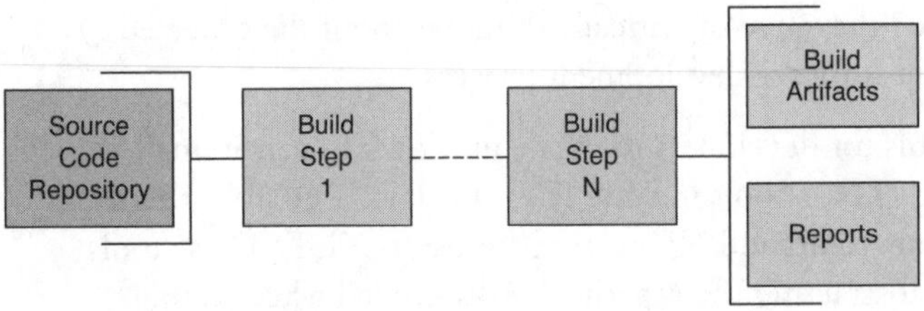

Figure 18-1 CI/CD build job progression

The CI/CD system can poll the SCM system for changes, or, more commonly, the SCM system can trigger the CI/CD system to generate a new build after each source code commit. At the end of the build, reports are generated. If there were no errors, the compiled code, known as *build artifacts*, will be stored at a location that is dictated by the CI/CD administrator. The testing tools and CI/CD systems contribute to an efficient DevOps environment. Buggy code is less likely to be deployed because errors are caught earlier in the development process and preventing technical debt from accruing.

Jenkins Architecture

Jenkins is an extensible platform with many plugins to support technologies and capabilities that it does not include out of the box. For example, despite Git being a popular SCM system, Jenkins only supports SVN and CVS by default. No problem! There are plugins to enable Git support so that you can use your existing SCM repositories.

Jenkins consists of one master and optionally one or more slave systems to accept jobs from the master. The master is capable of performing the build and reporting tasks, but for scalability purposes, you will want to consider a multimachine setup where the slave nodes perform all of the work. Figure 18-2 shows an architecture example of a Jenkins master with two Jenkins slave servers. Users interact with the master, and build instructions are sent to the slaves according to the number of executors (or concurrent build processes) that you have allotted to each slave. Whether the build happens locally on the master or on the slaves, the build artifacts and the reports are made available on the master server for users to access.

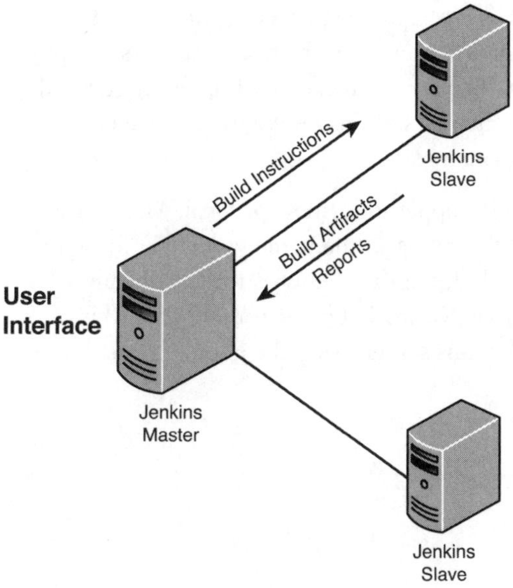

Figure 18-2 Jenkins architecture

Jenkins Deployment

Our test environment will consist of two servers: a Puppet master and an Ubuntu server that will serve as the Jenkins master server and run the Puppet agent.

> **NOTE**
>
> If you can deploy this test environment on a public cloud provider such as VMware vCloud Air, Rackspace, or Amazon Web Services, you will have an easier time utilizing an advanced functionality known as "web hooks" that we will discuss later.

We will leverage one of the popular Jenkins modules from the Puppet Forge (rtyler/jenkins) by running the following command on the Puppet master:

```
puppet module install rtyler-jenkins
```

Make sure to also download the NTP module if this is a new environment so that you can keep the Puppet master and agent server times synchronized:

```
puppet module install puppetlabs-ntp
```

Once you have the Puppet master and Puppet agent deployed properly, add the code in Listing 18-1 to your /etc/puppetlabs/puppet/environments/production/manifests/site.pp file on the Puppet master server. Alternatively, if you have an existing Puppet master and agent deployment from working with previous chapters of this book, just add the new package and class declarations to your existing agent server.

In my environment, my Jenkins server's name is puppetnode1.devops.local. Make sure to adjust the node declaration in Listing 18-1 according to the name you select for your Jenkins server. Notice that our sample code includes updated entries for the default node definition in site.pp as well. We ensure that Network Time Protocol (NTP) is deployed to both the Puppet master and the Jenkins server using the `node default` section of the manifest.

Listing 18-1 Jenkins Deployment Instructions

```
node 'puppetnode01.devops.local' {
  package { 'git':
     ensure => installed,
  }
  package { 'maven2':
     ensure => installed,
  }
  class { 'jenkins':
    configure_firewall => false,
    plugin_hash => {
      'credentials' => { version => '1.9.4' },
      'ssh-credentials' => { version => '1.6.1' },
      'git-client' => { version => '1.8.0' },
      'scm-api' => { version => '0.2' },
      'git' => { version => '2.2.1' },
    }
  }
}

node default {
  # This is where you can declare classes for all nodes.
  # Example:
  #   class { 'my_class': }
  include 'ntp'
}
```

The first two resources in the manifest ensure that the Git SCM system and Maven are installed. Maven is a Java build system that we will use with our sample Java application. One of the benefits of the Maven system is that it can automatically generate reports about build processes and generate deployment packages (jar files in Java terminology) for Jenkins to make available to users. These factors will help us have an easier time verifying build success or failure.

Next, we tell our server how to deploy the Jenkins package. Tyler did a great job of writing a module that makes Jenkins trivial to deploy and configure. There are only a few options that we need to set. First, we specify that the firewall does not need to be configured during the Jenkins deployment. Then, we include a hash of the Jenkins plugins that we need for our setup to run properly.

NOTE

It is important to be specific regarding the Jenkins plugins to install and the plugin version numbers. The Jenkins Puppet module will not automatically resolve plugin dependencies for you. Fortunately, the Wiki pages for each plugin explicitly list which plugins and version numbers are compatible. You can find the Git plugin's information at https://wiki.jenkins-ci.org/display/JENKINS/Git+Plugin.

We want the Git Jenkins plugin, and we have to make sure that the prerequisite plugins and correct version numbers are deployed. At the time of this writing, Git plugin version 2.2.1 was the latest release. The order of plugins in the plugin_hash does not matter.

The application that we will use in our build is a simple Java "Hello World" program that will be built by Maven. It is not necessary to fully understand Maven or Java because Jenkins will take care of all the source code build and report-generation tasks on our behalf. The source code for our sample application is hosted on this book's GitHub account: https://github.com/DevOpsForVMwareAdministrators/mvn-hello-world. Before moving on with the rest of this chapter, go ahead and log in to GitHub right now and create a fork of this repository. When GitHub finishes generating your repository fork, go to your copy of the repository on GitHub, and copy the HTTPS clone URL for it to a text editor for safekeeping. Make sure you select HTTPS and not SSH or Subversion! See Figure 18-3 for an example.

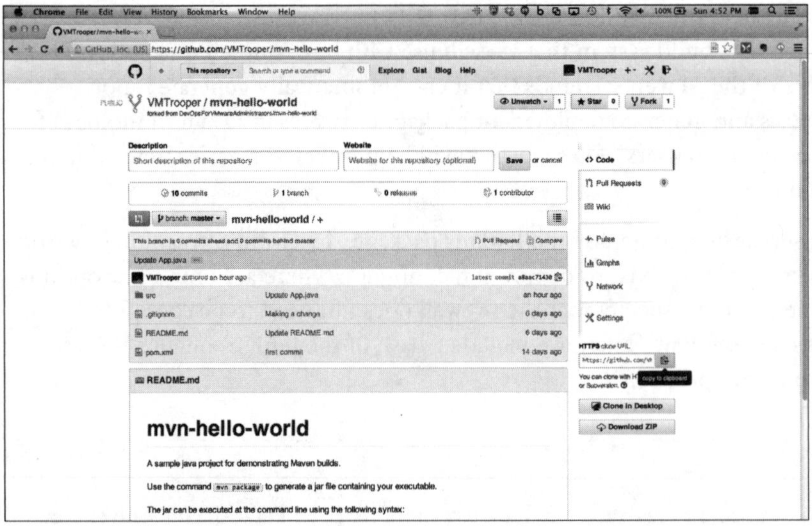

Figure 18-3 GitHub repository

Jenkins Workflow

Now that the Jenkins server is deployed, we will first take care of system prerequisites and then move on to automating our application build.

A number of things go into a Jenkins server configuration that we do not cover, including user credentials, security hardening, and so on. Instead, we focus on configuring the core settings required to get our build system up and running:

- The programming language we are working with
- The source code repository that we are building from
- The output of the build process
- The build process reports

Jenkins Server Configuration

By default, you can find the Jenkins UI on port 8080 of the IP address of your Jenkins master server. So, if your IP address is 192.168.10.10, enter the following URL into your browser: http://192.168.10.10:8080. Figure 18-4 shows the initial screen that you'll see when you first access the Jenkins UI.

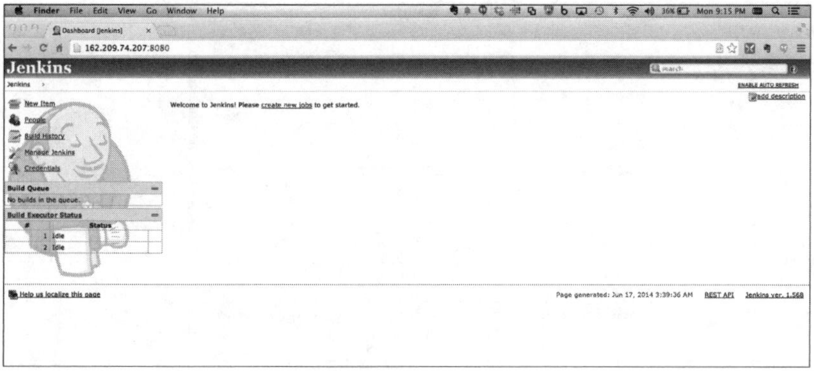

Figure 18-4 Jenkins system home page

The first thing we will need to do is tell Jenkins which of its Java development kits (JDKs) to use for its builds. You can verify what the path is on your system by using the following command:

```
update-alternatives --list java
```

On my system, this command produces the following output:

```
/usr/lib/jvm/java-6-openjdk-amd64/jre/bin/java
/usr/lib/jvm/java-7-openjdk-amd64/jre/bin/java
```

I used Java 7 for my testing, and so the path that I will use is /usr/lib/jvm/java-7-openjdk-amd64/. Jenkins can have multiple JDKs defined. However, we do not need that functionality for our test application.

Now that we have our JDK path, let's tell Jenkins where it is. Click the **Manage Jenkins** link on the left side of the screen and then the **Configure System** link on the screen that follows. Figure 18-5 shows the various system settings for the Jenkins system. We are only concerned with the JDK setting.

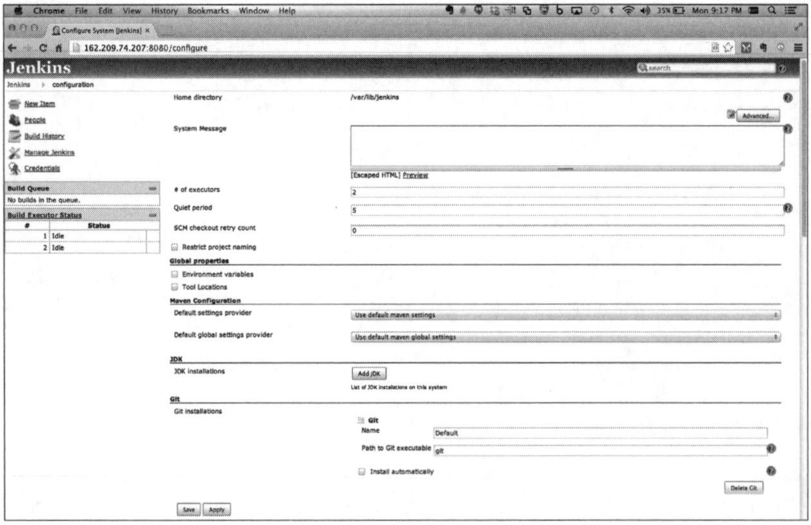

Figure 18-5 Configure the JDK path for Jenkins to use

Click the **Add JDK** button, and in the dialog that appears, click the **Install Automatically** option. Next in the JDK Name text box, provide a unique name for the JDK that you are using. This value is purely up to you. In the JAVA_HOME text box, paste the JDK path that we looked for earlier. For my system, this is /usr/lib/jvm/java-7-openjdk-amd64/. Figure 18-6 shows a configuration example.

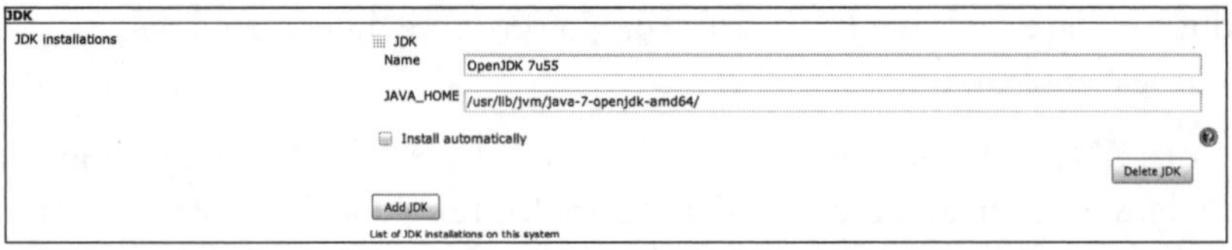

Figure 18-6 JDK settings example

Click the **Save** button, and you should be taken back to the home screen. Now, we are ready to define our first build job.

Jenkins Build Job

Click **New Item** on the left side of the screen. Jenkins will ask us for the name of our build project (the Item Name text box) and which kind of project that we want to create, as shown in Figure 18-7. We will use the "free-style" option to keep things simple. The name of your job does not need to match the name of your software repository. Click **OK** to move on to the rest of the build project's settings.

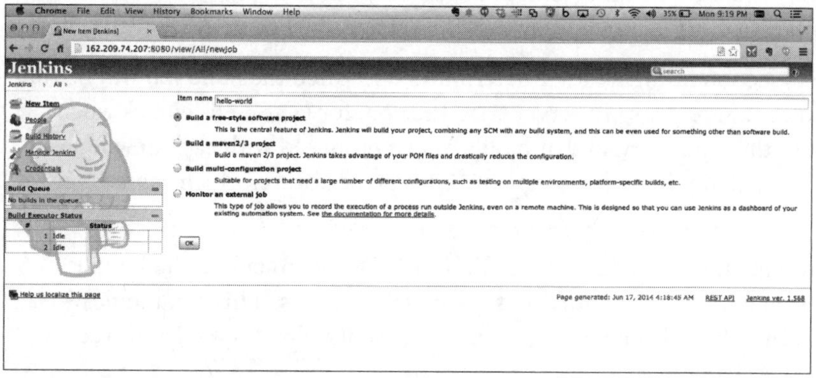

Figure 18-7 New build job dialog

We will now configure the Git settings by selecting the **Git** option in the Source Code Management section of the screen. Figure 18-8 shows an example.

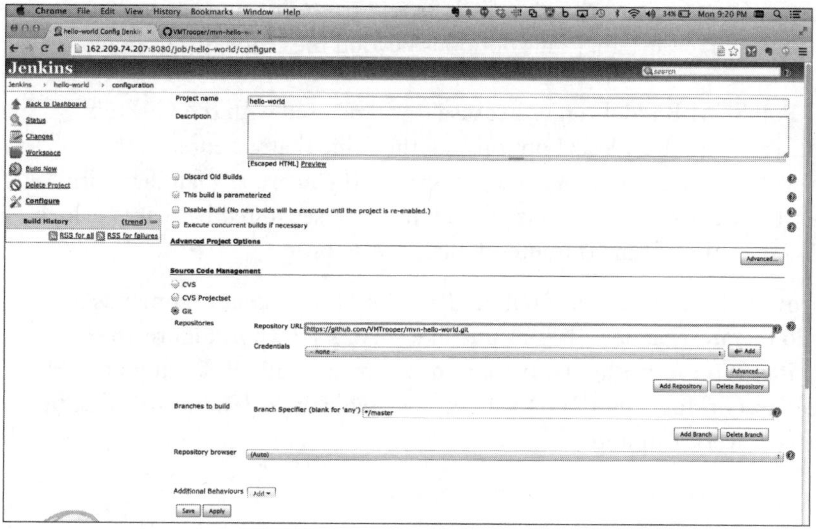

Figure 18-8 The project's Git repository

The only field that needs to be filled in for Git is the Repository URL. We will paste the HTTP clone URL for our fourth repository that we saved earlier in the chapter, and your link should be similar to the one pictured in Figure 18-8. No credentials need to be specified because we are using the HTTP link as opposed to the Secure Shell (SSH) link.

The Build Triggers section in Figure 18-9 determines how often the build job will be run. Ideally, you would configure your Git server (GitHub.com for us) to tell Jenkins when changes are made to the repository so that builds can be produced with each new repository commit. This capability is made possible by Git's hook feature, which can trigger actions on commit.

For our test environment, this would require GitHub to be able to talk to the Jenkins server's IP address on port 8080 to notify Jenkins of new commits. This communication will be possible if your lab environment is running on a public cloud provider, as recommended earlier in this chapter.

If your environment is all on local virtual machines (VMs), you still have a couple of options:

- Use the Poll SCM Build Trigger, which can poll GitHub as often as every minute to see whether there are any changes in the repository.
- Set up your own Git server using instructions from http://git-scm.com or by using a community project like GitLab. (This option is beyond the scope of this book.)

We will cover the Poll SCM Build Trigger because it will be used with the GitHub integration as well. Select the **Poll SCM** option, and the value that we enter in the Schedule text box will use the cron job scheduling format. If you are not familiar with the cron scheduler, there are five values that you can provide, separated by spaces, which correspond to different units of time (minutes, hours, and so on).

If your environment can be accessed via a public IP for GitHub to issue commands to (we'll see how to do that next), enter a large value like what is shown in Figure 18-9. This schedule signifies run every 3 hours. If your environment is all local, but your VM can communicate with GitHub, enter ***/1 * * * *** instead, which tells Jenkins to check the repository for changes every 1 minute.

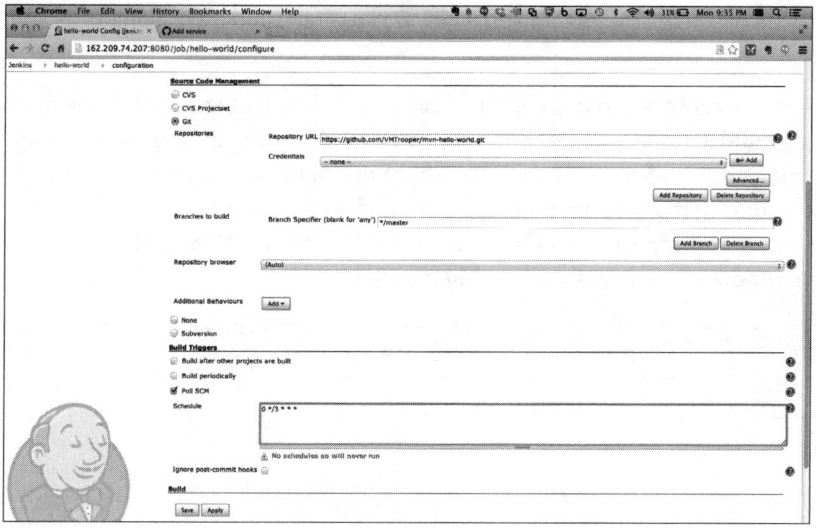

Figure 18-9 Jenkins repository build trigger

The build steps come next. In the Build section of the page, click the **Add Build Step** button and select the **Invoke Top-Level Maven Targets** option. The Goals text box allows us to specify a Maven command for the project. We will specify the **package** command, as shown in Figure 18-10.

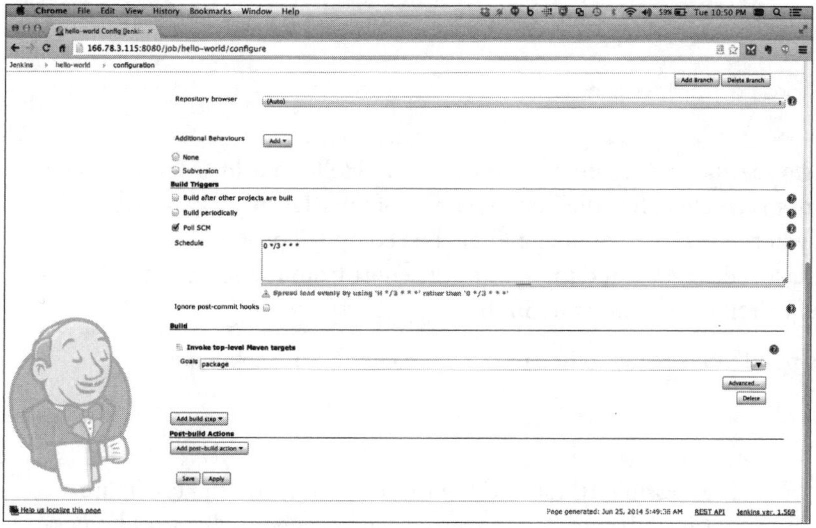

Figure 18-10 Jenkins build step

If you have multiple build or test steps that you want to run, you can define as many as you would like.

Now, how do we get our reports and our compiled binaries (a.k.a. artifacts)? Well, we need to define some post-build actions for that. First, we add a post-build action to Archive the Artifacts on the Jenkins server. Second, we add another post-build action to Publish the JUnit Test Result Report. After you have added both build steps, you need to tell Jenkins where to find the binary and report files. The values we will enter are ****/target/*.jar** and ****/target/surefire-reports/*.xml**, as shown in Figure 18-11.

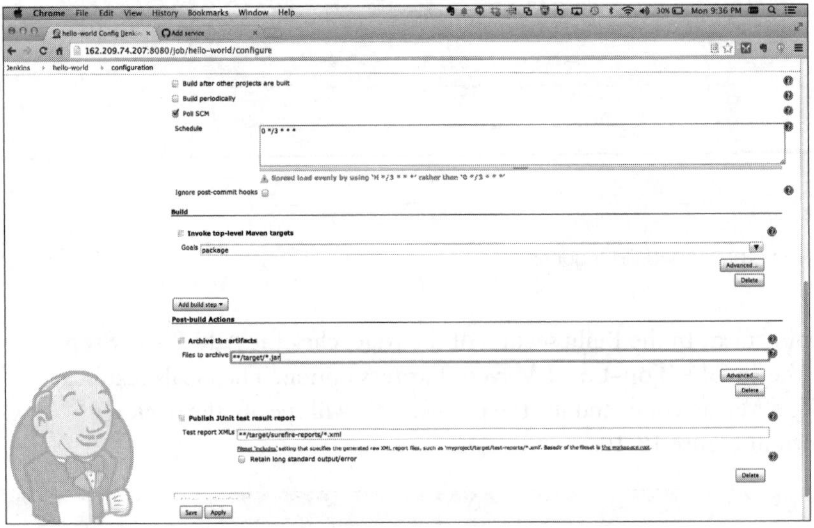

Figure 18-11 Jenkins post-build actions

In the paths that we specified, ** signifies the root of our "Hello World" Maven project. The target directory is created after the first execution of the Maven package command (`mvn package` if you run it at the command line). The compiled program will be stored in a jar file in the target directory, and the JUnit test report from the Jenkins build will be placed in the surefire-reports subdirectory in the target.

Your first Jenkins build job is ready to be saved and executed. So, click **Save**.

Git Hooks

If your VM has a publicly accessible IP for GitHub to speak with, you can configure a post-commit Git hook on GitHub.com. Go to your fork of the mvn-hello-world repository, and click the settings. Now, click the **Webhooks & Services** link on the left side of the page, and you should see the page displayed in Figure 18-12.

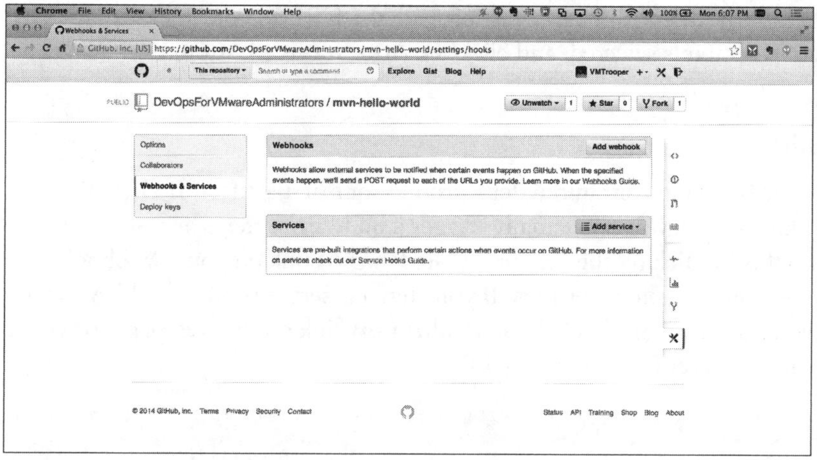

Figure 18-12 GitHub integrations for external services

Click the **Add Service** button and select **Jenkins (Git Plugin)**. Do not select the Jenkins (GitHub Plugin) option, because we installed the generic Git plugin on our Jenkins server. We chose the generic Git plugin instead of the GitHub version just in case you want to work with any other Git services out there, like gitorious, BitBucket, or a locally hosted GitLab instance (see Figure 8-13).

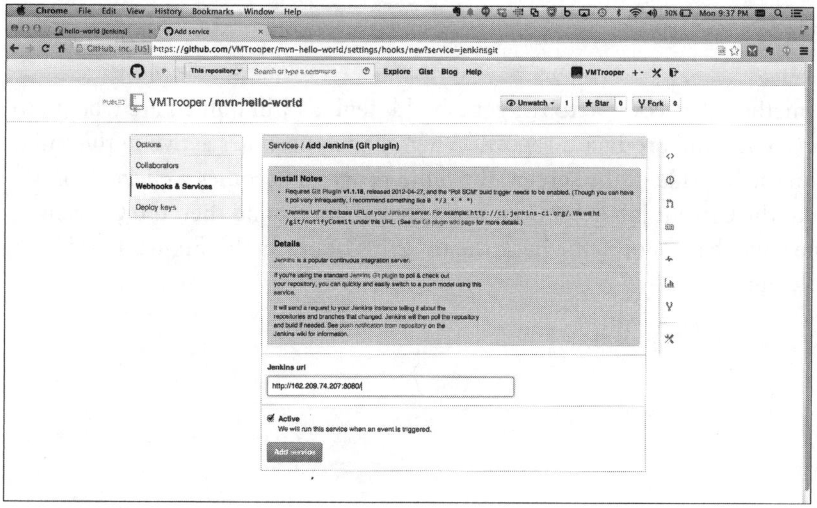

Figure 18-13 Git post-commit hook settings

The configuration is fairly straightforward. Just provide the URL to your Jenkins server, make sure the **Active** option is selected, and click the **Add Service** button.

Your First Build

Now that we have the build job configured, let's produce our first artifact. If GitHub can reach your Jenkins server, you can actually trigger a build from there by testing the service. You can do this by clicking the **Jenkins (Git Plugin)** link on your Webhooks and Services page of your repository settings. If your Jenkins server is on a local VM on a private network, you can alternatively click the **Build Now** link on the web page for your build job on the Jenkins server (see Figure 18-14).

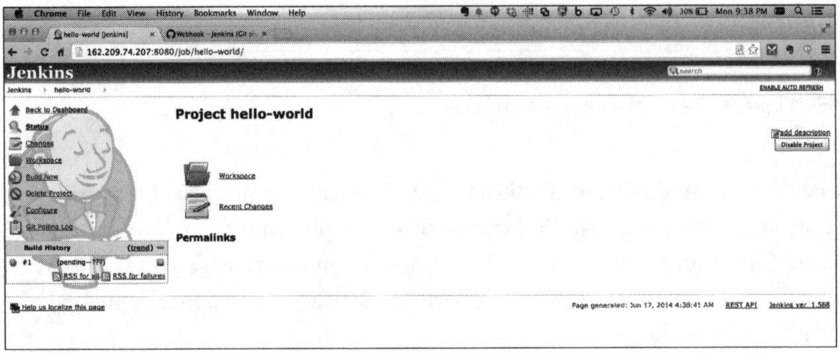

Figure 18-14 Jenkins build job page

Regardless of the method that you use to trigger a build, Jenkins will immediately begin to compile your source code and produce a report. When the job becomes active in the Build History window on the left side of the screen, the build progress becomes a clickable link that will take you to the current job execution. Let's click that link and then the Console Output link on the page that follows, to check the progress of our build. Figure 18-15 shows some sample output.

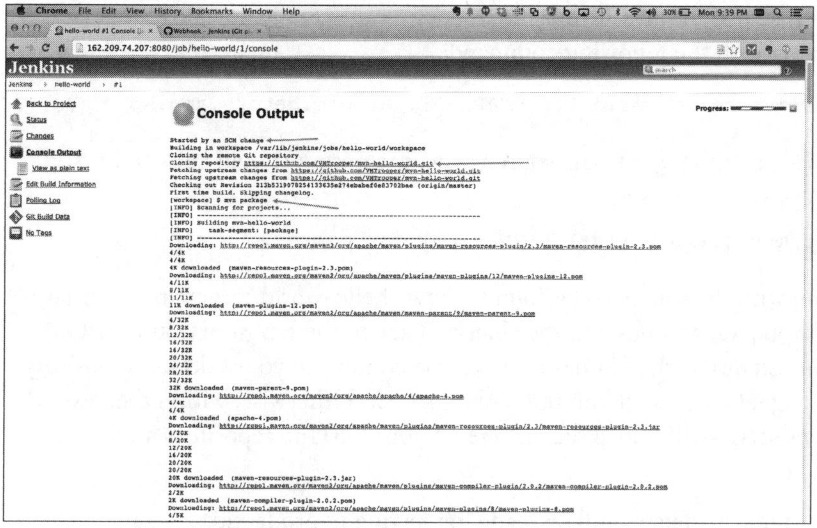

Figure 18-15 Jenkins build job console output

Notice that the first line of the build execution states the reason why the build is running. The Jenkins server first clones your source code repository. Then, it runs the `mvn package` command.

Click the **Back to Project** link when the build is successful, and there should be at least two additional links on the home page of the build project: one for the jar file artifact and another for the test result (see Figure 18-16).

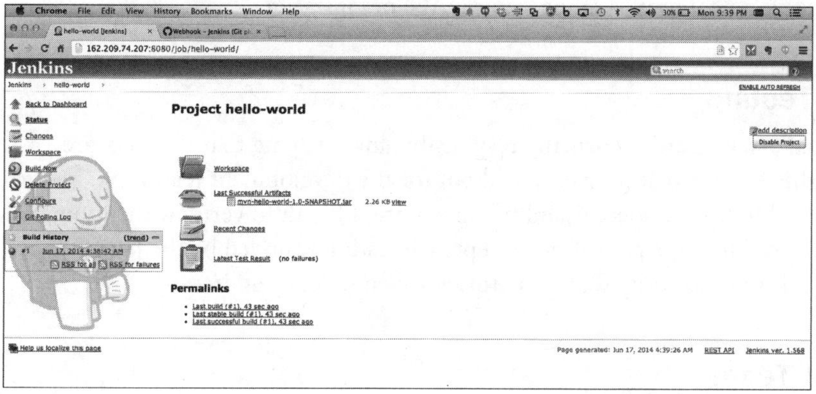

Figure 18-16 Build artifact and report after job execution

If you have Java 7 installed locally on your desktop, you can actually download that jar file and it should execute with the following command:

```
java -cp target/mvn-hello-world-1.0-SNAPSHOT.jar com.devops.app.App
```

If you have not made any changes to the source code, the output should be as follows:

```
Hello DevOps World!
java -cp target/mvn-hello-world-1.0-SNAPSHOT.jar com.devops.app.App
```

Try experimenting with the source code (found at mvn-hello-world/target/src/main/java/com/devops/app/App.java) and pushing the changes back to the repository on your Git server (GitHub and so on). If the Git hook works, the commit to your GitHub repository will immediately trigger a new build on the Jenkins server. Otherwise, within the next minute, the Jenkins server will notice the change on your GitHub repository and automatically trigger a build.

At this point, your build artifact would be ready for staging in production. So, an additional post-build action could be added to have Maven create a formal release and place the artifact on a repository server. If your group is practicing CI, the build will go through a final round of verification and be placed into production. If your group is practicing CD, the artifact will be placed directly into production.

Quality Assurance Teams?

Traditional software development organizations have dedicated quality assurance (QA) teams. Do CI systems obviate the need for QA talent? Absolutely not! Rather, our QA engineers can become a vital part of other teams in the organization.

Acceptance Testing

The product management team is normally responsible for verifying that the software releases meet all the features that they have laid out for the development teams. No matter how good automated testing is, some usability aspects are difficult to verify with automated tests. QA engineers can become part of the acceptance testing team led by the product management organization to verify that user stories are completely addressed.

Development Team

Some QA engineers may be interested in actually developing the product hands-on. In that case, they can be trained via peer programming or other orientation methods, to get up to speed on your organization's development practices and start contributing code.

Bug fixes may be a good place to start so that these new developers can identify coding conventions and learn the architecture of the product inside out while contributing to product stability.

Build/Test Infrastructure

If the QA engineers enjoy the software development process, but would rather focus on the testing process, the operations team can always benefit from their software development expertise to maintain the continuous integration infrastructure.

Summary

Software packaging and deployment can be a hassle and error-prone if done manually. Continuous integration/delivery systems like Jenkins allow you to automate the code download, compilation, testing, and packaging processes to remove human error from the equation.

References

[1] Apache Maven documentation: http://maven.apache.org/

[2] Jenkins CI documentation: http://jenkins-ci.org/

Chapter 19

VMware vRealize Automation in DevOps Environments

At this point in the book, there has been much conversation about the definition of DevOps. VMware's vision on this topic is that there is no objectively "true" definition, but instead we advocate conceiving of DevOps as a journey toward a state of cooperation and collaboration between the development and operations teams. Although there is no specific "tool" that defines it, a core component of DevOps, and also that of a true software-defined data center, is an extensible platform that augments the functionality of existing toolsets.

Topics covered in this chapter include the following:

- Emergence of DevOps
- Stable agility
- People, process, and Conway's law
- vRealize Automation
- vRealize Application Services
- Puppet integration

Emergence of DevOps

Based on our experience with customers, we see a pattern in how they mature with the cloud. There are typically a few stages on this journey, though these are not always taken sequentially:

1. Automate the virtual infrastructure.
2. Enable a portal to provide a service catalog; this is integrated into the consumption engine of the infrastructure-as-a-service (IaaS) components.
3. Enhance the value to the application teams by providing application blueprinting services, allowing the standardization of provisioning simple applications, middleware, databases, and complex multitiered applications.
4. Provide advanced, mature capabilities such as application release automation.
5. And finally, establish IT as a true broker of services.

The emergence of DevOps as a discipline unto itself is an exciting time for the industry. We are seeing opportunities to streamline business and IT operations to a degree we have never seen before, and there is no clear "winning technology" in the realm of developer tools. With a keen eye to this evolving landscape, VMware actively works to engage and integrate with many of the mature and emerging tools such as Puppet, Chef, Artifactory, Jenkins, Docker, and many others. Seemingly, there are new tools popularized daily, but VMware strives to keep its frameworks open to leverage these effectively and intelligently in the broader context of deploying and brokering services.

Stable Agility

Agility is a sexy concept. Rigidity is not. The IT industry moves at such a mind-bending pace that businesses struggle to find the perfect solution to meet their goals, and their goals are often in a state flux. Further, businesses are often asked to make purchasing decisions affecting the next three years or more. There is no crystal ball, so leaders usually (and correctly) look for flexible and extensible solutions that can adapt with business requirements.

But this is only part of the picture. A modicum of rigidity—or perhaps more generously, long-term stability—is critical to operating responsibly. Like an aircraft carrier launching F-18s, a solid infrastructure underpinning the data center is vital to the success of the mission. Some changes need to be made with great care and can often take months to plan properly. There are very good reasons why concepts such as change control exist in the data center: Many mistakes cannot be rolled back instantly, and outages affect the business directly, all too often in a cataclysmic fashion.

Conversely, many of today's applications change very quickly. For companies such as Netflix, new features, updates, and bug fixes can be implemented and pushed to production many times a day, seamless to the end user. Methodologies like continuous integration (CI) and continuous delivery (CD) are increasingly desirable and support the philosophy of *fail fast, fail often*, with the understanding that pushes of unsuccessful code can and will be rolled back immediately when required. This ability to change course almost instantly is the agility businesses typically seek, but it takes work to create the underlying structure to support this.

To follow the earlier analogy through, it is more than likely that the Navy would gladly employ a faster, more nimble aircraft carrier should they have the option. Indeed, if the underlying infrastructure is the aircraft carrier, virtualization and the software-defined data center enable just this kind of forward progress. The operation of that aircraft carrier, however, still needs to be carried out deliberately and with adequate planning. And no matter the upgrades, even the best aircraft carrier will obviously not outmaneuver an F-18; they are simply designed for different purposes.

People, Process, and Conway's Law

The preceding section alludes to some of the conflict present in many organizations today. I often see development and operations teams sitting across the table from one another, partitioned physically, logically, and conceptually from one another. Sometimes arms are crossed; other times, fingers are pointed. This should be concerning for an organization that seeks to operate as a cohesive unit.

> *Any organization that designs a system [...] will produce a design whose structure is a copy of the organization's communication structure*[1]

Application architects and developers want to move quickly and are generally not too concerned about the underpinnings of the frameworks upon which they develop; they simply want to fly fast. Hence, platform-as-a-service (PaaS) offerings are quite popular. Infrastructure and operations teams are often not able to adapt to the ever-changing needs of the developers due to the constraints mentioned earlier—namely, ensuring that the controls in place are adhered to for the greater good of the enterprise. Operations teams can thus be perceived as slow moving, contributing to undesirable phenomenon like Shadow IT; if a developer needs something done quickly, his or her credit card may short circuit an entire organization's efforts to control its intellectual property. Clearly, this needs to be addressed.

> *IT pros always and without fail, quietly self-organize around those who make the work easier, while shunning those who make the work harder, independent of the organizational chart.*[2]

At VMware, we champion the theory that changes to people and process can most effectively take place when these changes are reinforced with technologies that adhere to similar principles as the goal. One mechanism is the software-defined data center (SDDC): We make the aircraft carrier much faster by architecting infrastructure solutions completely in software to adapt quickly, automating processes wherever possible while being safe and responsible.

Another mechanism, which we focus on here, is a complementary method to the SDDC vision aimed to bring the application and the infrastructure teams together using a common framework from which they can both extract value, share duties, and work cohesively to achieve the goals of the business. This technical proximity fosters teamwork and contributes to a faster time to market with less friction. Let's look at some of these methods and toolsets in depth.

vRealize Automation

Consumers[3] of IT have evolved significantly in the past few years, due in no small part to the Apple-inspired proliferation of the App Store concept. Consumers of all kinds expect services on demand with minimal fuss. This, in turn, requires a service catalog underpinned by a measure of automation and governance to fulfill the request in a timely manner with adequate safeguards.

Formerly known as vCloud Automation Center, vRealize Automation (vRA) is a major component in the broader vCloud Suite that functions as the central hub for automation activities and governance while providing a user-friendly catalog of services. It is here that the consumer requests services through a portal and interacts with his workloads thereafter, as shown in Figure 19-1.

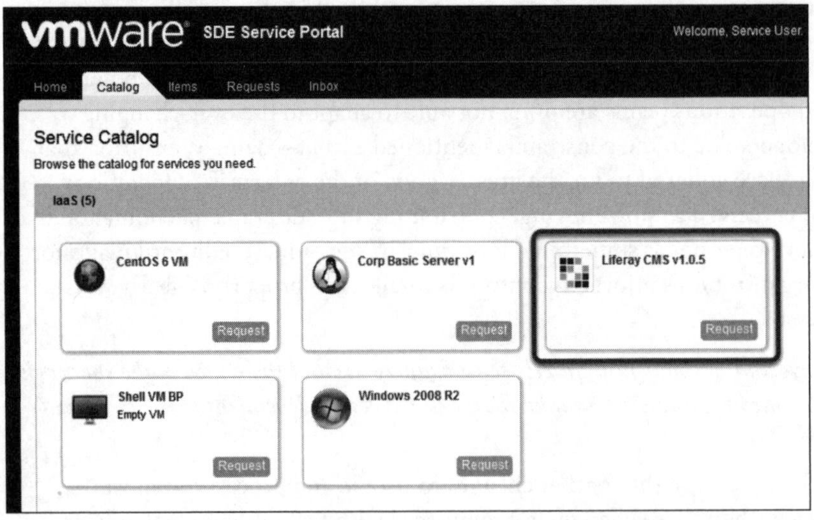

Figure 19-1 The vRealize Automation catalog of services

A fundamental value proposition of vRA lies in the extensible nature of the solution. Fading are the days when the deployment of isolated templates is sufficient to meet most businesses' needs. The template deployment itself is a small piece of providing a service; automation of IP Address Management (IPAM), firewall and load-balancer integration, assignment of backup policies, deployment of integrated multitier applications to heterogeneous internal and external infrastructures based on policy—this is approaching what it means to truly be a broker of IT today.

Anyone who has made the mistake of allowing an automated process to run without adequate checks and balances knows the value of strategic human oversight on processes. A robust and nuanced approval engine, completely customizable by the administrator, ensures that low-impact requests can be immediately fulfilled while resource-intensive or privileged requests can be flagged for manual approval at any stage of the machine's lifecycle.

But we are still talking about the plumbing of the infrastructure for the most part. How do we bridge the gap between the infrastructure teams and development teams?

vRealize Application Services

Part of the vCloud Suite, and tightly integrated with vRA, is Application Services (formerly Application Director, or AppD). Application Services provides a framework in which to build fully integrated multitier application stacks using an intuitive drag-and-drop palette to instantiate components and relationships.

One should think of this layer as an orchestration engine for deployments, a mechanism to create and deploy application blueprints that are standardized, flexible, and decoupled from the underlying infrastructure. Figure 19-2 shows a blueprint example.

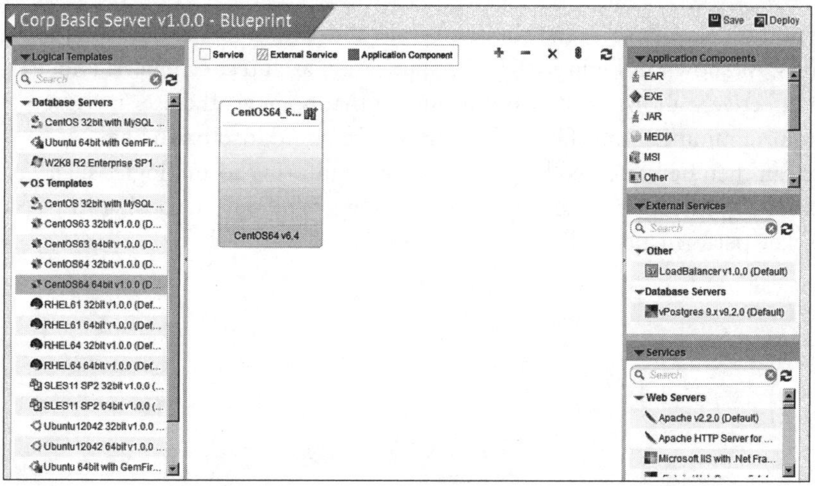

Figure 19-2 The Application Services blueprint framework

NOTE

The Application Services blueprint framework comprises the following: 1. The application blueprint's working space with a CentOS template. 2. Configuration details of this template. 3. This column contains templates for application components, external services, and native services. 4. This column contains logical templates that are wired to the cloud provider.

The objects brought into the palette are linked to repositories or shares housing the artifacts via a construct called a *deployment profile*. ISOs, war files, jar files, templates, executables, MSIs, and so on—these can all be leveraged as though they are native components in the application build process.

Ultimately, the build needs to land on infrastructure, and hence deployment profiles are tied to a cloud provider, allowing for the same blueprint to be used on multiple deployments in separate environments. This can be vRealize Automation, vCloud Director, or Amazon EC2. We will focus on the vRA integration for simplicity's sake, but it is important to be aware of the possibilities and the inherent portability of the application blueprints.

So, how does this affect deployment? Quite simply, each service fashioned in this manner and deployed from the service catalog is built fresh, live, and on demand. This allows application architects the flexibility to create and modify full-fledged integrated application stacks with complex dependencies, automate the build process, and expose this all as a catalog item to the consumer. This significantly reduces the time to value and request fulfillment and eliminates a lot of repetitive tasks that can easily be made in error; standardization and automation of builds ensure the stability of the end product.

A notable feature in this solution set is the ability to scale nodes both in and out using Application Services. As shown in Figure 19-3, the application architect can mark a node as scalable, which effectively allows on-demand scaling of that node via the user interface (UI) or application programming interface (API) with the required load balancing. This functionality can then be leveraged by performance monitoring technologies such as vRealize Operations (formerly vCenter Operations Manager) to scale according to workload or other key performance indicator (KPI) criteria.

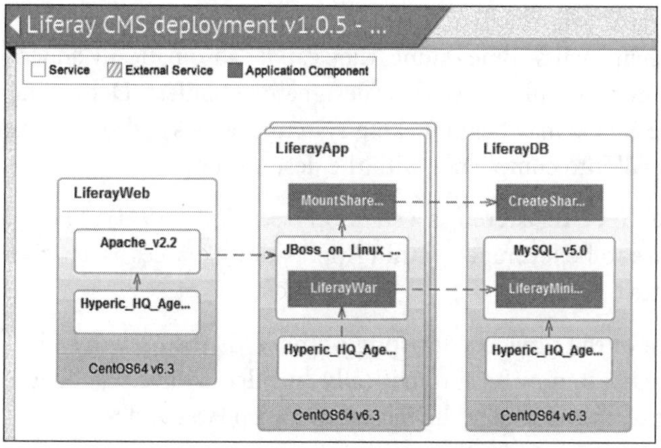

Figure 19-3 A complex three-tiered application

> **NOTE**
>
> In Figure 19-3, dotted arrows indicate the dependencies; the application will be built according to these. The LiferayApp is clustered, and therefore it can scale in and out on demand.

Returning to this notion of the palette in Application Services, consider further how we build applications. Remember, extensibility is a key tenet for VMware! Let's examine this further via the integration with Puppet.

Puppet Integration

VMware was an early investor in Puppet Labs. Partnering closely with them, the result is a complementary framework that is mutually beneficial to consumers of both technologies.

> **NOTE**
>
> Puppet has an Enterprise offering, but it is not explicitly required for integration with VMware solutions. However, you should always be sure to check with Puppet Labs to ensure you are in compliance with Puppet licensing.

Puppet utilizes a master/agent hierarchy that facilitates large-scale application and OS control via a singular interface. When agents come online, they can be automatically added to the Puppet master, at which point they will receive their designated manifest. Depending on the criteria of that manifest, the agents may begin making system changes and/or pulling down modules from the master to fall into compliance with the desired state.

Application Services allows Puppet to be registered as a solution (see Figure 19-4). This integration enables Puppet modules to be leveraged within Application Services as a native object via the drag-and-drop palette.

The orchestration and deployment of the service, consisting of the VMs themselves and the fully integrated application stack, can now be automatically enrolled with the Puppet master, allowing the development team to manage the instances for updates and to monitor for configuration drift and enforce remediation when necessary.

One of the net effects of this integration is a tighter coupling between the infrastructure and development teams—one of the core principles of DevOps. It becomes advantageous for both teams to work together because this framework is mutually beneficial to both teams.

So how does this occur? To register Puppet as a solution in Application Services, have a look at VMware KB 2068342. This KB provides up-to-date information in accordance with current versions of the solutions.[4] Ultimately, you must log in to the Puppet master and download and run the Ruby script provided in the KB. The following is an example to register with Application Services 6.1.

```
ruby RegisterWithAppD.rb -i Application_Director_IP -u User_Name -p
Password -t Tenant_Name -g Group_Name -d Deployment_Environment_Name
```

Let's walk through how this functions. First, Puppet is added to Application Services as a solution by running a quick Ruby script from the Puppet master.[5] You will then see Puppet registered as a solution, as shown in Figure 19-4.

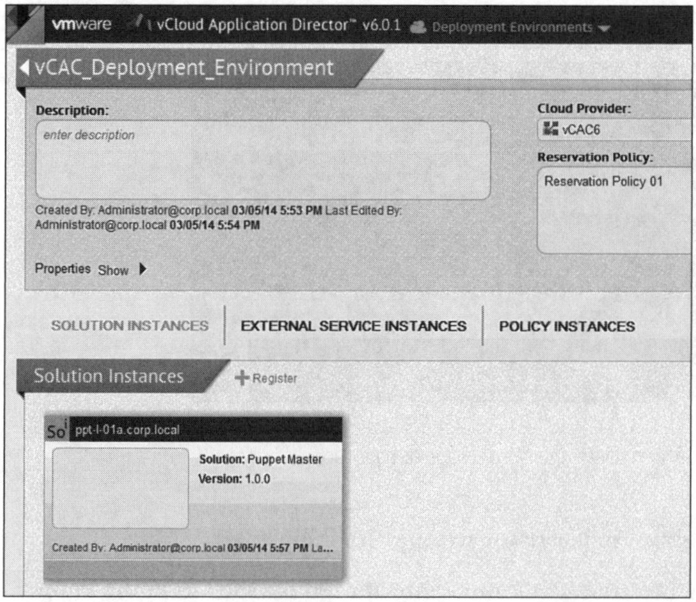

Figure 19-4 The Puppet solution registered within the Application Services framework

What occurs here on the Puppet side is that this integration modifies the site.pp file in Puppet, which is the main configuration file. The purpose of this is to include the directories of all Application Services nodes that are integrated with this Puppet master (see Figure 19-5).

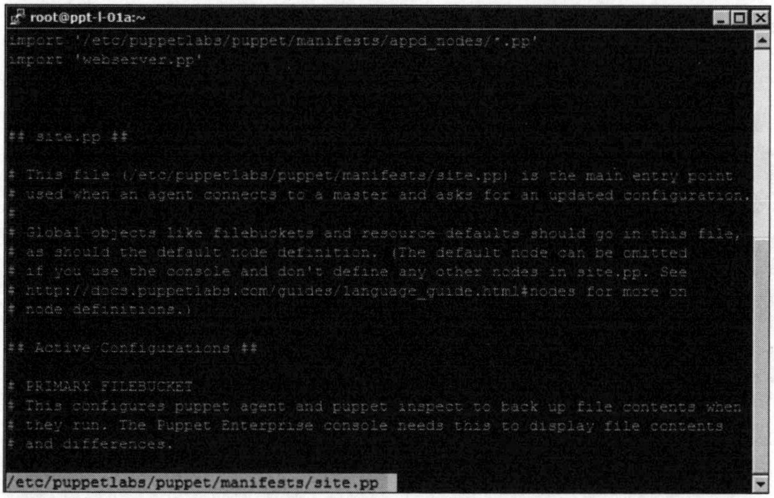

Figure 19-5 Integration with Application Services modifies the site.pp file. The two lines at the top of the screenshot are added post-integration.

Next, we need to import the Puppet modules into Application Services (see Figure 19-6).

Figure 19-6 Launching the Darwin client from the Puppet master

Perform the following to register Application Director with Puppet:

1. As per Figure 19-5, log in to the Application Director remote shell from the Puppet master by launching the roo shell client:[6]

```
java -jar ~/darwin-cli.jar
```

2. Log in with administrative rights to the Application Services framework:

```
Login --serverUrl https://FQDN:8443/darwin --username Admin@domain
--password PASSWORD
```

3. As per Figure 19-7, import the Puppet modules that you want available:

```
import-puppet-manifests --puppetPath /usr/local/bin/puppet --typeFil-
ter "^motd$"
```

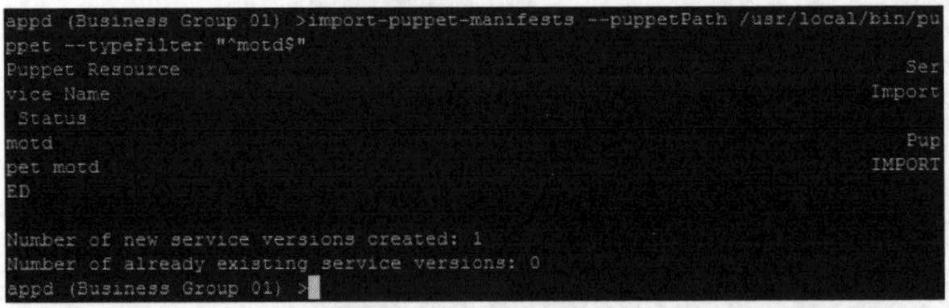

Figure 19-7 This allows the import of any modules that meet the regular expression `"^motd$"`, which in this case indicates a "Message of the Day" Puppet module. A wildcard could be used to import all the modules, but you should be careful of this because of the potential size of the import.

At this point, you should see a Puppet module has been imported into Application Services, as shown in Figure 19-8; the Puppet module listed in the Services portal in Application Services is MySQL Server. This could really be anything, however. Take a look at the Puppet Forge to get a sense of the community-built modules available for free.[7]

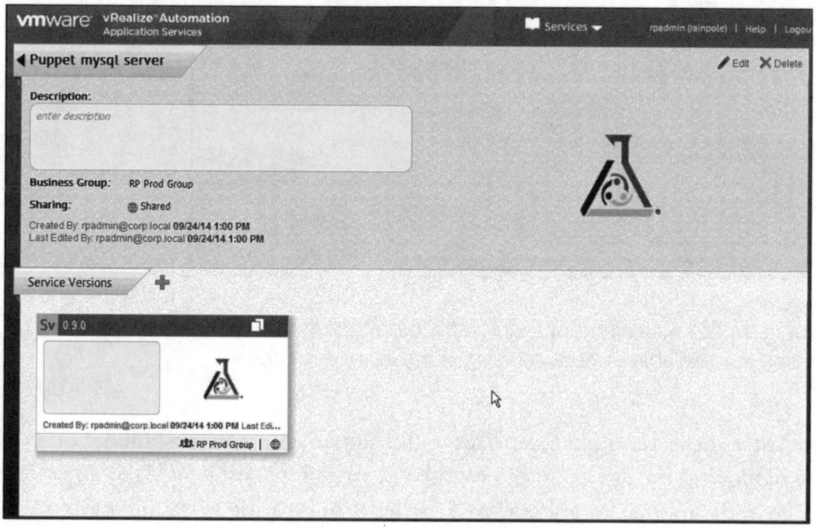

Figure 19-8 Puppet modules can now be leveraged natively as services.

Depending on the nature of the module, you might need to add some information to the module definition from within Application Services. The insertion point here allows variables to be passed from VMware, or other solutions, to the Puppet modules to customize and automate the deployment of the application. Again, this requires some coordination between both teams to ensure that the required variables are being pulled from the appropriate location and delivered to the application.

At this stage, the Puppet modules can be used natively within Application Services. As shown in Figure 19-9, the MySQL service appears as an object that can be added to the CentOS instance, or any other compatible instance, as many times as required by the application blueprint. Remember, because these are decoupled logical templates, they are very portable and flexible.

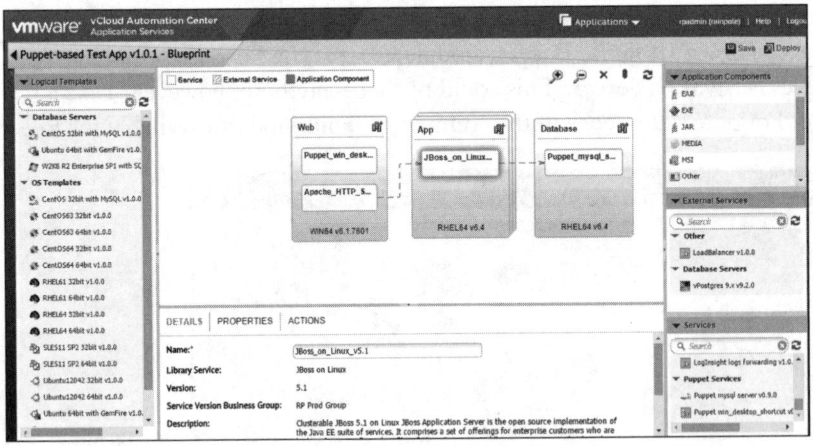

Figure 19-9 Puppet services now appear as elements to be flexibly deployed within application blueprints. You can see the available Puppet services in the lower-right corner.

Conversely, if you just want to leverage templates with Puppet agents preinstalled, you can do so easily by deploying the agent on the templated virtual machine (VM) at any stage. The real value in the methodology outlined earlier is in creating portable, multi-tiered, completely integrated applications that span multiple VMs while remaining easy to visualize and consume. After the initial setup, application building can effectively be offloaded to a team that knows next to nothing about Puppet, significantly freeing the Puppet admins from the build process.

The potential of this solution should be clear. The infrastructure team facilitates the creation and deployment of the master blueprint and presents the service to the consumer. The application architects control the application blueprints, designing anything from simple to highly complex application stacks. Once operationalized, the applications can then be managed, updated, patched, and controlled for configuration drift via Puppet.

Let's revisit another multitiered blueprint in Figure 19-10, post-deployment, based on a Liferay application.

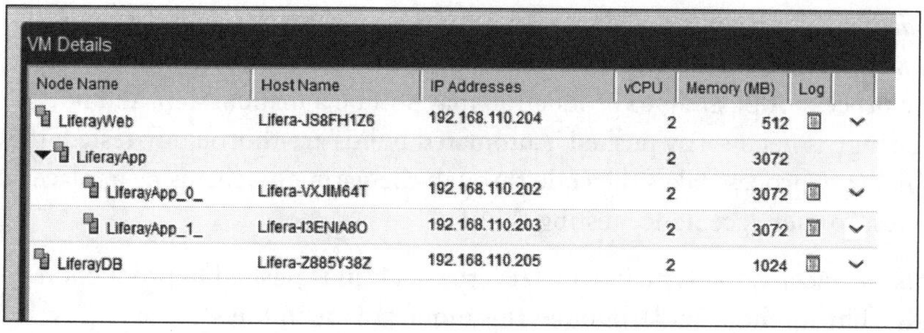
VM Details
Node Name
Host Name
IP Addresses
vCPU
Memory (MB)
Log
LiferayWeb
Lifera-JS8FH1Z6
192.168.110.204
2
512
LiferayApp
2
3072
LiferayApp_0_
Lifera-VXJIM64T
192.168.110.202
2
3072
LiferayApp_1_
Lifera-I3ENIA8O
192.168.110.203
2
3072
LiferayDB
Lifera-Z885Y38Z
192.168.110.205
2
1024

Figure 19-10 Visualizing a three-tiered scalable application stack after deployment within the Application Services UI

The inclusion of a scalable node (LiferayApp) is important here. Application Services will mark this node as scalable, allowing scale-in and scale-out operations to occur with a single click. To enable this, simply click the small server icon in the upper-right corner of the OS template on the palette (see Figure 19-9). This functionality can be accessed via the API as well, so look for VMware and our partners to leverage this functionality across solutions.

Further, the chain icon in the top toolbar (see Figure 19-9) allows for dependencies between applications to be specified; this ensures that the application will come up only after the database has completed installing, for instance. During deployment, you can observe the live progress of the build; in the event of failure, it's now trivial to determine exactly where the deployment fail and fix the issue.

It is a good time to mention that although we have focused here on Puppet integration, there are many more possibilities. VMware solutions can integrate with Chef, SaltStack, Jenkins… the list is quite long because this market is vibrant and growing by the day. VMware's goal is to facilitate an open framework in which the development team's tools of choice can function easily. It is beyond the scope of this chapter to go into each in detail, however, so we focus next on an emerging VMware technology that takes this process to the next level: VMware vRealize Code Stream.

Code Stream

Before going into specifics on the upcoming Code Stream solution, let's define some terms.

- *Continuous integration* refers to the regular check-in of code to repositories, and to the automation of builds and testing to ensure that bugs are found early and fixed with minimal churn.

- *Continuous delivery*, built on top of a strong continuous integration foundation, is a series of practices that ensure the latest code *could* be pushed to production at any time, but the process of pushing to production may still be a manual step, and not every code change is necessarily pushed. Automated builds are thoroughly tested; the continuous delivery process takes the code through the gating mechanisms in place from dev to test to user acceptance testing (UAT).
- *Continuous deployment* is the state in which every check-in is pushed to production automatically. The methods underpinning this mode are much the same as continuous delivery, but taken to the extreme. This mode clearly requires the utmost of confidence in the automated build and testing processes, as well as a business that could see the benefits outweighing the potential risks of this model. Etsy and Facebook might see this as an end goal, but it is likely not something a bank would want to pursue. It is, ultimately, all about the business needs.

Whether the goal is continuous integration, continuous delivery, or continuous deployment, Code Stream can provide a vital component in the overall solution by providing automation of pipeline development, leveraging existing source code management systems such as Git, build systems such as Jenkins, and artifact repositories. Code Stream is delivered as an onboard component in vRA, but it can operate independently, though the technologies are highly complementary.

Specifically, Code Stream is targeted to release managers or release engineers as an integrated component in vRA; apart from the core code, it is delivered with an onboard[8] jFrog Artifactory server that allows for UI-based pipeline creation, gating, and deployment to specific environments, while abstracting the artifacts present in the environment for easy use. This is a major step in achieving continuous delivery; automating pipeline control facilitates a seamless transition between development stages, ensuring adherence to best practices and standards while leveraging in-place or scripting tools for CI testing.

NOTE

In the 1.0 release of Code Stream, only custom scripts, vRA, vCenter Server, and vCloud Director are supported for provisioning and configuration. More solutions and integration points will become available in future releases.

From a people and process perspective, Code Stream facilitates the interactions between development and operations teams by providing a technical framework in which both teams participate to achieve a common goal: Staying integrated with the development teams, including release management now, while understanding the server and operations side, is key to ensuring the transition between stages occurs in a fluid manner. This workspace can be visualized and managed within the Code Stream UI, which again, is integrated in the vRA UI.

To visualize this in action, let's take a simple example of pipeline creation in Figure 19-11. The pipeline defines all the required steps required to deploy and test an application, including, if necessary, the deployment of the VM itself. As the steps in the stage progress, the pass/fail criteria determine the progression to the next stage. Stages can be added to the pipeline as needed, depending on the needs of the business. Each stage is fully customizable with action items that control each requirement of the stage.

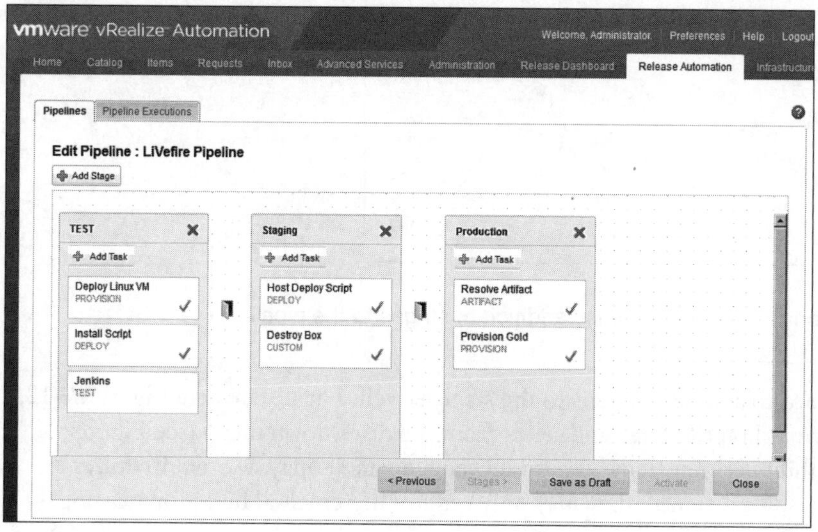

Figure 19-11 Code Stream's pipeline execution is an ideal framework for release managers to visually control the deployment process across lifecycle stages.

In the example in Figure 19-12, the development stage has four components: provision, deploy, unit test, and script test.

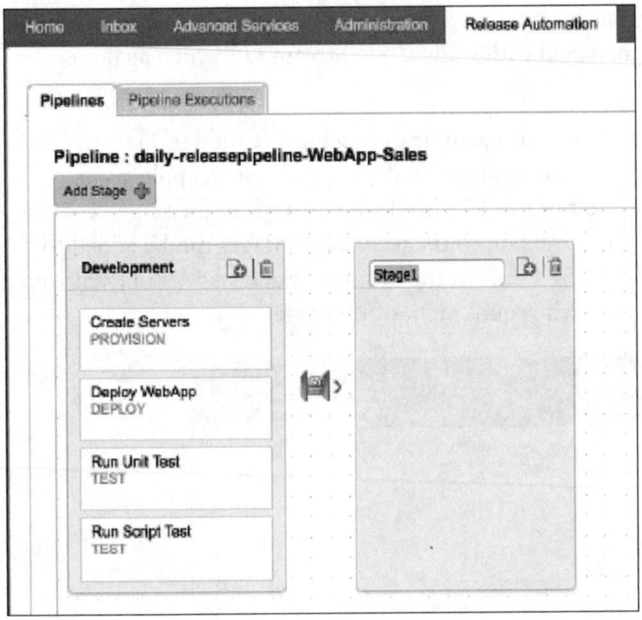

Figure 19-12 Code Stream allows easy addition of stages to the pipeline.

It is straightforward to add new actions to the stage as well. For instance, in Figure 19-12, just click the **+** symbol on the stage and select from the drop-down menu (see Figure 19-13). This flexibility is important because subsequent stages may not require fully provisioned servers, for instance; they may only require incremental builds on existing operating systems.

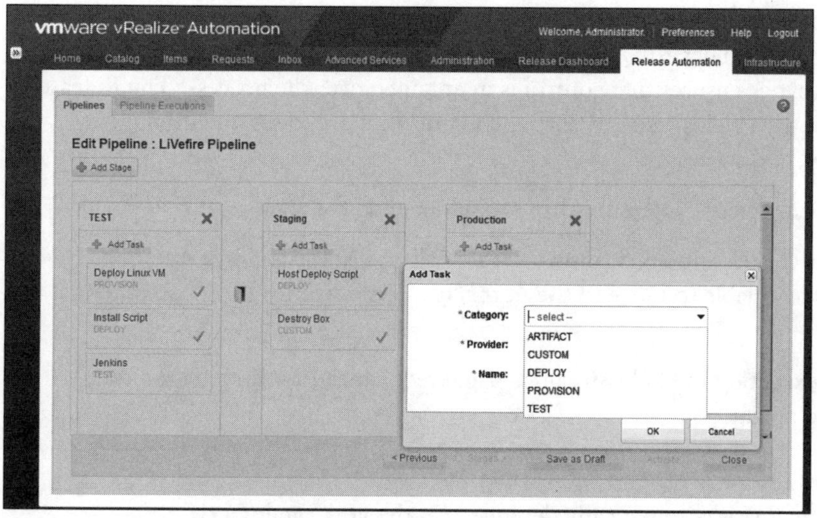

Figure 19-13 Steps can be added easily to the stage via the UI.

Similarly, the creation of gating rules is UI driven and integrated with vCenter Orchestrator (vCO), which also comes onboard the vRA appliance itself (although you are free to use any vCO server you want). This gating functionality, referenced in Figure 19-14, allows the user the flexibility to use simple logic to determine success or failure, funnel manual approval through the vRA mechanism, or build more sophisticated logic using vCO.

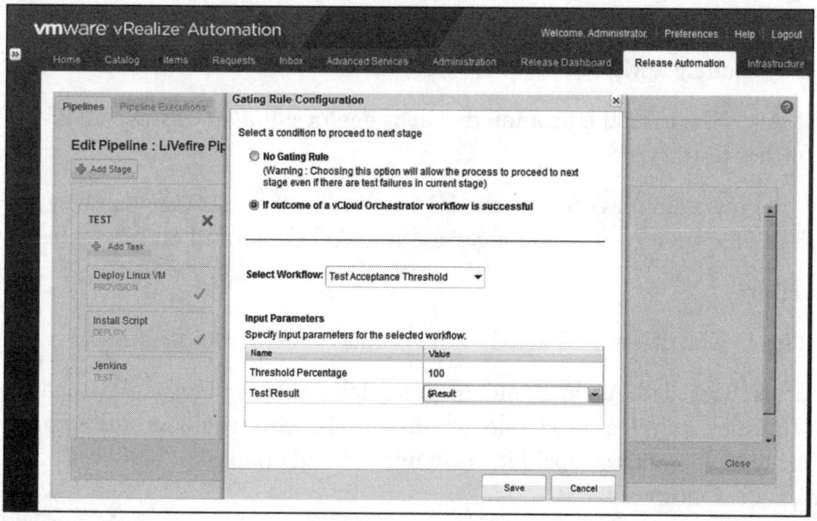

Figure 19-14 Gating rules can be added to manage advancement between stages. These rules can be based on the success of the previous stage, based on the outcome of a vCO workflow, manual approval, or a combination of these and other factors.

The Code Stream pipeline will then initialize, build, and test according to the appropriate stage, passing from dev to UAT to staging while governed by the gating rules in place. This governance ensures that control is maintained over the process. The Release Automation dashboard yields visibility into the many build processes, identifying key milestones, errors, and successes.

Let's run through a scenario to ensure that you understand the flow:

1. A developer checks some code into a Git repository. At this point, a number of methods are available to move to the next stage, so we will focus on one potential path.
2. A pipeline execution in Code Stream is triggered, which has three stages: test, staging, and production.
   - **Test**
     - A VM is automatically deployed via the vRA catalog.
     - Code Stream executes a build on the VM with the latest bits of code. This could leverage Jenkins, as well, to automate the builds.
     - An automated test is run via a tool like Selenium.
     - If this is successful and passes the gating rule, the pipeline will continue to the next stage.
   - **Staging**
     - Because this may be a "brownfield" deployment, the staging stage might not require a VM.
     - If this is the case, the promoted code is deployed on an existing VM for further testing.
     - If the preceding task passes, the VM created in the test stage will be destroyed because it is no longer useful. We have moved on successfully.
   - **Production**
     - The code/artifacts are passed to the production environment. Success!
3. The pipeline has succeeded. As this standardization takes shape, it is useful to analyze the pass/fail statistics, as well as use Code Stream to assist with troubleshooting the pipelines. The troubleshooting capabilities are not currently in the general availability (GA) product, however.

As is true with most VMware solutions, a pluggable design allows for third-party integrations into various repositories, build systems, ticketing systems, and more. As the solution matures, this ecosystem will become increasingly robust and interconnected. As mentioned, there is already tight integration with vCO (Orchestrator), which has a rich marketplace of workflows designed to augment automation projects significantly.

Summary

VMware is constantly evolving with the needs of our clients. The clear advantages in moving toward a DevOps-centric model have created an opportunity for us all to work closer together and foster a fluid, robust framework of people, process, and tools, enabling IT to deliver maximum value with minimal friction to the business—to become a true broker of IT services.

With vRealize Automation, Application Services, Code Stream, and the marketplace of integrated technologies, VMware is dedicated to continue playing a vital role as partners with our customers in this exciting journey.

References

[1] http://www.melconway.com/Home/Conways_Law.html

[2] http://www.computerworld.com/article/2527153/it-management/opinion--the-unspoken-truth-about-managing-geeks.html
To be clear, the term *consumer* in IT does not necessarily apply to the end user. An IT department's main consumers may be developers.

[3] http://kb.vmware.com/selfservice/microsites/search.do?language=en_US&cmd=displayKC&externalId=2068342

[4] You can obtain this script via VMware KB 2068342.

[5] Darwin-cli.jar needs to be downloaded from the Application Services appliance. You can find details at https://pubs.vmware.com/appdirector-1/index.jsp?topic=%2Fcom.vmware.appdirector.using.doc%2FGUID-D39A5F38-7EEF-43A3-8CF2-7ADA4C1E03F2.html.

[6] https://forge.puppetlabs.com/

[7] Note that Code Stream supports attaching to existing Artifactory servers as well.

Index

Symbols

A

B

C

D

E

F

J

K

L

M

N

O

P

Q-R

S

T

U

V

W-Z